The Woman on the Mountain

SHARYN MUNRO

HOURGLASS

An HOURGLASS book
An imprint of Exisle Publishing Limited

First published 2007

Exisle Publishing Limited
'Moonrising', Narone Creek Road, Wollombi, NSW 2325, Australia
P.O. Box 60–490, Titirangi, Auckland 0642, New Zealand
www.exislepublishing.com

National Library of Cataloguing-in-Publication Data:

Munro, Sharyn (Sharyn Therese).
The woman on the mountain.

ISBN 9780908988709.

1. Munro, Sharyn (Sharyn Therese). 2. Self-reliant living –
New South Wales – Hunter Valley. 3. Women
environmentalists – New South Wales – Hunter Valley –
Biography. I. Title.

333.72092

Designed by saso content & design pty ltd
Typeset in Bembo 12/17pt by 1000 Monkeys
Printed in China through Colorcraft Limited, Hong Kong

1 3 5 7 9 10 8 6 4 2

To my children, who have taught me most about love.

CONTENTS

CHAPTER 1

WHY I LIVE
'WAY OUT THERE'

WHEREVER YOU LIVE YOU need to feel safe, and in tune with your surroundings. I do.

Yet my place is a 90-minute drive from a post box, police station, shop or mechanic, let alone a Big M or a Big W or whatever other letter is considered crucial to modern survival. Half of that drive is over a dirt road, partly through a national park which verges on wilderness. I have no neighbours within sight, sound or coo-ee, or not in the accepted sense. My neighbours are the wild creatures who live in the national park.

I have a telephone, but I must take care of my own power, water, sewerage and garbage — and of myself, for I live alone. I had never intended to live by myself, way out here in the mountains; I wouldn't have entertained such a foolhardy idea. You'd have to be mad!

Perhaps I was at the time, four years ago, when I made the decision to end my second long-term relationship. My dad had recently died, and I was seeing the whole world differently. That break-up precipitated a second decision: stay here alone, or sell up and leave.

I'd first lived here in the late 1970s, with my husband and two young children. Our relatives and colleagues had indeed said we were mad, but we weren't alone in following our back-to-the-land urges, just a bit late. Woodstock was long ago, Jimi Hendrix was dead; we hadn't even thought of going to the Nimbin Festival; we owned a Kombi, but it was new and it didn't have flowers on it. We were far too sceptical to be hippies — but we did read *Earth Garden*.

For fifteen months we lived in a tent while we made mudbricks and built a small cabin, cooking on an open fire, carting buckets of water up the hill from a nearby spring, showering outdoors under a canvas bag. I absolutely loved the simplicity of it and the closeness to nature.

My husband used to work away from home for a few days each week, often staying away two nights, while the kids and I remained here, with no car and no phone. I was never worried — I'd done first aid, we were all healthy, and it was too remote for baddies.

But isolation tests a relationship, puts it under stress until any structural cracks show through the civilised veneer. When the marriage failed a few years later, I was as upset by the loss of my simple bush lifestyle as by the loss of my husband of twelve years. I'd married far too young, for the wrong reason — insecurity — and to the wrong person. For my foolishness I was then sentenced to thirteen years in the city, bringing up my children on my own, renting cheap, sad houses, and working at a crazy succession of jobs for which my Arts degree had not equipped me.

Every second weekend, if I could afford the petrol, we would drive the four and a half hours to our real home, which we always referred to as 'the mountain'. When the kids had finished school and were so involved in their own lives that I hardly ever saw them, I announced I was going back up there for good.

Amazingly, a phone line had been put in to that remote area by then, under pressure from nervous weekenders. So in 1994 my new partner and I installed solar power and moved to the mountain. With a computer and a phone line, I could keep doing the copywriting/ editing for the graphic design studio where I'd last worked. He would continue to do guitar repairs and restorations. The plan was that with no rent to pay, growing our own vegies and living frugally, we could make enough for thinly buttered bread at least. In the meantime we would pursue our creative interests, which for me was writing; for him, developing his own handmade classical guitar.

His plan worked — the Kellaway Classical Guitar sounds as beautiful as it looks.

My plan didn't get started for the first four years, as there was always too much else to be done that, being female, I couldn't ignore. We were together here for eight years, during which time this place had etched itself into my very bones. It wasn't really a choice with this break-up; there was no way I could leave. Understanding this, and my grief-stricken state, my ex-partner did not create difficulties.

Having owned the mountain for nearly 30 years, I belonged to it.

I'd just turned 55; I had arthritis, which, though under control, restricted what I could do physically. How I would manage, whether I could manage, I didn't know, but I was damn well going to try before I gave up my bush life again. The alternative was too depressing.

Unfortunately, the self-sufficient lifestyle here depends on things that require ongoing work and maintenance, much of which assume either strong wrists or a good relationship with things mechanical, neither of which I possess. There would be many days of frustration and foul language directed at sullen metal objects.

The isolation proved the easiest thing to cope with. Perhaps this is because I'm a writer, with my kaleidoscope brain full of people and places and situations demanding I get over here to the keyboard and get on with their stories — so I'm never lonely. Only once did I have an intense feeling of 'aloneness', which is not the same as loneliness. It was the first time I'd arrived back here by myself at night. I always tried to get back by twilight to avoid a nerve-wracking trip from town, peering for, second-guessing and dodging panicked marsupials. The Council slash the exotically rye-grassed edges of their long and lonely tarred road; many wallabies and wallaroos are enticed there to graze — and many are killed.

The feeling began almost as soon as I turned off the engine and headlights. Silence. Blackness. Emptiness. I flicked the torch beam about as I walked down to the dark house ... where no one was waiting. After the long drive in around the uninhabited forested ridges of the national park, it hit me: 'I am totally alone here — this huge forest doesn't give a damn about me! Anything could happen and nobody would know. What am I doing here? Who am I kidding? I'm not this brave ...' and a lot more in the same vein.

Sudden, overpowering awareness of what an irrelevant human dot I was in this vast wild world.

Rushing inside, I lit the fire, sobbing, sniffling, feeling extremely sorry for myself because I would *have* to leave now I felt like that. But as the familiar cosiness of my cabin settled around me like a child's comforter, the feeling passed. I suppose it had been a flash of panic.

Later, when I went outside and looked up at the enormity of the starry sky, undimmed and undiminished by city lights, I didn't feel overwhelmed. I felt I was in my right place, and grateful to be so.

I once had a similar panicky feeling on a small island, surrounded by sea and with no other land in sight. It was milder but more persistent, and during my stay I had to consciously keep it below the surface. My moment of panic here made me better understand what visitors often evidence when they finally reach my little mudbrick cabin. They've been driving for ages, have seen only one house in the last half hour, most likely have taken a few wrong turnings — and suddenly there I am, on my tiny patch of 'civilisation', a clearing in the midst of seemingly never-ending mountain forests. They feel intimidated. One city visitor experienced such anxiety that he had to bolt after only a few hours, instead of staying for the weekend as planned.

Yet if I were forced to live again in a city, town or suburb, I certainly wouldn't feel safe, or in tune with my surroundings. I'd be nervous, draw my curtains at night, lock my doors, lower my voice — and I'd feel like a fish out of water.

I'd pine for the tree-clad mountains stretching forever into the distance, the blue gums and stringy-barks and she-oaks just beyond my house fence, the hundreds of infant rainforest trees I've planted in the gullies, the wild creatures that are my neighbours — the wallabies and birds, the quolls and koalas, the snakes and lizards — I'd even include the leeches. I'd miss the sounds of cicada, mad wattlebird and bleating frog chorus, or me yelling 'Feedo!' at the top of my voice for the horses to come. When could I yell anything at the top of my voice again?

To illustrate how isolated I am here, and thus the degree of privacy to which I'm accustomed, when I put the phone down after finally getting it into my head that I was as shortlisted as you can get for the 2002 Alan Marshall Short Story Award — that is, I'd won ($2500!) — my first instinct was to rush straight out to the verandah railing and tell my world. Almost bursting with joyful incredulity, I screamed that all-purpose four-letter word so loud and so long that it hurt my throat. Tarzan would have been proud of my effort — but no one would have heard.

What would I have done in the city? Burst?

In the city I'd be hemmed in by a sea of roofs, hard footpaths and roads, fences too close, traffic too loud, other people's dramas or plaintive dogs too present and unstoppable. I'd avoid the front verandah or balcony like everybody else, skulk in private places of the garden if I was lucky enough to have one, and long for a vast canvas of sunset skies unbroken by blank-faced office towers, for vistas of green and blue with not a red-brick wall or red-tile roof in sight.

People often ask me, 'Why do you live way out there, so far away from everything?'

I usually simply answer, 'Because I can.'

I might continue, 'And it all depends on what you mean by "everything", doesn't it?'

I have email and phone contact (lightning strikes and floods permitting) if I want it, ABC Radio National to keep my brain ticking, and plenty of wood, water and sunshine. I can enjoy my home-grown vegetables, home-baked bread and home-brewed beer, great views, privacy and solitude interspersed with visits from family and friends. I am able to live in a natural environment, to take my proper place in what I consider the real world, the whole wild rich world around me — and I can always drive to that other 'everything' if I should need it.

So my final answer to their 'Why?' is 'Why not?'

Writers need solitude to write, but they also need opportunities for inspiration and observation, so as to have something to write about. Typically, you'd imagine a writer living in ...

- an ancient farmhouse in Tuscany, blue shutters, worn stone steps, sunny vineyards, rough red wine, the golden-green glow of olive oil ... and a village down the road; or

- a stone hut on a Scottish hillside, fireplace, flagged floor, cold

mountain burns and bracken, mist, brown bread, brown tea,
brown whisky … and a village down the road; or

*a charming cottage in the Cotswolds, low cosy ceilings,
blackened oak beams, thatch and roses, gooseberries and muffins
… and a village down the road; or maybe

*a top floor of a pension with a gem of a landlady, in any
European town with a literary history, grey slate rooftops, soft
feather bed, thick soup … and a village down the road.

Where I live there aren't any subtle interplays of human relationships to observe and dissect; there aren't any other humans.

There aren't any walled gardens, winding staircases or mysteriously
locked doors to set in play a train of speculation; there aren't any other
buildings.

There aren't any evocative ruins, hauntingly hollow shells, dry-
stone storytellers; there's never been any other buildings.

There aren't even any rusting ploughshares, although I found a
rusting crosscut-saw blade from the cedargetters of the 'red gold'-rush
days. I have written several fictional stories about earlier settlers here,
but mostly it has been the bush itself, my sense of this place, that has
inspired my fiction.

According to the census, I live alone. If a spy were to slink over the
ridge and watch me as I go about my daily outdoor business —
emptying the compost bucket, sipping coffee on the verandah, heading
up the hill to the loo, pegging out washing, shovelling up horse
manure, splitting firewood — he'd probably agree.

In reality, I share my mountain with many others, none of whom

15

wear clothes or comment on mine; none of whom have ever invited me to any of their social events, or even to tea, despite helping themselves to my tucker when they please; and none of whom seem to have any awareness of the respect due to me as a superior being by way of my only having two legs when they have four.

They have obviously read the sign on my property gate, 'Wildlife Refuge'. They know that means they take precedence here, but it's supposed to be within reason. They do let me occupy a small fenced-in spot in the middle of these 164 acres. They treat this as we do a cage at the zoo, except that familiarity does indeed breed contempt. They are very involved in their own societies. I am not invited to join; I'm merely an oddity that is tolerated — in my place.

Yet as a writer I must draw on the society around me, and since that is non-human for most of the time, much of what I'm writing gets classed as 'nature writing'. I don't approve of this division into genres by topic. If I write about people as a part of nature, what genre is that?

What I write from my mountain is thus not to do with the dialogues and dialectics of a society primarily concerned about the status of cappuccinos versus café lattes. I'm afraid others more in touch with that world must write about it. My world is unfashionable, timeless and teeming and intensely fascinating. It commands my interest, my passion and my pen.

So far as I am concerned, I am an observer of the world in which I live, just like Jane Austen.

And if most of my neighbours are wallabies, well, better Wallaby World than Wally World. I feel about the latter as people often do about here — it's all right for a visit but I wouldn't want to live there.

However, I wouldn't say no to a few months' writer's residency in one of those romantic places with a village down the road.

CHAPTER 2

GETTING OUT OF JAIL

LURKING BEHIND THE QUESTION of why I live like a hermit amongst the wildlife is a harder one: what caused me to be the sort of woman to answer 'Why not?' as I have? Until I saw from people's reactions that my lifestyle choice was considered quite odd, I hadn't thought much about this. To answer it, I needed to retrace my steps to find where the paths had diverged, where I took the turnings — or was pushed.

The most obvious conscious choice of direction was moving here in early 1979 with my husband, our five-year-old son and three-year-old daughter. But the world we left behind was also relatively odd. In fact, we lived in 'a village down the road' from Newcastle for the ten years before we went bush.

Minmi was an ex-coalmining town stranded in its own past, five miles of winding road and bushland beyond the last suburb. In its heyday, it had been a bustling town of 5000 residents, with fourteen pubs. When we lived there it had 200 people, no shop and only one pub, but the best sort — the local at the heart of the village.

Our home in this village was not your average house either. It would be hard to imagine a more extreme downsizing to a 3 x 4-metre tent than from the grand complex that locals simply called 'the old jail'. Built in the late nineteenth century, it encompassed courthouse, police station, three-cell jail and exercise courtyard, plus the residence, with accommodation for a special constable tacked on later. Not to forget the back-to-back outdoor double toilet — the most imposing proverbial 'brick shithouse' imaginable.

Of sandstock brick and sandstone, our five double chimneys overlooked multiple roofs over multiple wings and entries. Vast semi-circular windows of intricately patterned clear leadlight graced the two big rooms that had respectively served as police station and office, while the courthouse had tall double-hung windows whose lower sashes were multi-paned with rose, amber and green, for privacy. All the official rooms had cedar-panelled ceilings, and even in the residence the rooms had marble fireplaces, cedar doors, rosewood skirting boards and architraves, and tallowwood floors, and each of the many external steps was a single polished grey-slate slab.

Grand.

There was a separate kitchen/dining room building, as was the safety custom in the days of wood-fuelled cooking, linked to the main house by a breezeway. The latter also led to the heavy iron door, complete with spy hatch and massive iron bolt, accessing the jail courtyard, open to the sky except for iron bars, and thence to the cells. These had similar iron doors — creak of rust, clang of finality — no getting out of there.

Atmospheric.

Built in times when Australian rainforest timbers were plentiful and tradesmen were unstinted and unstinting craftsmen, it had my carpenter dad's approval: 'Ah, they don't make 'em like they used to.' It was unrenovated except for a few regrettable efforts by the only previous private owners, like painting over the soft pinks and ambers of much of the external walls.

Our renovations were basic but expensive. We did not touch the courthouse or cells, but the rest was totally rewired, and the floors sanded, polished and sealed. We renovated the bathroom and kitchen — the latter mostly done by Dad, who lived with us for six weeks while he built many cupboards.

A big cost was installing a septic toilet and self-contained drainage system, as there had been none. Until we could turn the old pantry off the breezeway into an indoor toilet, the backyard dunny still had one side in operation under the rather unsavoury pan fill and collect method — although I can't say the new septic's frequent odour of boiled cabbage at the back door proved much more appealing. When the outhouse was partly demolished I saved the kauri full-width seat and lid, and it graces my pit toilet here. It's very smooth, as you'd expect after being polished by more than a century of warm thighs.

However, when I swapped teaching for motherhood, our income was halved, so for our last five years there we were restricted to low-cost, high-labour jobs, like stripping doors and patching and painting the lime-plastered walls. A few pot plants and hanging baskets turned the exercise yard into a pleasantly sunny, protected courtyard, accessible also from the lounge room via an iron-barred door.

I'd had to promise not to get pregnant until we'd repaid the loan for the total purchase amount of $6000 (truly!) and even that loan was only possible through personal string-pulling by my in-laws. In the 1960s a wife's income was not taken into account and women could not borrow. The Pill had arrived, but if bank managers knew about it, they weren't letting on.

We loved living in this semi-rural, anachronistic village. We loved the sense of history, the pub just down the road, the publican and his family, and many of the pub-frequenting villagers. I'd joined the Ladies Darts Team, and so got to know another world of women, vastly different from that for which my convent school and university had prepared me. As the locals gradually educated us into acceptable behaviour, we made friends and had many great post-pub parties in the courthouse. I remain in touch with several of those friends, all of whom have left the village, and with whom those party memories still raise more than a giggle.

So long as you didn't mind everyone thinking it their right to know your business, the reward of village life was that your neighbours cared. For instance, I'd be asked at the pub about the owner of the green Mini that had been parked outside our gate on the weekend. 'Stayed overnight, didn't he? Live far, does he? On his own, wasn't he? Not married, then?' No chance of getting away with any illicit affairs round there.

On the way home from hospital with each of my babies, we had to stop by the pub so the new baby could be passed round the bar, along with the Commonwealth Bank tin money box — a miniature bank building — for the equivalent of the traditional donation of a sovereign 'to give the nipper a start in life'.

I would push the big cane pram, a family heirloom that I'd desecrated by painting bright orange, over the bumpy dirt road for a walk, or to fetch the mail from the post office — there was no mail delivery. As I passed, people would appear at their gates or fences to ask how the baby was doing. Was he over the croup that so-and-so had told them about? And proceed to give me the benefit of their experience with croup or wind or babies in general.

Here I feel obliged also to confess that I painted a beautiful, borrowed, antique cane bassinet and stand with gloss enamel 'Aquarius Green', a rather acidic lime. It was the era of the musical *Hair*, 'the dawning of the age of Aquarius', plus that's my star sign — but neither seems a worthy excuse in retrospect.

Once I'd become a stay-at-home village mum, I started a local playgroup. The large courthouse room was perfect: chipboard panels from the tip attached to the walls for pinning up blank newsprint paper for painting; overflowing boxes of dress-ups from St Vinnies; ice cream containers of violently pink, green or yellow home-made playdough, sparkling with the coarse salt we added on the mistaken theory that then the kids wouldn't eat it; old carpet to protect tender baby knees from the wooden floor, and that didn't object to having the above paint and playdough trodden into it; wooden fruit crates, covered with paper, as tables; an old couch or two for the weary mothers from which to referee the toddlers or feed the latest infant.

It was fun and games interspersed with tiffs and tears. I introduced excursions, which were welcome on the proviso that we were always back in time for some of the mothers' daily hit of the TV soapie *Days of Our Lives*. In the long summer holidays, to give the older kids in the village some activities and stimulation — and the mums a break — I ran craft workshops in the courthouse.

All this interaction meant that from babyhood my children never lacked for playmates, even though we didn't have near neighbours. Their birthday party photos show the wide age range of local children, mainly girls, who liked to visit. They came partly to experience the novelty of differences — of this impressively large and solid house compared to the small, flimsy, and mostly askew miners' cottages in which they lived; and of our lifestyle, with so many books, and original paintings and pottery, a strange world where television did not rule.

Hence when we moved to 'the mountain', my kids swapped a busy social life for each other and the wallabies, just as we did. At least living somewhere without even a corner shop had partly prepared me for bush life, since I'd got into the rhythm of keeping a vegetable garden producing, which is harder than it sounds, and I'd become used to shopping only once a week.

My decade in the old jail was relived over and over again recently as I wrote my first novel, *A Taste for Old*, set in a similar ex-mining village in 1972, when, like Australia's government, it was on the cusp of big changes. 'It's time' ran Labor's winning slogan, but unlike the nation, my village didn't think it was.

In researching its history, I came across a National Trust website for the renovated jail complex when it was last for sale. Much extended, it had become a function and reception centre and restaurant. The playgroup room had become a billiards room — not so different in purpose. As one of its past uses, what I assume was my playgroup was incorrectly described as a crèche, hardly the word to describe our rough DIY set-up. The old place now looks very posh, more redolent of renovation than of history, and has clearly had much more capital sunk into it than we ever could have, or would have wanted to.

The hollows worn into the slate steps of the old jail had meant more to me than the grand cedar ceilings, because they held a greater sense of history. The building as I knew it was intriguing, mysterious — far more than just a house — and the village was similarly imbued with layers of past lives and events that triggered my imagination. Had we stayed long enough in the jail we'd have ended up with a showpiece, an impressive and historic home, worth a lot of money. So what? It wasn't a lifestyle destination I wanted — renovating for years, then showing it off, lunches and dinner parties — all that seemed shallow. Aldermen were threatening imminent 'progress', housing developments all the way from that last suburb to our village. Houses on the hill overlooking us? Neighbours just over the fence? Our village turned into a suburb? No thanks.

Although we'd planted over a hundred trees on our large block in the middle of bare paddocks, they would not give real privacy. Also seeking more space, and a greater connection to land than our garden could offer, we bought 100 acres near Merriwa. We camped on it in our new Kombi van every second weekend. Despite spending most of our time collecting and burning prickly pear and trying to stop the kids disappearing down wombat burrows, we loved it.

Soon we wanted to reverse the time balance, to be living like that for five days a week and going out to earn money two days. As we'd never risen above student levels of consumerism, nor had any desire to, there was no need for a big income.

Fascinating as I found that Merriwa block's sandstone ridge vegetation, its flowering small-leaved shrubs, its ironbark and wattle trees, its lichen-encrusted rocks and its sandy wombat world, I knew it was too dry for me to be happy living on it full-time. Although my childhood's Sunday-night-only baths had been due to lack of tanks that didn't leak rather than lack of rainfall, I never wanted to return to such water restrictions if I could help it.

We started looking elsewhere, but too often the block on offer was a fenced-in island of degraded land with perhaps one rocky patch of remnant bush, and surrounded by other similar blocks. Rural residential jails. My privacy envelope had expanded and I needed real bush around me that I could walk through unhindered. Eventually we found this mountain, much more remote than we'd intended, but by then we knew how hard it was to find anything so natural closer to civilisation. And it had high rainfall.

Both the old jail and my mountain have links to the past and a strong sense of place. I can't imagine living in a place devoid of these qualities, scalped and sanitised free of them, such as a new project home in a new subdivision, no matter how well landscaped, no matter how great the facilities. There would be such a separation from reality as I understand it that I'd feel as if I was constantly short of something vital, like air.

Conversely, I often wonder how people used only to such lives would cope should they be suddenly placed in the position of what millions around the world know as normal, with a sheet of tin, one pot, one spoon and a ragged blanket as 'Home and Contents'.

I imagine that for a day or two they'd behave well, as if they were on a reality TV show, but when no one called 'Cut!' as their nails chipped, their hair grew greasier, the loved one began to smell like a human animal instead of deodorant, and meals became minimal fuel for the energy to find food and water the next day, rather than an occasion for display … what then?

Somewhere in between the riches and the rags is a sustainable way of living that we need to adopt if our grandchildren are not to find themselves without a choice in the matter. That requires urgent attention to global warming, yet what we hear from our major politicians is still as irrelevant as the hollow 'pock!' of their party ping-pong.

Unbiased scientists worldwide have been calling for immediate action, but only a few enlightened governments are acting. The UK is way ahead of us — *and* it signed the Kyoto Protocol, the international agreement to reduce greenhouse gases. Major polluter, the US, did not. Nor did follow-the-leader Australia, shamefully the world's highest per capita greenhouse gas emitter. While a small contributor in the global perspective, it all adds up.

A global problem requires a global solution, as the UK Stern Report, released in October 2006, pointed out. It put the cost of ignoring climate change in economic terms, which is a language the US and Australian governments will at least listen to. They have both reckoned there's no point in signing Kyoto if the developing polluters, China and India, don't — but why *would* they sign, and act, if the big boys don't? To me it sounds much like the US stance on nuclear weapons: 'Do as we say, not as we do.'

Here, after years of denial, our federal government suddenly changed its tune in late 2006. As water restrictions bit deeper, and unseasonal snow followed unseasonal bushfires, and after millions of dollars of agricultural drought relief had to be announced, it became politically correct to admit the existence of climate change. With a federal election looming in 2007, the token mumblings and token fundings began — but did not extend to a national target for greenhouse gas emissions or penalties for the polluters, to putting a price on carbon.

Hats off to Arnold Schwarzenegger for leading California to major cuts in greenhouse emissions, for disregarding his president's head-in-the-sand policy. Other US states are following. Here, South Australia is taking genuine steps — its premier called climate change 'a bigger threat than terrorism' in 2005. But for the overwhelming majority of politicians the issue is driven by the polls rather than a sense of urgency, with no one in power standing up to say, 'Hey, Rome *is* burning! Let's quit fiddling NOW!'

They're still debating what would be the most popular tune to play next.

They're still putting profit before the planet and its people, tinkering at the edges of the problem while trying not to inconvenience Big Business.

After all, they don't want to be accused of being greenies. 'Sorry, kids,' ancient ex-pollies might say to future generations scrabbling for food in a dried-up and drowning world, 'we were too busy with Economic Progress to stop climate chaos.'

Yeah, right. I wonder if they'll hold tribunals for crimes against the human race, against the planet?

My dad found it hard to understand us giving up our 'riches' stage of that grand house for a second-hand tent, especially when we weren't even going to run cattle on the land we'd bought instead. What else was grass for? When he saw this place, he reckoned it'd be quite a good block — if we cleared most of the trees.

Attitudes to land aside, Dad influenced several major directions in my life. When I was seven he moved my mother, my twelve-year-old sister and me from the house he'd built in the fibro heaven of Rydalmere, a western Sydney suburb so new in the 1950s that we'd kept a milking cow in the paddock next door. From then until I left to go to university at sixteen, home was a 10-acre orange orchard and market garden, at Erina, near Gosford.

The saying, 'You can take the girl out of the western suburbs but you can't take the western suburbs out of the girl', could be true, since my older sister did not transplant well, and moved back as soon as she left school at fifteen. My voice usually betrays my working-class westie origins — no one would accuse me of sounding posh, of being from Potts Point or Pymble. The move put the country into my soul for good. Dad got me out of the suburban jail first.

My parents were poor when I was growing up. It was the norm to look in the shed first for bits and pieces that might be cobbled together to fix anything that was broken, from a saucepan to the tractor. Going to town to buy a new part or new item was the last resort. We were taught to make do instead of making demands, to recycle and repair. With hindsight, that was sustainability in practice, and I've never lived otherwise since.

Mum had only reluctantly agreed to move to the farm to keep Dad out of the pub, a standard Aussie blue-collar male's after-work habit, but one that had been a major source of argument. They must have got along better for a brief time, because within three years I had two new sisters. But the farm was a financial failure and Dad was forced to restrict it to weekends, and return to carpentry. And to the pub after work — where he got his contacts, he said. The arguments resumed.

Since he was never hard enough to be a businessman, hated asking for money owed, Dad would take a case of peaches in lieu of payment. That sort of thing would drive my mother, struggling to find money for basics, into a fury. It wasn't easy for them to keep me on at school for an extra two years so I could win a scholarship and go to university. This was a first in our family. How and why I was different — a bookworm — I don't know, but I was finally allowed to be so, which in those days was not an assumed right. The thought of having to do 'Commercial' and be a secretary was a fate worse than death to me.

I do remember making a statement of choice about being different in one way, when I was fourteen. Having given up hope of myself as ugly duckling ever being transformed into beauty, one Saturday morning I bought a pair of thick stockings, multi-coloured, zig-zag patterned. They were eye-catching, to say the least. This was 1962, when teenagers hadn't long been invented, and rebellion as an intrinsic part of that stage was hard to put into action in a small town, especially for a convent girl. And Gosford *was* small then.

The stockings weren't blue, but they were about as far out as I could go to proclaiming myself an intellectual instead of the only two local options: a surfer chick — peroxide blonde, tanned, bikini, boobs, bad boyfriends, sex — for which I wasn't qualified; or a nice girl — short perm, twin-set, sensible skirt, fortress step-ins, armoured bra, nice boyfriend, no sex, so early marriage — for which I wasn't inclined.

I can see those stockings now, and me eagerly trying them on my stick-like legs as soon as we got home from town. Dad took one look, chuckled, and said, 'I'm afraid they don't do you any favours, love. You'd look nicer in ordinary ones.'

'I don't care,' I replied, in full teenage angst, 'if I can't be beautiful, I'm at least going to be noticed. I don't *want* to be ordinary!'

Perhaps I was heading down this path to oddity because I spent much time on my own, as my schoolfriends lived in town. My companions had been the books I devoured, like the C.S. Lewis *Narnia* series, since I'd discovered Gosford library at age nine. But my heroine lived in the only books my family owned and thus the only ones I could re-read. These were four age-mottled and tattered titles from the *Anne of Green Gables* series, by L.M. Montgomery, 1920s and '30s editions, having belonged to an aunt of my mother's. Anne related to nature in an excessively romantic way, she wrote stories, she was neither beautiful nor ordinary, and she had an attic bedroom. I'm still hoping for the attic bedroom, but for the rest … she made me.

By the time I got to university, a little frog in funny stockings didn't make much of a splash in that bigger pond. Newcastle Uni then was very industrially focused, and there was only one small subpond to which I was attracted, the Arty one, where the girls had long hair like Joan Baez, the men had beards and shorter, but never short, hair — like Oscar Wilde, or Mick Jagger — and they all wore corduroy, wrote poetry, debated philosophy, listened equally knowingly to Bach or Bob Dylan, and drank flagon red wine, lots of it. There were strange rules, unwritten and unspoken, and many of the girls were beautiful *and* intellectual. How to win here?

I never worked that out in time, and the attempts were painful. I took refuge in marriage between university and my Diploma of Education year, partly so I wouldn't be sent off, alone, to the country to teach. Our group dismissed marriage as a piece of paper that could always be ripped up if it didn't work out. No big deal. If only I'd had more courage …

Many of the choices I've made seem to have been unconsciously influenced by that early desire not to be ordinary. I always wanted to leave more than a record of a mundane, even if well done, daily routine. At ten, I used to agonise only over whether it would be as an artist, an author or a ballerina. In some ways I'm writing this book to show that it is possible to belatedly clamber back onto the path to fulfilling dreams.

Was my desire not to be ordinary just the unrealistic ambition of an egotistical malcontent? Or the striving for meaning in life by a creative but undisciplined mind? Naturally I'll choose the latter. Others apparently know the answer, for they nod sagely, 'Ah, an Aquarian — that explains it.'

On my 49th birthday I vowed to take action to regain that creative path, so as to be able to greet 50 with pride and pleasure. By then I knew that life did not usually drop gifts into the laps of we poor sods, no matter how talented. Success, happiness — they all have to be worked for. Even then we might miss out, but the trying brings unforeseen benefits.

Firstly, I would get serious about writing. I did not want writing to be just another 'if only' at the end of my life. I'd been dabbling with short stories for too long. I would start treating them as work, getting them up to scratch and sending them out to competitions. Only when they were acknowledged as top standard would I try to get them published. I had my first major win two years later.

Secondly, I would stop dyeing my hair, whose Scottish black had begun greying too soon, after the insanity of my marriage break-up.

When I did, there were unexpected side effects, like suddenly becoming invisible as a female. No more wolf whistles. I'd have cherished those last two uncouthly shrilled syllables if I'd known; I might even have taken a bow.

So by 50 I was ready for the perception of my older age by others, which mattered less and less because I was writing often enough to know I *was* a writer, so I was excited at the years ahead of plunging into that addictive world. The next 50 years, I told myself, re-polishing the thought that Elizabeth Jolley wasn't published until her fifties.

Now I learn that she only got about half her 'next 50 years'. My heart hurts whenever I think of her in a nursing home, suffering from Alzheimer's. All those lost lovely words.

It reinforces my resolve to stay on the path, and it reinforces the message I learnt in September 2002, to maximise 'now'. For if Dad's lifestyle choice made me a bushie instead of a westie, his death made me a hermit.

CHAPTER 3

CLOSE TO THE ELEMENTS

HERMITS OFTEN HIDE OUT on mountains, but I have a particular excuse. My Munro ancestors came from the edge of the Scottish highlands, so it's in my blood to find valleys rather claustrophobic.

My mountain is about 1000 metres in altitude. In recent years I have discovered that the Scots call any mountain over 3000 feet (914.4 metres) a 'Munro', as apparently a Munro first listed such peaks in Scotland, and people who climb them are called 'Munro baggers'.

Perhaps this also explains why I'm so self-critical — a perpetual bagger of this Munro?

The mountains I face are over 1500 metres. These ranges being so high, we catch a lot of rain. In the 1970s we were told that around 1500 millimetres was the annual average, but an average can allow for great extremes. Our little family had moved here permanently in January 1979, having spent the previous six months visiting, checking out the best sites, noting sun angles and prevailing winds, testing soil. We'd arrived in our overladen Kombi, towing an overladen trailer. Unbeknownst to us the mountains had received about 100 millimetres of rain in a deluge the night before.

We slipped and fishtailed on the dirt road, just made it over the last flooded creek crossing, got bogged and were towed out twice, then were finally trounced by the last steep rise before our gate. Abandoning the trailer, we slid the Kombi back down the hill, took a mighty run-up, and managed to get up the hill and inside the gate. There we left it, since our own track was newly bulldozed, and of soft and treacherous clay.

In the drizzle and near dark we stumbled down the track carrying a few essentials. Although we kept telling the kids that this was an adventure, we felt plain miserable. The tent had been erected on a previous trip, so we made a cold dinner and crawled into our beds. At least the tent didn't leak, but it was not an auspicious start to our new life.

We had to wait two days for the rain to ease enough for us to ferry our gear down, a laborious operation that took another two days. The wheelbarrow, laden to three times its height, was very handy for this. However, to get it over the uneven track and up the inclines, my husband had to run at them, so care of the contents was not his priority. On one load, when we took off the plastic covering, the entire barrowful appeared to be coated in peanut butter, until we worked out that my big glass jar of flour had broken, as had a large bottle of soy sauce above it.

Later that year it became drier than we could have imagined, although the spring in the gully near our camp kept up its small flow from somewhere deep underground, unaffected by surface drought. Yet despite the extremes dealt by the elements, that first year here, living mainly outdoors, remains the happiest of my life.

About seven years ago I found my diary from that year — the only year I have not either stumbled to a halt by March or missed many days. As I'd used a blank page book, I wasn't restricted in how much I wrote each day, although the entries got shorter and the handwriting more illegible as the year went on.

Re-reading it, I am astonished at our pioneering energy — digging trenches for the house and for laying water pipes, carting rocks for foundations, making mudbricks, erecting fences, digging around and under and burning out huge old stumps, turning a tussocky paddock into a garden, planting vegetables and herbs, fruit and nut trees — and still I was enjoying cooking and teaching the kids, and getting to know my new world.

We may have had our feet in the dust but we remained civilised; we ate and drank well, and never missed reading to the kids at night. Here's a diary sample, from my 31st birthday evening:

> *Made dough for bread tomorrow. Had ratatouille (after* Dr Dolittle). *Clouds over far mountains amazing while heavy mist in valley below like a river. Now (9.30) in dense cloud here. Played Respighi cassette tonight as birthday treat — and Mildara Chardonnay Champagne (quite a strong taste).*

Playing the tape was a treat because it used up the batteries far more quickly than the radio did — and we needed our daily dose of ABC radio. Later we would get smarter, and clip a lead onto the car battery.

For dining, under the spreading arms of a white mahogany tree we had set up a card table and canvas director's chairs, with holes dug in the ground for the uphill chair legs so diners didn't roll down the slope when eating, as several unwary visitors had done. As they were a little tipsy at the time, they rolled easily and didn't hurt themselves, although the sight was so funny that the sides of the callous and equally tipsy spectators ached for some time.

Our chosen clearing had appeared to be a gentle slope but actually was relentlessly unflat, as each small area that needed to be level soon proved. Everywhere involved walking uphill, to or from, and we got very fit, especially carrying buckets of water up the steep incline from the spring. That was excellent for deportment too; only my straightest back would keep the buckets from bumping into the slope ahead and spilling.

My cooktop was an old fridge rack balanced on four rocks, my cooking equipment was disposal store cast iron — camp oven, frying pan and saucepan — and one heavy aluminium soup pot. (I know, I know, it's toxic — I don't use any aluminium now!) From our Merriwa camping weekends I'd developed quite a collection of recipes for one-pot or one-pan dishes. For those weekends I used to cheat a little to compensate for the absence of bench space, like making the dough and rolling the balls for chapatis at home, in which form they'd happily sit until I was ready to flatten them and cook over the fire to accompany the Saturday night curry. Now I had the luxury of the card table as a bench.

The camp oven, buried in hot ashes and coals, worked well, but I could only bake one thing at a time in it. We bought a rusty fuel stove for $10 and set it up close to the big tree above the 'kitchen'.

The first time I used it I wrote:

Took a long time for oven to heat up but finally cooked pitta, pumpkin pie and two veg. strudels in it. Flue melted its joins and blew off.

Here's another baking morning.

Lit fuel stove — baked cookies first, then two loaves bread, then prune loaf, then Rieska [quick rye bread for lunch]. Used top to warm yoghurt, de-candy honey, cook chickpeas, etc. All done by 12.30. We got sand and rocks for last trench. Finished that by evening.

Was that me, that so-organised, energetic young woman? Where did she go?

In this primitive kitchen I was making soft cheese and yoghurt, since I could buy unpasteurised milk from the dairy about three-quarters of an hour's drive away, where the tar road started. The top of the $12 kerosene refrigerator, near its rear vent, proved to be an ideal warm spot for yoghurt to 'clabber' or bread to rise. Although eating meat didn't bother my family, cooking it bothered me, and they were happy to eat only vegetarian food at home — it was also much easier to keep fresh safely.

After 32 years I am still a vegetarian; and that flower-painted kero fridge now sits on my verandah, to be pressed into back-up service when I have visitors, like my son, who like their beer colder than I run my small 24-volt fridge. Unfortunately all the dairies are gone, as in the 1980s a large state dam drowned the main valley through which we used to drive from town.

We had thought hard about whether we should have a milking cow and keep poultry, to be really self-sufficient. But we decided against 'farming' animals, mainly due to my dilemma about the unwanted male calves or chickens that would inevitably be produced. To give them away would have been sending them to the axe en route to oven and dinner table — second-hand guilt, first-hand responsibility. No.

On the very first night that my husband stayed in Newcastle for work, I had a sense of adventure, being alone in the bush, but wasn't at all scared. I read the kids to sleep in their double-decker stretcher, then sat out by the fire for a while, listening to the night noises. Feeling tired, I went in and made up the 'double bed' on the old carpet with which we'd covered the tent's plastic floor. This process was simple enough: a double sleeping bag laid over two side-by-side single foam mattresses that were stacked up during the day as a 'lounge', to make walking space beside the kids' bed, as the tent was very small. I fell asleep peacefully.

I was awoken by the most fearsome, fierce, ferocious, frightening noise I had ever heard in real life. It seemed to be inches from my ear, just the other side of the fragile canvas wall. I knew there were no savage man-eating animals in the Australian bush, no bears, no tigers, and yet to my movie-fed brain the sound was as if both of those had bred with a rabid dog to produce this offspring. Such a noise had to be accompanied by bared, sharp teeth. One slash of a claw and my children and I would be exposed to this monster of the night!

Well and truly scared now, but acting the grown-up, I grabbed the torch and rushed to unzip the tent door to the tiny annexe of mosquito netting, where we had stored tools and the kero fridge. Here I seized a hammer on my way to unzip the outer netting door. (Note: circular zips are not a quick or silent way to get out or in or to surprise an intruder.)

The noise had stopped long before I emerged into the darkness; the torch beam revealed nothing but the gum tree, looming, and the canvas shower bag, swinging. I zipped my way back to bed and lay in trepidation until nearly dawn. The kids woke me shortly after.

Later that day I lit the fire and boiled the billies for the kids' shower. We had four billies made from large ex-Golden Circle pineapple juice tins, with fencing-wire handles. From a fairly horizontal branch of the grey gum beside the tent we'd erected a pulley system for the shower bag, which had a luxuriously adjustable copper rose. Four thin poles supported a hessian modesty panel that still allowed great views to the far mountains, and bush rocks prevented muddy feet.

I let down the bag to fill it — a bucket of cold water and two billies of hot water gave a surprisingly long and satisfying shower. I tipped it up to empty out any leaves first. Instead, a handful of black pellets fell to the rock floor.

At that stage I was unfamiliar with the various calling cards of my neighbours, so I couldn't say who'd left these. Next night, and most nights afterwards, the night monster came to loudly mark its territory, wake us up, walk along the branch of the grey gum, shit in the shower bag, and depart. 'Take that, you ignorant upstarts, you intruders, you!'

On his return, my husband, who'd grown up in a leafy suburb, had known the noise immediately and had laughed at my terrified descriptions. It was 'only' a possum. Perhaps because we'd had a dog and no trees near the house on the farm where I grew up, I'd never heard one.

After a short time of our tent living, the night monster possum began including us on his route earlier in the evening, so he too could sample the dinner. Any dish placed on the ground or on the washing-up stand would be lumbered up to with his full-nappy gait, inspected, and usually cleaned up. Rice was very popular. No matter if the dish happened to be beside our feet; we were of no importance. We didn't mind because he then ceased to wake us in the middle of the night, and no longer felt the need to mark his territory in our shower bag.

The unpredictable weather often caused us access problems until we got a four-wheel-drive vehicle. Being an ex-teacher (Secondary and Infants) I'd been classed as a registered 'school', and on the two days when my husband was away I taught my son. Because we felt it important that he mixed with other children, he went to the nearest school three days a week.

That meant leaving here at 6.45 a.m. to make it to the school bus, which turned round near the dairy, at the end of its run. The bus would then take him to the one-teacher school 27 kilometres away. Getting to the bus on time was difficult in winter, when the day began and ended in the dark. The night before, I would boil the billies and fill a large thermos or two with hot water. This was enough for a civilised start, providing a warm wash and warm Weetbix.

It was understood that if my son didn't show up we were probably rained in. My daughter started the next year, and both my kids loved that little school. The teacher was young and friendly and funny; his wife, a teacher in town, was a delight. We became friends with them — I still am. He reckoned that my kids' enrolment meant they finally had enough pupils to form a cricket team. He also tells the possibly apocryphal yarn of how the school's rural area was then so quiet that a car passing was such a big event that the kids would stop a cricket game to watch!

In the May of that year we were truly rained in. My entries complain of the tent starting to leak at the seams, of difficulties lighting the fire, of me holding an umbrella over my husband while he tried. We had a gas lamp and bottle, so why on earth hadn't we bought a gas ring?

By the third day of nonstop rain I wrote:

Awoke to feel the carpet risen on a bed of water under the tent floor. Colder today. Bread low, no biscuits left (plain) — very little cake — so lit fuel stove (with kero) and baked soda bread, wheat biscuits, Anzac slice, bran muffins and cooked a curry. Once going, easier than the fire. Drains all full and flowing. Not game to look in toy tent. Kids fractious for the first time.

No doubt I did all that cooking under an umbrella too.
Two days later I wrote:

Five days and nights is a bit much!

That weekend the teacher turned up on his trailbike, bearing brandy like a good St Bernard, to check on us.

We were starting to have setbacks from more than the weather as the realities of our bush idyll sank in. A few days after the sun finally came out again I wrote:

Find it hard to believe we only have this many bricks (608). Seem
to have been at it for ages. Also the bloody possum last week ate
all capsicums! Also hearts of cabbages nearly ready. It took him
ages to discover them but he made a mess then.

We had netted the perimeter of the vegetable garden to 1.8 metres but hadn't worried about putting netting over the top against climbing critters. We didn't think we had to, as the possum had left it alone for months — until the vegetables were worth his trouble. But there was worse to come. In August:

Near dark when got home — about 7 — discovered that cows had
walked our garden fence down (netting) and eaten every scrap of veg. and
seedling and trampled all new seed beds, new rhubarb crowns etc.
Completely bare so suddenly! Fence on N-E boundary very important
now — like a lot of other things round here. Very depressing.

The cattle belonged to the original owner, who'd never needed fences since he'd owned the whole area, and he didn't see why he should start fencing the cattle in just because he'd sold some of his land. They wandered far and wide and many had been doing so for years; our intruders were, in effect, wild. Whenever I saw them anywhere near our clearing I would race towards them yelling like a banshee, waving and throwing sticks at them. How I didn't break a leg in my frenzied runs across the rough ground I don't know, but our territory had to be claimed — and reclaimed.

We were told that to keep cattle out, a fence needed to be of barbed wire. As we were due to go away on holidays, that partial boundary fence had to be finished first. In cold rain, with scratched and sore fingers, leeches in our boots and water down our necks, we worked to get it done. It was extremely unpleasant — as far from idyllic as possible. On the last day, I left my poor husband to run out the final roll of wire while I went to pack.

Barbed wire rolled on him and cut his hand; he fell in the nettles
— very steep gully; hard work. We chased cows out.

As the year edged on, the little cabin grew walls and the tent grew holes, but by November we had forgotten what wet days were like. The country had dried out terribly and storms were bringing wild winds and lightning — and fires further along our ridge.

Our big double dam, with its island in the middle, was finished, and filling, ready for us to pump up to our new cement tanks on the ridge above us, but we hadn't yet laid the pipes, as the pipeline routes were rockily off-putting.

To raise the alarm about the fires, we drove down to the dairy and rang the Forestry Commission for help, since they were our main neighbour. They came. No fire trucks or tankers for us then, just manpower with wet hessian bags, or rake hoes and backpacks if the Forestry had spares. Their back-burning measures took out 50 per cent of our property and the fires were still not completely extinguished everywhere. We hoped we were safe.

Yet the very next week they flared up again.

*Fires surrounding us by noon — burning all along previously
burnt edge below fruit trees and above and beside our camp.
Ranger called in to check all OK. Will return to fell a burning
dead tree later. Very smoky. Hard to see what is happening.*

Just in case, I placed a big tub of water in the middle of our
ploughed area in the wide clearing, for the kids and I to hop into, with
a blanket kept soaking there ready to put over our heads.

More storms brought a little rain:

Ceased to worry about the fires except for the trees alight — rather dangerous.

Violent electrical storms continued into December, but at least we
now had the pipes connected and water on tap, with great pressure
from the downhill gravity feed. We were preparing for Christmas. The
weather was 'extremely windy and dusty — unpleasant'.

Then the smouldering embers inside the old logs in the forest were
blown into new life. The Forestry men were called back up and, along
with the two only other locals and my husband, they battled the fires
for the next six days. Nobody had Christmas that year.

20 December:

*They fought all day but wind very fierce and gusty. By evening
huge willy-willies of flame leaping through trees.*

My husband was off early each day with the men, fighting fires to
the back of us. My daughter was unwell.

22 December:

By 4 pm he hadn't come home for lunch even. Spotted new fire in valley below (in front of us); tried to walk to find men to tell of other fire — too far to push her in stroller so came back home.

A local arrived en route to save his house in that valley and said both valleys were ablaze.

Huge brown cloud of smoke from there — whole valley full of dense smoke. My husband came home briefly with an injured possum to be nursed, singed, etc. ... didn't return until about 10.30 — very tired.

23 December:

Wind getting up from the west — worst for us. I watered garden and got heavy-duty hose up ready to spray tent. Possum took off in the night so must be OK. Had drunk a lot of water. Fire racing up valley again. Still burning below us — I keep checking it — wind on edge is fierce — would be a bad one if it was whipped up that slope.

Bulldozer sent in to make trail; fire crossed it, also the creek, their (valley) road and the top road. Kids gone with M. [my friend from that valley, who took all our kids to town] as safer. I will stay to keep an eye on our block. Many big trees over track — burning as well — had to detour several times off track. Many confused wallabies jumping from one burning side of track to the other – so bad for them. Also no feed at all between this fire and the last, as no rain since then so no green growth even yet.

Even previously burnt bits blazing away. They have apparently
called in the Army and the Civil Defence to help. Other fires
about to join up with this one — a real disaster.

But it had only been declared so when the fires were threatening pastoral country. Proper properties.

After that experience I started our local fire brigade. We would not be so helpless next time.

It was six weeks before any green showed in the stark black-and-white landscape of all the ridges and valleys we could see. Then it was bracken, no use to the animals. The fires had crowned all through the forests, so many baby animals and birds were incinerated, tragedies revealed when the big old hollow trees fell. Sometimes there were orphans, like a baby pygmy possum, that we tried unsuccessfully to save. And for months after there were sporadic mighty crashes echoing over the ridges as burnt-out trees gave way.

It would be 22 years before we had another such major and unstoppable fire.

Reliving that first fire through my diary has made me realise that one reason why I am so close to my place, my country, is that we have been through so much together. Writer and scholar Nonie Sharpe says indigenous people believe country is sentient; northern coastal people told her that new people must become known by country, must mingle their sweat with its water, so they become bonded to country. Fire can do this too.

My diary stopped at the stage when our cabin roof was about to be put on. There were still many gaps, such as gables and windows, but the mouldy, wind-battered tent was leaking so badly that we had to dismantle it and re-erect it in the house for a little while. As the cabin was finished and more functions moved indoors, I recall very vividly my sense of loss.

The fuel stove was installed inside, so no more outdoor cooking. I'd been used to washing up in a dish on a tin stand, outdoors; now, as I stood at a sink with at least cold running water, indoors, I felt trapped, deprived. I kept looking out the window — what was going on outside? Were the thornbills feeding past here yet?

I was cut off from my world, and I didn't like it.

CHAPTER 4

AN INTRODUCTION TO SOCIETY

I SHOULDN'T HAVE COMPLAINED about my over-civilised sink, for I was soon to be cut off from the natural world in a far more drastic way. The ensuing thirteen years of exile in Sydney were not happy ones. But reliving the bad times can wait a little longer; I'll approach them from the blessed position of my daily life now, back here, alone, and as contented as I have it in my nature to be.

That daily life is shaped and coloured more by the world around me than by my own solitary doings, which, apart from my writing, are not all that exciting. For example, it's a big event when the cake of soap in the shower is at long last almost finished and I can choose a new one. Don't laugh — it's important. Will I really feel like sandalwood for a whole month, or would green apple be wiser?

All the activity is generated by my local society, a wild bunch, even harder to get to know and be accepted by than our jail's villagers. It's taken years, but I'm gradually learning how to get my own way, almost, without doing them any harm. Civilised conservation, I call it, or having your cake and eating it too — before the wallabies do. And if there are disputes they usually win, having the majority.

I'd like to introduce some of them. The most noticeable group, because the most populous, are the Red-necked Wallabies. As I said, it's Wallaby World, and by Miss Austen's social code, theirs would be considered a very middle-class one.

When I first lived here, there was no house fence to separate us from the locals, and there was already a wallaby in residence in the large clearing in which we chose to build. She had absolutely no fear of us or our vehicle; we were as irrelevant to her as to the possum.

No matter what we were up to or how close our actions brought us to her, she did not shy, merely interrupted her grazing for a brief instant to look. This was her patch. If we wanted a share tenancy on it, that seemed to be fine with her. She would often sleep during the day between two large stringy-barks, right next to where we'd erected the kids' play tent. Even the noise and erratic movements of a three- and five-year-old at play did not cause her to do more than flick an ear in their direction. I hadn't realised until then that their ears turn like individual periscopes.

Wanting to preserve such innocence, such lack of fear, we applied for our block to become a dedicated wildlife refuge. I thought the sign might deter shooters up from town for a 'bush bash', not to mention staghorn and orchid thieves, and it would at least tell dog and cat owners that their pets were only welcome here if under control.

Only much later did I understand that this 'innocence' is actually arrogance.

It was a strange feeling to be building where no others had. Pioneering, yes, but also intrusive, as it was clear to us that the wallaby and the possum had prior claims on this specific spot. As no doubt did others less visible to us. We thought we adapted to each other well, but everything we did had an effect; and later, as we fenced to protect our gardens, we also fenced them out from part of their regular beat. It didn't seem much to ask of them to relinquish, but since we couldn't actually ask, we simply imposed what we wanted. These days I feel less sure about the morality of takeovers and invasions of any type or degree. Going soft — or getting wise?

Since I've become the sole human resident it's quieter on my side of the house fence, so I hear more and, without the distraction of human company, I see more. The wallabies have always known their place here. It was me who was confused. All these years they've patiently waited for me to muddle about, and fail, in my ignorance of how everything must work together here. But they've finally got the message through to me — wallabies rule.

As they graze all around this clearing, even from my house I see a great deal of their social and family affairs being carried on right under my nose. If I look up from the computer, through the window in front of me I can see quite a lot of wild 'street life'.

Sometimes I feel as much a voyeur as my maternal grandmother, my Nanna, who lived in the same rented semi-detached house in a main street of Muswellbrook for 40 years. In old age, having broken her leg and needing to walk with a stick henceforward, she was too proud to be seen 'hobbling about like an old crock', and no longer went out. So she would sit behind the lace curtains of her front room and watch the world pass by on the footpath a few feet away beyond the fishbone fern 'garden'. Surprising what she found out this way: who was pregnant (again!), who was drunk last night coming home from the pub, who was looking poorly, who was getting too big for his boots, who had the nerve to show her face in public, who was going to the dogs, who had walked past with her nose in the air but was no better than she should be … !

I will try to be less judgemental, although I am quite as fascinated by the goings-on.

The Mothers' Club members meet on a north-facing grassy slope just outside my fence. In the morning sessions they sunbake without a care for danger or dignity, their legs sprawled apart, leaning back on their tails to expose their pale furry tummies to the warmth of the early sun. In the hotter afternoon sessions they take to the shade of the edging trees, stretch out wearily, lolling sideways in languid odalisque poses, yet with heads erect to keep an eye on their restless young who catapult about like overwound clockwork toys.

These toddler joeys are always on the verge of overbalancing, so fast do they bound and so inexpertly do they wield their disproportionately long tails. In mad circles, they race into clumps of bracken, disappear, then spring out again like jack-in-the-boxes further along. Definitely ADHD.

As any mother will tell you, life's a lot easier before the kids become mobile. As the pouch-bound joey grows, it's not unusual to see mother and joey eating in tandem, the big-eyed baby 'practice grazing' on what it can reach from the safety of the pouch as the mother slowly levers her way across the grass. If she stops and sits erect to check me out, the baby might withdraw until all I can see poking out are its black nose and eyes, ears hidden inside the furry parka hood of its mother's pouch.

Bigger joeys, spending more and more time out of the pouch, each try their mother's patience by interrupting her grazing to demand a drink of milk. When she decides that the guzzler has had enough, she pushes it aside and resumes grazing. At other times I see a mother holding her wriggling joey still with one dainty black paw while searching for fleas in the soft baby fur with the other. The joey cringes exactly like a child does when you want to wipe its face or comb its hair. 'Aw, Mu-um!'

When the alarm goes up for the group to take flight, which they do in a very helter-skelter, every-wallaby-for-itself kind of way, these toddlers often rush to get back into the safety of their respective pouches, but it's a terrible headfirst scramble and squeeze, and usually the mother takes off with a tangle of tail and long black feet and paws still hanging out. Or else the joey doesn't notice her leaving, and when it suddenly becomes aware that it's alone, goes hurtling off in any direction. Pure panic — just like any three-year-old in a department store who looks around and can't see Mum.

As they're allowed to remain in the pouch for about ten months, they're quite big by the time the mothers evict them. Only then will the females give birth to the babies they had waiting in the wings, so to speak. Even with new ones in the pouch, they still suckle the expelled older joeys until they are well over a year old. New and old joey have a special teat each, from which they receive custom-designed milk. How clever is that? Once a joey is weaned, it's about ready to start its own breeding cycle. When they do, such new mothers seem too small, are hardly much bigger than their growing offspring.

The young males front up to each other with typical teenage bluff and bravado. They 'have a go', play at boxing, cuffing each other over the head. As they still can't balance on their tails, which they need to do if they want to use their big back legs to kick forward like the grown-ups do, they're always falling over, looking foolish rather than impressive. I laugh, although I do feel for the oft-wounded vanity of adolescence.

But worse lies ahead for these young bucks.

The begetting of wallaby babies is preceded by a most elaborate and apparently difficult courtship. A peculiar hoarse grunting noise signals that an approach is being made by one of the males. I look up and invariably see the female object of desire patiently moving forward, attempting to keep grazing, while the would-be lover keeps hopping to get in front of her, trying to halt her progress, to make her notice him.

He rubs his face and neck against hers if she'll let him, and leans under her to sniff if she's on heat. But mostly it seems to be just a long, slow, fruitless procession across the paddock — her ignoring him, levering along on her hind legs and tail; him levering along behind, grunting away ineffectually, his little penis hopefully at the ready, pink and pointed, curved like a new moon.

I've never seen a female do anything but reject these advances, so perhaps the fellows are poor judges of when she's ready, but they must succeed sometimes, as there are always lots of joeys about. And it would appear that she has to be willing. Perhaps she gives in well out of my sight, but I'd be surprised if she bothered to hide from me since I don't rate much higher than a fencepost with this lot.

The most memorable courtship was heralded by violent crashing through the bush, and constant grunting, sounding more like wild pigs than wallabies. Going closer to the fence to see what all the commotion was about, I saw one female flying from the very pressing advances of a big male, with five other young blades also in hot pursuit! Someone, presumably the dominant male, was grunting very loudly and vehemently.

She must have been on heat to attract such a crowd of panting males, all jostling to get close to her. Their tender crescent dicks were all exposed, their balls on strings hanging low — so vulnerable, I thought, given the blady grass and tussocks and fences they were belting through.

The main suitor was having a harrowing time, as not only was he trying to persuade her, but whenever he managed to get her to stop and listen for a minute, the other blokes would sidle closer and he'd have to keep one eye on their movements, making little rushes at them to hunt them off, coughing warningly at them, but never succeeding in getting them to keep their distance for long.

Then suddenly she'd make a break for it and they'd all follow, over the dam wall, round the side and through the edging bush again, cracking fallen branches and skimming through fences, clearing the tussocks in desperate bounds, she saying 'No!' all the while, emerging once more onto the open grass to pull up, panting, for yet another stand-off session.

At first I watched all this with some amazement, keen to see what would happen, then with diminishing interest for a while longer. When my legs were going to sleep from standing still for so long, I gave up, as it appeared that neither the fair maid nor the definitely-not-faint-of-heart young blades were ever going to. I went back to my vegetable gardening, and for ages after could hear them racketting about. Talk about playing hard-to-get!

The Red-necked Wallaby is a pretty species, sweet-faced, with a gentle look. Their fur is grey, dusted reddish-brown on their backs and heads, with black around their ears and down the middle of their rather triangular faces. They have a paler front, and neat black paws. At quite early ages they are recognisable as the more muscled, broad-shouldered, proud-chested males and the daintier, more rounded females. Within the sexes many have small distinguishing features — a whiter cheek stripe, a tatty ear, a darker back — but more often it is behaviour, 'personality', that marks them. More inquisitive, more set in ways, more solitary, more bold, more nervous ...

There are other inhabitants who hop but they have no more to do with each other than they do with me. The wallabies are by far the most numerous but I also see wallaroos and kangaroos. It took me a while to recognise which was which from a distance, but the easiest giveaway is how they move. The wallabies lean more horizontally, lower to the ground, when they go racing by, compared to the kangaroos and wallaroos, who maintain a more erect carriage.

As time went on I came to know them so well that I can't imagine how I was ever confused. I suppose it was rather like the racist-flavoured platitude about Asian people, lumping all those varied races and nationalities together — 'They all look the same' — hopefully uttered only until the speaker's ignorance is relieved by actually getting to know some individuals.

The wallabies' bigger cousins, the wallaroos, are the Common or Eastern Grey Wallaroos. They prefer rockier country, such as on my lower escarpment. In the Austen social scale, they'd be working-class, peasants, a bit rough — common! The first pair I saw passing through surprised me by their great difference from each other in colour, the male being nearly black and the smaller female pale grey. This is apparently typical. They were both much shaggier of fur and stockier of build than my wallabies, and for years that pair were the only ones I saw here. Since the 2002 fires, I have seen a small family of them, usually drinking at the little dam we put in below the house, but also grazing. They are still quite wary of me.

The Eastern Grey Kangaroos used to be seen higher up on my ridge, but since those same fires a group of them hangs around here a lot. By anyone's standards, they're upper-class — naturally grand, majestic in stature, the males as big as a pony, daunting when they stand fully erect. It's a chastening experience to see them lope down my track towards the house, only to stop and look imperiously down at me over my yard gate. All that's missing is the monocle.

We're used to seeing big domesticated animals like horses and cows in the landscape, but given that we don't have elephants or giraffes, these are the biggest native creatures I'm ever going to see. When they're feeding nearby I often get a fresh shock as one of the males straightens up. The sheer size of him!

They're all handsome, with admirable carriage. Straight backs and necks, heads held high as they bound across the paddock or through the trees. The females are smaller, but retain the well-defined facial bone structure of the species; they never look like wallabies. In their dusky greyish-brown coats, paler front fur, black highlights of ears, nose and paws, and their large dark eyes, they are always elegant.

Their young are just as cute as the wallaby babies — big-eyed, fluffy, uncoordinated, given to twisting themselves back-to-front to scratch at fleas or ticks, or leaning back at an odd angle to scrabble at their tummy fur, or corkscrewing themselves vertically into the air, just for fun. Like the wallaby joeys, they sometimes play at sparring with their mothers, who are very tolerant, literally turning the other cheek until they've had enough, when they give the annoying child a cuff and move on. The joey shakes its head several times, as if to clear the stars it's seeing, then comes back for more.

I am pleased that the kangaroos now ignore me almost as much as the wallabies do, if I move steadily. As I'm seeing several family groups now, not just one, I'd say they're here to stay. When I opened the yard gate the other day, a female kangaroo grazing very close by remained so unconcerned that her joey, who'd been dozing on the grass, stayed right where he was instead of panicking.

Only recently, for the very first time, I have seen a Swamp or Black Wallaby and her joey near my yard. Dark-chocolate velvety fur, small head, usually seen in the ferny forests on the shady southern side of my ridge. I assume the drought is sending them foraging further afield. They eat bracken, so I hope they start on mine.

I'll learn more about these newer neighbours when they're fully at ease with me, when they understand how this refuge works. That is, they're the occupants; I'm just the cleaner-upper of introduced weeds and bouncer of introduced animals. And protector.

When a wallaby stands still and looks me in the eye I cannot understand the kind of person that would see this as a chance to shoot it. I don't want to be classed as the same species as humans who take pleasure in shooting such beautiful and harmless animals, those who like living creatures as targets — not for food or self-protection, but for 'fun'.

Here all native animals are protected from shooters. It is not so everywhere, despite what the laws say; especially with some weekenders who like to play at being tough bushmen, huntin' 'n' shootin'. Since it's usually very late on a Saturday night when I hear the distant shots, the toughness is probably out of a bottle and I fear for both their discrimination and their accuracy.

I feel like warning my resident wallabies and wallaroos and kangaroos, anything big enough to be a target: 'Don't go down to the woods today' — stay up here with me. I could add, 'And be glad our state forest is now a national park', for they are allowing amateurs — 'almost professional but!' — to hunt and shoot feral animals in their/our state forests, without supervision. I'll bet my local weekend shooters would like a go at that.

They are calling it 'conservation hunting'. Who do they think this spin is kidding? Not the wounded feral animals that will escape to painful deaths, and the wounded or killed native animals hit 'by mistake', and their babies that starve as a result. Not to mention the odd bushwalker or birdwatcher accidentally potted — but they're probably greenies anyway, so no great loss to the state.

Feral animals — deer, cats, dogs, pigs, foxes, rabbits, cane toads, camels, brumbies, introduced birds like starlings and Indian Mynahs — *are* a problem, but they didn't ask to be brought here any more than our convict ancestors did.

If the criteria for extermination were ongoing damage to Australia's natural environment or displacement of the indigenous species — the destruction of their habitats, food sources and health, even to extinction — I think we'd be top of the hit list of introduced species. We'd hope the culling was humanely done, wouldn't we?

For me, the validity and relevance of the books of the world's religions are not indisputable. In fact, the Bible's insistence that God gave man dominion over all creatures seems to me to have caused a lot of our problems. Instead, I keep to one rule, and try to follow the admonition of Charles Kingsley's *The Water-Babies* character, Mrs Doasyouwouldbedoneby. I know Jesus is reputed to have said much the same, but I like the pithy rhythm of Kingsley's language better. If everyone managed to treat others as they'd like to be treated themselves it'd be a pretty nice world, don't you agree?

Mrs Doasyouwouldbedoneby had an offsider, Mrs Bedonebyas-youdid, but I found her rather Old Testament vengeful and didn't take her up to the same degree.

Although mightily impressed by Mrs D's simple rule as a child, I only thought of it in the context of human relationships. I'm now extending it to all creatures, even — almost — to leeches, based on the premise that being different from humans is not a reason for superiority and exploitation, but rather for learning more.

We used to kill whales before we realised how intelligent and complex they are, how more like us. 'How can they!' we now say of pro-whaling nations. But I don't feel that the right of a species to survive ought to depend on its degree of similarity to us, or on whether it's of any use to us. It's an intrinsic right, as part of the whole wonderful natural world — biodiversity. We simply don't know enough about how all things were designed to work together — ecosystems — and we usually don't find out until it's too late.

As Dr David Suzuki says, '... we tear at the very web of life that makes the planet habitable.'

This blind blundering is nowhere more evident than in clear-felling our native forests for wood pulp to send overseas. Recycled, plantation and alternative fibres can be used instead, and yet we allow this madness to continue. We lose the plants and animals that lived in those forests and we lose the trees that would have been hard at work absorbing CO_2 from our atmosphere, helping to save us from worse climate chaos. Which is clearly not as urgent as the lining of foreign pockets by the cheaper wiping of bottoms, foreign or otherwise.

And we think we rule the planet because we're so clever.

It is said that cockroaches will survive a nuclear war. Imagine if they ended up the dominant species. I'd hope they'd not be wanting revenge for all those baits and sprays! But I wonder if they'd even consider the remnants of the human race worth keeping. After all, we're greedy, aggressive, dangerous, and so stupid we foul our own nests, overpopulate, and self-destruct. What good are we?

With that humbling thought held firmly in the back of my mind, I'd like to think that many of us are atypical humans and that we do care enough about our world to stop wrecking it and start healing it. I'm not a misanthrope, even if I did choose the daily society of animals over that of men.

And believe me, I tried both.

CHAPTER 5

LIVING FOR WEEKENDS

BEING FORCED TO LIVE in Sydney, amongst millions of other humans, after living here with just 'my family and other animals', as Gerald Durrell put it, was a culture shock from which I didn't really recover, since I always saw my life there as temporary.

With hindsight, I was barely holding myself together. The marriage break-up had turned my world upside-down, and as a single parent it was a desperate financial struggle. The kids and I were restricted to visits here at best every second weekend, depending on whether I had petrol money or a suitable vehicle. I was without the consolation of this place where I belonged, and the lack of physical work seemed to leave me out of kilter with myself. There was only stress and worry and no release for it.

I began smoking again, which I hadn't done since first becoming pregnant. It didn't help, but somehow chimed with my desperation. I'll stop when I'm happy, I promised myself. Which I did, just before I moved back to the mountain again with my new partner. It's pathetic, I know, but I started rolling the smokes once more when *that* relationship began to sour. They were roughly nine-year cycles, I've calculated, but this time I stopped far sooner, determined not to be so pathetically dependent.

It helps being so far from the temptation of town. Such a strong addiction is always hovering, waiting for the next stressful situation. It's ironic when I think how hard I persevered with the damn things as a student, to overcome the nausea, so I'd fit in, look cool. If only we'd known …

Often it rained on our precious mountain weekends, which we thought most unfair. We'd either leave Sydney on Friday evening or at dawn on Saturday. Sometimes the kids would bring a schoolfriend each. If we'd arrived at night, the visitors wouldn't know what the outdoors was really like until next morning. I've never forgotten the pre-breakfast comment of one nine-year-old, whose home was an inner-city semi on the main Rozelle shopping street, with no front yard and a tiny cement rear yard. Taking in the paddocks, the surrounding forest, the mountains stretching away into the far distance, she said, 'Gee, you've got a big back yard!'

I've found four pages of scribblings from one wet autumn mountain weekend in one very wet mountain year. I'd forgotten them, but the freshness of detail, lost if left to memory alone, says a lot about those years of estrangement …

Rainbound — a weekend feature of life at the mountain as a visitor — without the compensation of fine weekdays; those are wasted on Sydney days spent indoors at work.

I light the fire in the fuel stove after arriving and unloading — go through the acclimatisation, the transition ritual of reading the Saturday papers I've brought with me, drinking coffee by the stove, letting the glimpses of dripping trees and low cloud swirling amongst the trunks slowly make it sink in — we are not in Sydney.

By lunch the papers are read. I start to think about the cabin I am in; what plans we had, what we didn't do. By mid-afternoon am feeling relaxed; have a beer to prove that it really is a Saturday, and start to plan anew. Line the roof, plug those holes, and even — build that extension. I go back through the Classifieds and pretend I have the money for those cedar leadlight doors or that load of slate.

I love cooking up here — it feels a pleasure rather than a rushed duty. Because it's dark so early, we have eaten and the kids are nodding off by 7.30 — even though they will stay up to 11 in Sydney, driven in one-hour bursts by TV shows. The dim candlelight and the physical day they've had all make it seem later.

They ride — trailbike and horses — regardless of weather. I watch them from my spot by the stove, through the low-set window put there specifically to see up the track. My daughter, in her brown Drizabone and Akubra hat, walking her horse leisurely ... then my son, after the usual repairs to his second-hand bike — a stranger in wet weather gear and monstrous helmet, flying off in a spurt of mud ...

I let the quiet wash over me. The fire crackles, the wind drives the fine cloud droplets onto the tin roof so it sounds like rain, and faintly the trees above me on the ridge line tell me that it is really windy up there — but it is just a faint roar, nothing threatening or disturbing.

I browse through all my books — some as old as my first memories — and choose the one I'm going to read this trip.

As the wet weekends continue I stop being angry at the wasted time, the jobs not able to be done, and begin to look forward to the time on my own, to the peace that I don't feel in Sydney even when I am alone. It's a lack of restlessness, a feeling that I am in my home, safe and unworried.

I love it when I can work physically up here — but I'm no martyr any more, so if it's cold and drizzly I don't try. Through

my window I can see the odd wallaby feeding his way up the hill;
kookaburras on their favourite horizontal branch, keen eyes
sweeping the ground for titbits; or flocks of ground-feeding birds
like the crimson rosellas, or the tiny fat tits hopping and twittering.

Our resident shingleback lizard rustles out from under the kero
fridge to investigate, and remains fixed, pretending not to notice
me, till he gets up the courage to waddle (he plainly thinks he's
darting) across the room to safety under the sideboard. As the
winter sets in, we won't see him at all — I wonder where he goes
to hibernate? We used to find whole families of these fat hiber-
nating lizards curled up together under a sheet of tin or amongst
stored beer bottles — they remained in rigid crescents when we
picked them up to relocate them. Ours doesn't seem to have a
family — he has been alone in our cabin for years. I hope he
knows there is a world outside it. [He was actually a
Cunningham's Skink.]

The stove has been going all day and [with the fire door open]
is glowing and cosy to look at — not as good as an open fire, but
still a pleasure. My feet in double socks resting against the oven
door, adding a log now and then, re-adjusting the kettles as they
boil, turning the bread in the oven so it won't burn — enjoying
not having to jostle with the kids for the warmest spot and it not
yet so cold that your back freezes while your front toasts.

I like the way our track meanders between the trees and up
and over rises and dips on the side of our hill — I like coming
here and suddenly seeing the cabin as we lurch over the last rise.

Right now a Scarlet Robin has landed on the tank — there
must be a pool collected on the top — it's pivoting and swaying as
it drinks. The tank stand is getting green and mossy from the

dripping of the overflow this wet year. Sometimes I have to run the
tap to lessen its burden and it always feels wicked to be wasting
this water — but this year has not been like other years.

At night we'd play board or pen and paper games by candlelight, the kids idly scoring the candles with a matchstick, toying with the flow of wax. They'd make hot Milo drinks, adding so much powdered milk that it was thick enough to eat. I'd have a cask of wine on hand. When my daughter and I could no longer bear it that my son had to win, and he usually did, we'd clean our teeth at the kitchen sink, make a last trip outside by torchlight, and be asleep by 8.30 at the latest. But we didn't bother much about time up here. Time out.

Even when we lucked on a fine weekend, it wasn't often that I could get the kids to stick around and help me with maintenance, let alone start any new projects, and anyway I had no money for materials. When my son was about fourteen, and tall enough to reach the underside of the tin roof from my ladder, we did manage to gradually and very roughly line it with reject plywood, blue builders' foil stapled on top in an attempt to keep some of the heat in or out. The battens were ancient hardwood, and we only had hand tools, so nailing the sheets to them from below was a painful process.

The ply is better insulation than nothing, but not much. Every now and then there's a creak as a nail pops out and a sheet of ply partly loses its grip. Well, it's gravity isn't it? Should have been screwed.

A few friends, mostly new ones, helped me over those years. One loses track of some possessions and some friends in a marriage split-up. I found it hard to be around cosy couples and avoided them until I was stronger.

Fences were fixed, water pumped and wood cut with help from

visitors, especially one stalwart family friend, Nigel. The wildlife and the horses ate everything except the bay tree, the jonquils and the ferny asparagus leaves. I was often depressed at the place's abandoned air, but I was often depressed anyway, at my own sense of failure, at having lost my way. Only the children kept me going.

My Sydney jobs were meant as fillers until I felt up to the stress of teaching. After six frustrating weeks of job seeking I'd realised that an Arts degree was a handicap, stamping me as inexperienced and overqualified, despite my protests that I'd do anything. No one even wanted me as a waitress, because I was over 30 and hadn't done any since my uni days.

I'd taken the first job offered, in the storeroom of an architectural hardware firm. Bob, the storeman, the archetypal rough diamond with heart of gold, had originally been very unhappy about having a woman on his patch, but we became real friends. Over two years I worked my way up from the storeroom to scheduling and being a consultant to architects. I also made a friend 'upstairs': Susan, the accountant, a single parent like myself, extremely intelligent, with a dry and rather wicked sense of humour.

I did apply for a teaching post, but it was several years before I was offered one. Then it was way out west where I'd be the only French teacher, and I'd never taught that, although I'd been trained to teach both French and English, my majors at university. The kids were settled in their city school, had made friends, and there was the impossible distance from their father — and the mountain. I said no. Farewell to any prospects of secure work and pay, of working hours that matched school times, of school holidays without the worry of who to mind the kids.

I moved into better firms, in various commercial fields, advising on and specifying fantastically expensive designer furniture, lighting, door hardware, bathrooms, fabrics — with increasingly top-of-the-range products. I took Susan with me into one of those companies, since she deserved better pay and respect than she'd had in the chauvinistic place where we'd met.

How come I could do such unlikely jobs? Well, I had a good eye for line, colour and composition; I was intelligent and practical, I picked up new things fast; being a working mother of two, I was a good organiser, so a good project manager; and I was honest, so clients trusted that my advice was not biased for a sale.

I learnt to read plans, and did a few partial courses to flesh out the knowledge I gained from reading — a year's correspondence course from England in architectural ironmongery, in which I got a distinction; a term of fronting up to Tech on a Friday with electrical trade apprentices to learn about lighting sources; two terms of Tuesday nights at Tech to grasp the basics of mechanical engineering drawing.

A woman in the midst of such all-male groups was considered a joke, as was my presence on commercial building sites. I didn't mind the workers whistling, but I did mind the bosses smirking when I entered the site office. They stopped when, for example, I drew a screwdriver from my handbag and got them out of an urgent deadline problem, with big penalties at stake, by opening up a mortice lock and changing its function and hand on the spot.

Meanwhile the kids and I were living in student-type rented dumps that I filled with other people's reject furniture. As Rozelle and Balmain shot up the trendy scale, so did the rents. We'd soon needed three bedrooms, and moved many times in those thirteen years, 'downsizing' in a vain attempt to keep the rent to no more than half my wage. A grotty old house was better than a sterile flat with no yard, no earth, where I'd have really gone mad. I changed jobs to earn more.

The advantages of Balmain's pubs and cafés, like the theatres of Sydney itself, were lost on me, as I could never afford to go out unless someone else was paying. Every dollar had to be kept for its budget allocation.

As a client dithered over gorgeous curtain materials that cost more a metre (wholesale) than my fortnight's rent, or an elegant sliver of Italian leather, slung on chrome sticks, labelled a chair, and worth a year's rent, he or she would often turn to me and ask, 'So what do you have in your home?'

'Oh,' I'd say, shrugging my shoulders nonchalantly, 'a rather eclectic mix, actually.'

I saw inside many upmarket Sydney homes. I never wanted to live in any of them, harbour views notwithstanding. They were too impersonal and artificial, and way too big. It was out-of-control consumerism, as far from the simple life as one could get. I mean to say, *five* bathrooms, not counting the outside one by the pool, and even if only three of them had gold-plated taps and black-marble floors?

By my second job I'd moved up the scale enough for a company car to be part of the deal. I argued for a four-wheel-drive Subaru instead of a Commodore, so they could be sure I'd get back from the mountain on a Sunday night. The only problem was having to wash the bush weekend off it before taking it to work; I had much the same problem with my inner self.

I had several men friends — consecutively, not concurrently — and initially only went out every second weekend when the kids were with their father. They were mostly journalists, a profession which, at least in those days, carried the occupational hazard of drinking too much alcohol. Hanging out with them inevitably involved me doing the same, although I could never match their excesses. After all, they were in regular training. But it was no way for me to regain emotional stability.

When the kids began going less often to their father's, and I began wishfully thinking of father figures and happy families, I twice made the mistake of thinking a relationship might become more permanent. The reality was disastrous and brief each time. Conflict with my kids was unacceptable; we were better off on our own.

As the kids grew, so did the expenses, but unfortunately not the financial help. There was never enough money to meet demands, from big ones like a school excursion to the snow, to middling and too-frequent necessities like a new pair of sneakers, to the terrible weekly stretch of $10 each for music lessons. Being constantly worried about money made me more of a ratty mother than I wanted to be, or than my kids needed.

To supplement my earnings, I tried waitressing in an Indian restaurant a few nights a week, until I realised that my son was not meeting his Year 10 assignment deadlines. He needed supervision. Instead I took up proofreading at home, for a small desktop publishing company.

Then my current day job company closed my branch. They'd imported exquisite Italian designer door furniture. This job had at least given me a brief flash of luxury, in a rushed trip to Port Douglas and the Reef, and my first and only helicopter ride, showing the Italian principals around, since we could communicate in French — sort of.

Janet, the manager of a nearby trade-only fabric showroom, took me on, knowing I needed an income quickly. It was several steps down in pay and position, but they were fabulous English and French fabrics —Warner, Liberty, Osborne & Little, Pierre Frey — and I loved handling them and learning about this whole new field from Janet, who was only a few years older than me. Like Sue, she had a mischievous sense of humour, and also became my friend.

But it couldn't pay enough, so as the desktop company expanded,

I took the offered full-time job. I'd already been organising sales literature for wherever I was, designing the brochures, writing the copy. Here I learnt how to use a Mac computer and do 'typesetting' and layout. But, having made the classic mistake of being involved with the boss, I lost the job when I no longer wanted the relationship to continue.

That was all very unpleasant, but after fifteen years the scars had faded, so when he came across my name on the Internet as a prize-winning writer, he made email contact. Now in Tasmania, a publisher, editor and reviewer, graphic designer and artist, and as articulate, erudite and witty as ever, Fred's a valued friend and dependable e-correspondent — especially when I get desperate for 'proper English'.

But back then, being jobless was a frightening prospect — no income, even for a few weeks, with rent to pay, nothing in the bank and two kids to support. I made quirky flyers and hand-delivered them to potential employers, although my lack of official qualifications, plus being in my forties, made my chances slim. Only one replied. Weavers, a design and production company, offered me temporary work, which led to a permanent job. Soon I began to do their copywriting as well as layout.

I still do some freelance work for Weavers Design Group, mostly turning corporate-speak into readable prose for newsletters, brochures or website copy, often for their credit union clients. So although I have no money, or loans, I am quite knowledgeable about finance!

Weavers were very supportive. In a way it's as if I remained part of the company even after I'd left and moved back here for good. They used to call me 'our woman on the mountain', as one says 'our man in New York', although the connotations of gumleaves and gumboots were probably less impressive.

They had to tolerate a long and turbulent teething period in those pre-email communication days. We were using a program called Carbon Copy (I think) where my computer linked to theirs via a primitive modem. I'd try to get the modem to work on my dreadful phone line, waiting for that magic sound, the electronic gargle of a successful connection. Someone had to sit at a computer at their end to receive it, and stay there to respond, even if it was unbelievably slow. I'd be sitting here trying to get it through, never sure if the person down there had given up, or wandered off to make a coffee or take a phone call. To find out, I'd have to disconnect and ring them, as I only had one line. Then we'd have to start all over again. Hair-tearingly not ideal.

I think that was when I first discovered the release to be derived from screaming Charlie Brown one-liners — 'A-a-a-a-rgh!' — from the verandah.

Unfortunately it was before I discovered Hunter techno-genius and problem solver, Greg Norris, of Singleton Comptech Support. He has saved me from nervous breakdowns and loss of income umpteen times over the years, often talking me through to a solution over the phone. I may be a techno-dill, but I simply could not function here without his unflappable support. The curlier the problem, the better he likes it, which is just as well, since I toss him quite a few.

But at least I was living and working here, even if conditions weren't ideal. My partner was perfecting his guitars in his separate workshop, which had a pot belly stove, necessary to keep the humidity down for the timbers and for gluing as much as to keep him warm. Meanwhile I'd be shivering at my desk at the other end of the cabin from the combustion stove. Working on the computer, I'd be wearing fingerless gloves, beanie, thick socks and boots, tights, leggings, long woollen skirt, singlet, skivvy, woollen jumper, vest, cardigan and shawl, with a rug over my knees. Dead elegant — and cold. I cursed again the uninsulated roof.

After a few years he bought and installed a wood heater up my end of the house. Each winter I am grateful to him, as I am for the hot shower, even if that's still alfresco! Earning a living from here was the overriding critical issue for us both and we only just managed — and sometimes we didn't.

Having once subscribed to *The Owner Builder* magazine, I often looked through my back copies for ideas or information. The last page, 'The Back Porch', was for readers to volunteer their musings, so I sent in what I thought was a humorous piece on our unfinished building projects. I included a short note which mentioned I was a writer.

The then editor, Russell Andrews, liked it; he rang and asked if I'd write for them. That was about eight years ago, and it's been the major source of my small income since, and the most pleasant. Owner builders are a subculture of terrifically energetic, persevering and inspiring people who combine creativity with practicality. I find and follow up leads on interesting owner-built homes, preferably sustainable, ideally handmade. I interview the owner builders, take photos and write the articles, one or two per bi-monthly issue.

Yet it's always hard to make the initial phone call, which after all is cold calling, even though most people welcome the idea of sharing the story of their efforts. Then it takes bravado to leave my hermitage and front up, apparently full of confidence, to people I've never actually met. Sometimes I feel out of sync, wonder if I'm raving, having been on my own so long. Yet with many of my subjects I have much in common — environmentally, artistically and philosophically.

And I've made friends amongst them, mostly only seen when I return to their regions for another story. Robert Bignell, who took my official author photo, is one who lives in the Hunter. We were sitting outside his Old Brush Studio, watching the waterbirds on his lagoon, having a coffee and sorting out what was wrong with the world, when he said, 'Hang on a tick', and nipped inside. I avoid cameras, but he's a professional, so he snapped me suddenly and sneakily, which is why I have a rather odd look on my face. His excuse was that the light was too good to pass up.

Close friends are rare in my experience — and precious. One of the reasons I'd been determined to return to the bush and live the life I felt was right for me was that I'd been forced to accept the fragility of the future. The only two female friends I'd made in Sydney had died.

Susan, younger than I was, stumbled and fell for no apparent reason one day at the office; she was found to have a brain tumour. I watched her fight against dying, sharing it when she'd let me. It seemed particularly unfair that it was her clever brain being attacked. She was justly angry — and brave.

Janet, so shy of internal examinations that she never had pap smears, was finally diagnosed with advanced cervical cancer. We'd been swapping wind remedies, which didn't help because her problem was secondary bowel cancer. I shared her battle to the end too, more closely, at home, hospital, hospice. Janet was scared — and brave.

Then just before I moved back to the bush I learnt that my old friend Tony had liver cancer. I'd known Tony for 30 years; my ex-husband's best friend, once. He'd let the friendship with Tony drop, but I hadn't. An ABC journalist, Tony had made a happy second marriage, with Jo. When I first went to Sydney to look for work they put me up — and put up with my teary marital post-mortems. We'd had less contact since they moved to Tasmania.

He and I grew closer through letters over the two years of life that he fought for and won. He read my first attempts at short stories and I read his new poems. I went down to Sydney whenever he flew over for treatment, and the last time, knowingly to say goodbye. I managed to bring him up to the mountain twice. He knew it from the early days. 'I always thought this was one of the great escapes,' he said.

How Tony dealt with his cancer was typical: he involved himself totally with his specialist's radical theories and treatments; enrolled in French at uni (so he could read Proust in the original, he said); started writing poetry again — he had true talent but life had somehow sidetracked him; and took surfing lessons. From my desk I can see my favourite photo of him. On a beach, he's dripping wet, grinning through his greying beard, wearing a purple and black wetsuit. Hey, Tony.

His encouragement kick-started my formal writing. His dying made me even more determined not to be similarly sidetracked by daily life.

Chapter 6

Shelter — Somehow, Sometime

A FEW YEARS AGO, short of an *Owner Builder* story, I wrote about my own place, 'Confessions of a Bad Muddie'. Looking at archival photos of me making mudbricks, in shorts and Indian shirt, or flared jeans and cheese-cloth top, 1979 seemed long, long ago. My floppy straw work hat was actually a relic of my civil ceremony wedding, where I'd worn a cream trouser suit that hadn't even been bought especially for the occasion.

The lack of frills and fancies and romantic notions in my wedding was a fair indicator of the relationship. I didn't know any better at nineteen, having been brainwashed into thinking that romance was an invention of *Woman's Day* and Mills & Boon, and quite beneath any thinking person. I've learnt a little since then about romance.

After visiting over 100 home-made houses, I've learnt a lot more about building. I still can't explain why my husband and I did such an erratic job. Maybe because it was mud, and not 'proper' building materials, so it felt more like play?

We came here with G.F. Middleton's classic *Build Your House of Earth* as our bible. It was so confidence-inspiring that we lurched into building our 8 metre x 5 metre one-room mudbrick cabin (meant to be Stage 1) with great enthusiasm untempered by any other

71

knowledge or experience. It was also untempered by taking his advice to practise on something small first.

Yet nearly 30 years later the cabin is still standing, giving me shelter plus offering a perfect example of what not to do when building in mudbrick. It will outlast me, and maybe those who inherit it. And as every one of the 1475 bricks was pressed into the moulds by my hands, it's very personal — another bond with this place.

The old bloke who sold us the land said he'd bulldoze a track in and level the house site as part of the deal. We got him to push the topsoil layer forward, and that became my interim vegie garden. A foot depth of the clayey subsoil was pushed sideways into a pile that gave enough material for our bricks, as well as a play 'mountain' for the kids. They were desolate whenever we had to dig into one of their elaborately constructed labryinths of roads, tunnels and quarries, when they had to dismantle their 'sheds' made of sticks and bark, and relocate their Matchbox toy vehicles.

Building seemed so simple. I cut the tussock grass for straw to add to the mix, and carried buckets of water up from the spring, where the water trickled out of a clay slip in the hillside into a small hole that we'd edged with rocks. Clear and drinkable, and always a wonder.

Over a pit we'd dug, we'd balance a chickenwire and timber screen. My husband would shovel the dirt onto that and I'd rub it through the 'sieve' with a piece of wood, which gradually wore to a smooth ellipse.

We'd lift off the netting frame and my husband would hop in as the mixer. He'd be barefoot, as gumboots would refuse to part company with the mud base after a very short while. I'd start adding the water and straw.

When it was the right consistency, he'd fill the barrow and wheel it over to the rows of hessian-covered platforms that we'd set up for brickmaking. We couldn't do it on the ground because the ground wasn't flat enough. In fact it was sloping enough for a full barrow or two to get away from him en route.

I'd kneel beside the oiled timber double mould. With bare hands I'd spread and poke and pat the mix to fill the corners as he plopped the shovelfuls in. I'd stand to level the top, then ease the mould off, when, ever-magically, the bricks would emerge, just sitting there, slightly quivering, glistening dark grey–brown. With a stiff brush, in the tin bathtub of water, I'd quickly clean the mud off the mould and we'd do it again, and again. I can still feel the icy water on the wrinkled-prune skin of my fingers, and the gritty mud under my nails.

We'd cover the bricks to slow down the drying at first and in a day or two we could stand them up. A few more days and we could stack them. Mudbricks *were* simple!

At first we'd panic if we saw rain clouds moving across the valley towards us, and would race to pull across and weigh down black plastic over the piles of bricks, or later, the rising walls. If we did, the rain would not reach us; if we didn't, it would be a downpour. Eventually, tired of wrestling with long strips of windblown plastic, and with the elements, we gave up. The bricks coped better than we did.

Our legs and arms became very strong: mine from carrying water uphill, his from tromping and shovelling mud. At the end of a batch, we'd trudge up to our camp to make a fire for desperately needed coffee. Covered in flakes of drying mud, our heads drooping with weariness, aching arms hanging heavily at our sides, we felt as Neanderthal as we probably looked.

But we had the brickmaking sussed. We got quite efficient at laying them too: slap the mud mortar on thickly; wriggle a brick down into it, mud squeezing out; catch that with the trowel and use it for the next brick — easy.

It was what we made as we laid the bricks that didn't prove so easy. We broke two of the three basic rules in the old proverb 'Give a house a good hat, a good coat, and a stout pair of boots and you can't go wrong.'

We went wrong.

The hat was good, as it should be, given that the olive-green corrugated roofing and its supporting timbers were the major new materials bought, taking a great deal of the $2000 our cabin cost. The mud was free and the recycled doors and windows were dirt cheap! To my everlasting regret and mystification, we didn't insulate that roof when it would have been easy and we had the money.

The boots were bad. My excuse is that the site was meant to be flat. The old bloke can't have had his eye in the day he 'levelled' it, as, although it was closer to level than before, one front corner was more than a metre lower than the diagonally opposite one.

Not only would more bricks be needed, but stepped footings instead of flat. With all the hassle of working these out to fit brick lengths, we forgot about reinforcing the footings. We just threw rocks into the trenches and poured cement in to fill. In the next drought year, as the clay shrank, the unreinforced stepped footings cracked. The walls did too, but only up to window and door sills, and they were only skinny cracks. I filled them, and that's how they've remained.

Keen to start laying our mudbricks, we'd also forgotten about the cement-stabilised mudbricks that were supposed to be laid first; we just rolled out the dampcourse and slapped on the mud. What saved the base of the walls over the years was the brim of the hat; we'd at least done as told in extending the eaves.

As for the bad coat, I don't know why we didn't render the walls like the book said. Some render recipes used cow dung, and they emphasised that it had to be fresh! Maybe that put me off all renders. I also now see that our bricks were too clayey, and yet I'm sure we did tests on the soil. We were proud of the 'natural' look of the bricks and didn't want to cover them up, but why didn't we do even a light rubbing over to smooth the craggy bits into the inevitable cracks that such clayey bricks developed?

Perhaps because we'd never seen anyone else doing mudbrick, only read about it. Or perhaps because, with the tent disintegrating, we just needed to move in. When mere mortals do this, things remain at that stage for a long time, if not forever. But it could also have been because our relationship was starting to break down, the bush dream showing signs of becoming a nightmare. We'd probably ceased to care. Sorry, house.

The lack of a good coat most greatly affected the western wall, our bad weather side. Since that gable end was intended to join up with Stage 2 of the house, we even used an internal quality door. It was, after all, going to be an internal wall one day soon. 'Soon' still hasn't arrived.

The first big summer storm raked that western wall into millions of corrugations, most obviously in the mortar but also in any dips in the bricks. Succeeding storms over twenty years deepened them. It looked dreadful, but it was only superficial damage. Mudbrick walls are tough.

When I moved back here, my new partner and I immediately added a front verandah, almost as big as the cabin, and slapdash enough to be the subject of a tongue-in-cheek article for *Owner Builder*, 'The Nah Mate Building Standard'. I grew deciduous vines to cover up the roughest bits, as well as for summer shade under the clear roof inserts in front of the doors and windows. I practically live out there in warm weather. It's popular with a few of my wild neighbours too.

After a while it got too hard managing overnight visitors in the one-room cabin, so we decided to build some quick bedrooms by adding a narrow skillion off the back wall, tucking into the bank behind. Except the bank turned out to be mostly bedrock, a slow crowbar job. The new back wall was built up in rock against the bank, well protected from damp.

On top of the rocks is a window wall of diamond-paned scavenged sash windows, halved and turned on their sides into Tudor-type casements. Through them I can watch the crimson rosellas feeding on the blue flowers of the rosemary or the pale orange claws of the grevillea, only a foot away, at my eye level — one of the advantages of building into the hill. Beyond them rise the smooth trunks of the blue gums above the track.

The eastern end was built up in rock to low window height, that is, my bed height. A slab of white mahogany from a large fallen branch made a broad sill for two double casement windows from our magpie collection. I love casement windows because they can open right back, disappear, and let the outdoors flow in. From my bed I look out to the distant mountains, and in winter I often wish I felt just a little unwell, so I could lie on my sunny bed and read without guilt. Those nuns have a lot to answer for!

As no heat gets through my old western wall on the worst summer day, the new one had to be of mudbrick, on top of rock. Making mudbricks for this, I could feel every one of the twenty years' difference in my muscles. Mixing the mud in a wheelbarrow was heavy going, and by the time I'd added the dried grass, I could barely drag the larry (like a hoe blade with two round holes in it) through the mix.

This time I enjoyed using mud in a more free-form, sensual way, to meet the uneven rocks and around the green bottles inset for decoration and light, moulding, wetting, smoothing. When the bedroom addition was weatherproof we removed a central window in the back wall of the original house and I cut through the wall below it with a bush saw, for the internal doorway. It felt sacrilegious to be doing this.

Dampening it first, wearing an old leather glove, I did rub down the new mud wall. It was easy, and made such a difference that I turned again to the adjoining original western wall. This looked even worse by comparison, and was a great embarrassment now I was writing for *Owner Builder*. People expected me to not only know what to do right, but to have done it. But I, me, grey-haired mature me, hadn't done this; some young ignorant thing had, all that time ago. Yet it was clear I had to fix up her mistakes or I'd get no peace.

I tried hosing it down and rubbing, but it was old and stubborn and behaved like stone; the bumps needed rasping before they would merge into mud again and fill the dips. This was extremely hard on the arthritic wrists; I could only do a little patch a day, and some of the ruts were so deep that all I could do was blur them, but it looked much better.

Last Christmas, panicked by expected first-time visitors whom I feared would be justifiably critical, I also rubbed down the walls on the verandah, which was far easier work. Although not weather-damaged, their crannies had been expanded by wasps taking mud for their nests, crannies which would not have existed if I'd rubbed the walls in the first place. Mud is so forgiving.

Sometime, I will do the remaining east wall, and then paint them all with linseed oil and turps, which also should have been done in the first place. Maybe next autumn, when it's cooler, and my wrists have recovered …

The bedrooms' windows are still not sanded or sealed or re-puttied; we were keen to move in, and my partner assured me that he'd take them off one by one and finish them, later. 'Later' is a very stretchy word. Now I have them on my own running list of things to do sometime. Later.

At least since I've been on my own I've got round to hiding the silver foil backing of the addition's roof insulation, after staring up at it for years, counting the tape 'bandaids' where the bush rats had got in once and made holes in the foil. Unable to afford lining boards, I bought cream hessian and tacked it up. It sags a bit and resembles a poor man's seraglio, but it's an improvement.

And I can see the spiders clearly against such a pale background, which is a comfort at night. In the warmer months, last thing before I turn out my reading light, I always look up; it's surprising how often I spot a spider. No doubt if I hadn't looked, it would have gone about its business and disappeared by morning. But once I know, I have to put it outside — what if it dropped onto my face!

When I was young, we used to scream for Dad, who'd splat spiders against the wall with the broom. Big hairy spiders make very large and fleshy splats. Ugh. Now I'm more civilised, and braver. Well, I have to be; there's no one to scream for.

Before I tackle the job, I turn on all the lights, open the window in readiness, and have the torch handy in case the creature escapes into the shadows — I'd need to know where to. Standing on the bed to reach the low 'ceiling', I place a large glass over the spider, then slide a piece of card between the rim and the hessian, to make a lid. This is tricky because the hessian isn't rigid. The reason why I must use clear glass and not a mug is so I can see, to be sure I've got it and that it's not running up my sleeve instead. Then I can empty it out the window. Ugh. I'm shuddering now at the spider-up-the-sleeve thought.

My other good building deed in the bedroom was to put the missing timber stripping around the windows, so the wind no longer whistles through. It involved rather a lot of bent small nails, but it works.

I realise that, when I had a male partner, building was his province by natural right, as mine was the cooking and the gardening. All I could do was try not to nag as the years passed and the jobs remained unfinished under the endless time pressures of being self-employed. Alone, I was free to have a go.

And there's always plenty to have a go at, in all different materials. Metal is foreign to me, probably because I have no experience of or tools for it, but wood, mud, rock and cement don't scare me.

Take the cellar, which was the one benefit of the unlevel site. It keeps the home-brew cool, and there's a trap door in the floor for fetching replenishments. However the bush rats had created a maze of tunnels between the rocks in the footings — into the cellar. Snakes hunt rats, and snakes like cool places. I'd twice seen a Red-bellied Black Snake escape into those holes. I couldn't make myself go down there, despite my stocks having run dry. Late last autumn, with any snakes theoretically asleep somewhere else, I finally filled the holes with cement. As I had to crouch and crawl along under the verandah to do the front footings, it wasn't pleasant, but the cellar is safely usable again.

I'm quite proud of myself when I can finally cross something like that off my list. I try to do at least some small thing in the yard or the house each day before I start writing and am hooked. Some days the 'small thing' takes half the day, since housekeeping here is really farm maintenance.

If I do something that wasn't on a list, I'll add it to one, just so I can cross it off and give my efforts due recognition. It's a way of convincing myself that I'm being a practical manager even if I am a female with my head elsewhere most of the time.

Every now and then I get an urge to do something beautiful and unnecessary to the house, and I lurch into carrying out a 'project'. Last winter I covered a high fixed window in the gable end with those iridescent flat-based glass pebbles sold in bargain shops. I glued them on with clear silicone into a vaguely Arabic cum Art Nouveau pattern, in cool colours, as it's on the west.

Acknowledging this nest-decorating binge behaviour, I make sure I buy the materials for such small creative projects as soon as I can afford to after thinking of them, so as to have them here when the urge takes me. It's a long way to a shop.

After the rear addition, I thought myself pretty posh. It was now practically a four-room house, if you counted the pantry squeezed in between the two hobbit-size bedrooms — hobbits also build into hills. Posh too, because I'd painted old and new interior mud walls with cream organic paint to seal them and to reflect more light.

When visitors arrive I usher them in the front door and turn them on the spot as I point out kitchen, dining, lounge, study, office. Five steps more and they're in the bedrooms. They say it's 'compact' and 'cute', 'charming' and 'quaint', and I agree, as, apart from running out of walls for bookshelves, it's perfect for my needs.

The only room I'm really missing is a bathroom.

My ex-partner wasn't keen on boiling billies for a hot shower after a hard day's work. We replaced the old fuel stove with a reconditioned slow combustion one that came with a hot-water jacket. He put a tank on the roof and did the copper plumbing, taking the pipes out through the mud wall at the back of the stove. That being the most direct place to put a shower, he did. Four star posts and a strip of blue woven plastic as a windbreak, and a wooden packing pallet with rubber over it for a floor, and I had my first plumbed mountain bathroom.

It was also what first met visitors' eyes when they drove up to my house gate. Other disadvantages, especially on a wet night, were that it had no roof, and to get to it I had to walk right round the outside of the house. Showering by a hung torch was a bit risky when other creatures might have taken up residence since my last shower — spiders, especially in the folds of the face cloth; frogs; lizards; snakes; and, once, an echidna that emerged from under the pallet while I was washing my hair. With shampoo in my eyes, I couldn't quite see what it was and my scream terrified us both.

But plastic disintegrates. Bathroom model 2 was a three-hour job that lasted three years. My partner wired wood to the old star posts to extend the height. Sheets of rusty corrugated iron were screwed to these to form a roof and modesty panels, leaving it open above chest height for occupants to see out — and for the wind to take the shower spray far out of their reach. Visitors rhapsodised over the views and said we mustn't ever change a thing — but they could afford to be enthusiastic, since they'd go home to a viewless but sealed, warm and steamy bathroom.

Bathroom model 3 is my current one. My then twenty-something son needed to convalesce here after an operation, a follow-up from an earlier motorbike accident. On crutches he'd have had trouble getting to the shower. So, in advance, he got hold of a fibreglass three-sided shower shell, free, from a renovation job, and built a timber frame for it at the eastern end of my verandah. The plumbing was re-routed, and a bamboo blind was hung for the 'dressing room', as a token divider between the open top, open front 'bathroom' and the rest of us sitting beside it on the verandah.

It is less than ideal, as it blocks my morning sun and that view from the verandah, as well as reducing the light in my kitchen area. There's also a problem when a gusty westerly wind is blowing, as the shower curtain snatches a quick icy embrace — 'A-argh!' — in between the calm periods when the water actually feels hot. In winter I have very, very, very long showers, as I can't bear to turn the hot water off, knowing that when I do, after a fraction of a second of residual steam, I must open the shower curtain and freeze, naked at 5 degrees.

Like all the other bathrooms, this one is only temporary. Only in its fifth year, in fact. Sometime, somehow … oh, and a bath to lie down in, please. There are times when I'd trade a sunset for that!

The last building project here was begun the Easter after I'd gone solo. Two of my sisters agreed to help me build a little cabin as a permanent home for Dad. Below is a shorter version of a piece I wrote about this for *Bonzer* online seniors' magazine. It helped me put the experience in perspective, and so eased the pain …

DAD'S PLACE

No reason why we three women couldn't do it, if I kept the plan and method simple. My sisters had no building experience, but we knew Dad wouldn't care about rough edges and wonky lines. As he'd been a carpenter by trade, I thought it best not to use timber — might make the mistakes too obvious, even for an easy-going bloke like him. Considering fires, and what was handy, a stone cabin seemed best. Between us we'd manage the heavy work.

I'd chosen a spot by the Cootamundra Wattles, near some big rocks that would make perfect beer-o'clock sitting spots. My sisters arrived, and liked the site. We set to work. City-based Sister One looked so funny in my spare gumboots and old felt hat that I wished Dad was here to see. She was to pass materials to me, while Sister Four was assigned to mixing cement.

We levelled the site, and boxed in for the brick and concrete slab. Our arms were aching by the time we'd mixed and trowelled and smoothed, but satisfyingly so. Sister Four went to make tea for smoko while Sister One and I watered and covered the setting concrete.

Next day we started the walls, leaving enough of the slab exposed for an all-round verandah. He'd want that to enjoy the view. It was a small cabin, but we fitted in a window on the eastern wall, for morning sun, and the door was on the sunny north. The stones we used had come from Port Macquarie, where they'd retired from their second farm, a cattle property in Northern New South Wales.

Dad loved an open fire, but Mum had put always her foot down about the mess. We made a big chimney on the west; narrowing to a freestanding column, it was a challenge, but ended up only slightly askew.

On the last evening of their visit we drank to Dad as we admired our work, joking about what he'd think of it. He'd surely laugh at us girls as builders, especially Sister One — the one who hadn't transplanted to the country, who never went anywhere without make-up, and for whom a broken nail was a disaster. But for him she'd got dirty without complaint.

They had to return home, leaving the roof to me. Cutting tin was too hard, so I was using ferro-cement — cement over chickenwire and hessian. Dad would shake his head, but it would be watertight.

Then came the hard part. All the roofing materials ready, I went to get Dad. He had to move in now, because neither door nor window of this cabin would open: my roof would close it forever. As I carried the grey plastic sealed box I could hear small shifting gritty sounds — tiny bits of Dad, more real than ashes.

He fitted snugly in his cabin. I draped the hessian over the wire. I couldn't see the box any more. He was gone. I hated doing *this. 'Sorry,' I sobbed, as I worked the cement into the hessian.*

Interment is so … final.

When it was done, I sank onto the rock nearby, relief filming over the hole in my heart as the clearing echoed to what is known as 'a good cry'.

Rest in peace, Dad.

I walk by Dad's place almost every day. Hey, Dad.

When my granddaughter visits, she picks flowers and arranges them on his verandah and tidies up the pebbles in his garden. She has a special fondness for her Poppy. Although she was only two when he died, she was extraordinarily empathetic at his bedside in those last hours.

Dad would much prefer his cabin in my horse-cropped pasture to being one in a row of metal plaques in a neat memorial rose garden. The only complaint he might have is the lack of a few beefy Herefords in the landscape …

'S'pose she's still one of them vegetarians; glad the younger two got over that stage! Dunno how a man could make a living out of cattle if even his own daughters weren't eating meat!'

Yep, I'm still a weirdo, Dad.

CHAPTER 7

KEEPING UP WITH THE QUOLLS

WHILE CERTAIN PEOPLE MIGHT consider me weird, I pale in comparison with some of my neighbours, who also fail to observe the proprieties. They're rather lax about boundaries too.

My house yard's netting fence was intended to keep the larger native animals out of my garden, not to provide the smaller ones with a playpen for their young, as it does. One of these smaller animals — although not exactly small, being large-cat sized — is my co-tenant, a female Spotted-tailed Quoll. She has lived and bred in my shed for about eight years. Quolls climb, dig, tear and pull, so no fence would have kept her out of anywhere she'd chosen to live.

I'd never heard of quolls until I came here. Everyone knows about the threatened Tasmanian Devil and the presumed extinct Tasmanian Tiger, but the Spotted-tailed Quoll hasn't made it into the popular press, despite being a member of the same family as the Devil, far more distinctive with its spotted coat, and a much fiercer carnivore.

There are four types of quoll, two of which are extinct over much of their previous range. We're so good at this extinction business that Australia holds the world record for wiping out the most mammal species. And we've done it in only 200 years.

The Western Quoll once roamed over a vast area of inland Australia but is now only found in Western Australia's south-western tip. The Northern Quoll seems to be still doing well in the Top End, perhaps because of its 'pugnacious disposition'. The Eastern Quoll is thought to have disappeared from the mainland states, but it survives in Tasmania. Sightings are occasionally reported in remote places like my mountains; I was sure I'd seen one myself years ago, on the edge of this clearing. It sat up on its hind legs and looked at me — it was smaller and daintier than my shed tenant, and had no spots on its tail. If I saw it now I'd be better informed to identify it.

In wild-edge areas like this it wouldn't be surprising to find supposedly extinct creatures surviving here. A few locals insist they've seen a Yowie.

If I have anything to do with it, the fourth type of quoll will not become extinct, since that's *my* quoll, the Spotted-tailed Quoll, also called the Tiger Quoll or Tiger Cat — which is rather silly, since it's leopard-spotted, not tiger-striped. Described as 'the most combative creature of the Australian bush', you'd think it would capture the public's imagination, wouldn't you?

These quolls have no natural predators; they are bold and smart. They're still seen in the mainland's eastern rim and Tasmania, but with competition from foxes and feral cats, and with logging and clearing reducing their forest habitats, their populations have been greatly reduced and 'may become so thinly distributed as to be unable to survive', warns my Australian Museum *Complete Book of Australian Mammals*.

So my quoll needs my refuge. The quoll family stink out my shed, pee on my step, and nightly leave their distinctive droppings, often full of undigested fur, on my verandah. They're not the nicest of neighbours. As the song says, 'I don't eat animals and they don't eat me' — but I'm glad my meat-eating quoll is smaller than I am.

These quolls have been described as 'very ferocious' and have a bite grip second only to that of the Tasmanian Devil — they can bring down a wallaby, I heard on the radio. The first time my small grand-daughter saw our quoll, I was taking her outside for the ritual pee on the grass before she went to bed. From the steps she caught the quoll in the torch beam. 'Grandma!' She drew back, clutched me. The quoll bared her teeth at us. 'What is it? Will it hurt us?'

I assured her it wouldn't, and the quoll disappeared into her halfway house — a tin-covered stack of timber near my house, but my granddaughter was rather nervous as she bared her plump and vulnerable little bottom. I must say it occurs to me too, in similar situations, since I learnt about the wallaby. Chomp!

The quoll and I respect each other. Like me, she's a compromising creature. It's not that she's becoming tame — far from it! But she does tolerate me and my pitiful scratches of civilisation in her extended territory. She lets me into the shed to fetch things, stays out of sight as I hold my nose and forage about. I usually call out 'Coming through! It's only me!' as I enter. If we surprise each other, she silently shows her teeth and disappears. I acknowledge this as her claimed space; I don't want her to move elsewhere and be at risk.

She renders my shed almost unusable during her breeding season, since quolls don't separate their sanitary and living arrangements, and like their food best when stored long enough to be putrid. Unfortunately she has chosen my horizontal stockpile of second-hand doors as the centre of her domestic arrangements. I don't know what I'll do if I ever get round to more building — buy more doors I suppose. I expect they'd be ruined by now anyway, sandwiching as they do small bones and scraps of furry skin and less identifiable remnants of meals past.

Her moving in here was the result of false advertising, as she came in response to my ex-partner's attempt to keep ducks. She got the lot, mother and six ducklings, despite a fortress-like netted run. But pickings for her since from my vegetarian household have been extremely lean.

Yet she never gives up hope. On the verandah is my old garbage 'bin', a simple metal holder for a supermarket bag. She jumps in, scrabbles around, selects, and jumps out. I hear her every night, and if I shine the torch on her through the window above, she takes no notice. Her boisterous kids make so much noise they often don't hear me open the door, so sometimes I surprise two pink-nosed little faces peering in astonishment over the edge of the suspended plastic bag, followed by an explosion of spots as they make their getaway, gambolling off like runaway rocking horses.

The quolls prefer strong cheeses like Blue Castello, and even though I think I've scraped the wrappers clean, they find them worthwhile. Anything dairy-based will do, or even substitute-dairy, like tofu. Spinach and ricotta lasagne, dropped on the floor and dumped on the compost, was popular, but bliss is an oily tuna tin when I've had visitors. It gets passionately and noisily licked from one end of the verandah to the other.

Normally all wildlife sightings are a source of pleasure, but in summer, which is bringing-up-baby time here, I get a bit overrun with the patter, or clatter, of little paws. I always thought my quoll had twins, as each summer, from dusk till dawn, I'd seen just two spotted bundles of mischief cavorting about the house and yard while she went hunting. They're fully furred, although less spotty than their mother, old enough to be left unattended — in the playpen.

She pushes the boundaries a bit, since I was supposed to have the house. The line around my territory has retreated to the inside of the house. The verandah is definitely quoll country. This last generation is far less wary of me — the quoll kids have darted under my chair as I sat on the verandah after dinner, even with the fairy lights on above me.

I shut the front windows at night ever since two of them got inside into the sink (I admit it, I hadn't washed up). They made a terrible racket cleaning up the dishes. When sprung by the torch, a flurry of spots leapt out the window, which I quickly shut before hopping back into bed. I soon realised that only one had got away, as an almighty din soon began; one had got confused and leapt down behind the fridge, where, once recovered from the shock, it was banging away at the coils trying to get out.

Yet the lines are blurring. Apart from the rare days when I have to enter her shed, I'd only seen her gadding about at night or at its very edges. I knew my windowsills were part of her regular patrol, but one misty afternoon she appeared at the window in front of my desk. She was less than an arm's length from me.

I froze as her wet pink nose sniffed the glass, her dark eyes apparently scanning but not registering me. So close, I could see the fine raindrops glistening on her whiskers and rich reddish-brown fur, spotted with white to the tip of her tail; I could see the knuckly bends and sharp claws of her neat and clever paws as she clung to the window, and the deceptive daintiness of her pointed carnivorous face as she craned forward and up to investigate.

She whirled away to leap to the top of the shower cubicle, where her spotted tail, which is as long as her body, hung down over the edge.

'No,' I silently assured her, 'I don't need doors — or a shed really. Well, not all of it. But I do need more wonderful wild ones like you.'

For although there are laws, there's no practical way to protect the creatures in my refuge from unrestrained dogs, wild or weekender. One day my quoll came home late — midday — and along the track, which was unusual. She was moving slowly, awkwardly. Then I saw why. On her back she was carrying one of her offspring, who was far too old for that, almost as big as herself. But this was a rescue operation for, as she passed close by, I could see that the young one had a large area of raw flesh on its hind leg. Only a dog could have done that.

Too exhausted to make it to the shed, she took it to her halfway house. I put a container of water at the entrance to it, and hoped for the best. I was very upset, as I'd found a young quoll drowned in the horses' water tub a few days before. That had been bad enough — and I put a plank in there to make sure that any other creature that fell in from then on could climb out — but, if she only had two, this must be her last young one!

Next day, I saw a patch of brown and white just outside the timber stack; it must be the injured one resting in the sun, I thought. I tiptoed round the back to see better. There were six of them! Sleeping, curled together like kittens, a spotted furry carpet. The mother must have brought them down from the shed to keep the sick one company. I was delighted that she felt so secure with me; they were only about 5 metres from the house, right next to my woodheap.

I then read that the average litter size is five, but they play in pairs. And they are very playful, taking turns to keep me awake at night with their thumpings and crashings, chasing each other over my tin roof and along the windowsills. I grit my teeth and remind myself that all kids must grow up and leave home sometime.

But having seen the result of a foray beyond the netting, I wish she could keep them in the playpen forever. Or that I could net the whole property. Quolls can climb, dogs can't.

So each morning, as I sidestep last night's quoll contributions on the verandah or steps, or pick up the scattered garbage, I don't complain. In fact, if I haven't seen or heard from her for a night, I get worried. What is she up to? Is she OK?

This summer, I've seen no young ones, and the shed is not as smelly as it should be with an entire family. I am beginning to think that one of last year's young males may have taken over, ousted his mother from her shed and surrounding territory. They are mature at one year, and the males are more heavily built than the females. Without comparison, I can't be sure, but the current garbage-raking quoll seems a bit boofier, less delicate of feature than mine.

Late last winter I saw a big male sniffing through the orchard, in the middle of the day, which is very unusual. Whatever he was doing, he ignored me as he worked his way up the hill. I had assumed he was *the* male for the mating season, as each year one tracks down my female and creates a ruckus in the shed for weeks. But he may have been the usurper. I'd really prefer a female to share with, but I wasn't asked. I found I missed the kids this summer, noise and all, so I hope she comes back.

The quoll kids used to cover the night shift in the playpen until the baby magpie got dropped off. Each year I get at least one of these, and they've all been whingers. I don't blame the mothers for dumping them here as soon as they can, but 6 a.m.'s not fair.

This summer's magpie junior was no exception.

'Wah! Wah! Wah!' he whined, nonstop, as he waddled about the lawn. He'd be momentarily distracted by a piece of hose or agricultural pipe that he'd try to extract from the ground, but then the whining would resume. She'd drop in often to check on him and shut him up with a worm or two, then fly off, with him clumsily trying to follow, and whingeing even louder.

When he outgrew his mother, he followed her in short bursts of flight round the yard, but on the ground he loomed over her, looking cocky, and ever asking 'What's for dinner? When's dinner ready?' How well I remember that hollow-legged teenage stage.

Then the Crimson Rosellas turned up and for a week the lawn and lower branches were full of young ones, still green-backed for camouflage and still totally ignorant of the musical whistles of their parents. With heads bobbing and beaks open, all they produced was a constant rusty chorus of 'N-y-air, n-y-air, n-y-air!' Their nasal tones kept me expecting the Bugs Bunny follow-up of 'What's up, Doc?'

But without doubt the slowest developers are the kookaburra kids. My place has many older trees and good nesting holes — I have lots of kookaburras. In the breeding season, there are dozens of young ones about, sitting in groups from three to six, turning every raised object in the garden into totem poles, and all muttering. They have a totally flat delivery and are hopeless at learning the words, as all they have is a creaky 'Hah, hah, hah, hah …' ad nauseam.

Listening to their progress is more painful to the ear than violin practice, for they saw away relentlessly throughout the next trainee stage, 'Oo-wah, oo-wah, oo-wah! Oo-wah, oo-wah, oo-wah!' It seems to last a month, despite plentiful demonstrations from parents and relatives of how to get all the rises and falls of the proper song right.

This was the first year I've been aware of the King Parrots using the facilities, but, seeking the source of a single scratchy repeated note, like a stuck machine that needed oiling, I found a mother and baby in a small tree in the yard. The young one's head was still green, not yet the vivid scarlet of his mother's; he was leaning forward with his beak open, emitting that one note, without a break. Perhaps they were just visiting, but I suspect she was trying to get rid of the kid, drop him off so she could have a brief respite from his relentless demands. Only he wasn't having any of that and kept following her from branch to branch. She gave up; some kids just don't take to day care.

I heard him continuing the carry-on further up the hill. Not that the adult call is at all musical, but at least it's more varied.

Perhaps the different species are checking out the playpen for next season, since, also for the first time, I had a visit from a Yellow-tailed Black Cockatoo mother and child. I get groups of these big cockatoos in damp weather, but this time there were just two of them, sitting in the branches of the big stringy-bark uphill from the toilet.

Set amongst the rocks at the foot of this stringy-bark I keep an upturned triple-decker old ceramic insulator full of water, so thirsty birds often provide a little entertainment and aid contemplation. The toilet deliberately has no door; it is open on its eastern face, as little weather comes from that direction, and the morning sun is pleasant on bare knees in winter.

The two cockatoos didn't look much different from each other, dark brownish-black, with lemon cheek patches and tail bands, but I recognised that forward lean of the body, that whining tone. One of them was a young one, and it sounded like he was sawing down the tree without taking a breath.

I've just realised that I keep assuming these demanding young birds are masculine. Funny, that.

While the baby boom lasts, the oft-given comment of how peaceful it must be up here in the bush is met with a short and bitter laugh. 'Huh!' I say, quoll spots passing before my eyes, and outside the juveniles start again, 'Hah, hah, hah, hah …'

Even when the babies have grown up and been shooed off to find their own territories, it's never silent here. At night the orchestrated cacophony of frog voices, high and low, long and short, in the small dam down the front, merely provides a continuous background chorus for the hoarse, prolonged gruntings of koalas and the boomings and mournful calls of night birds.

When we first put this dam in, to have 'water views' from the verandah as much as for bushfires, my then partner decided to bring some tadpoles over from the big dam, which is out of sight. And earshot.

The following summer we thought we had a flock of demented sheep out front. It was, almost. Bleating Tree Frogs. The frog book notes that 'Large numbers of this frog can produce a deafening noise.' Indeed they can — my partner thought he'd go crazy, that he'd have to drain the new dam. Yet he got used to the noise, same as city dwellers don't notice four lanes of traffic roaring past below their unit balconies, or jumbo jets skimming their rooftops. Now I'd go crazy with that!

But once summer's over, the frogs calm down and the wild-child rearing should be done for the year. Right at the end of summer, I was thrilled to spot eight White-headed Pigeons fly up from the rainforest gully and land just outside my gate. I'd seen one or two before, but this was a rare sighting. Through the binoculars, one of them seemed more grey than white. As I noted the event on the calendar, I heard a noise at the low window. I turned. There on the sill was the greyish pigeon. A young one? I checked the yard. Yep, all the grown-ups were gone. The word about the playpen had spread to the rainforest.

I can only hope that the Brush Turkeys don't hear of it by next summer.

CHAPTER 8

BUSH MATTERS

ON THE FARM WHERE I grew up, the only 'wild' place left on it was a small patch by the creek, flood-prone, so not worth clearing. That patch of gums and wattles was for me the heart of our place, and pushing through its privet edges marked my entry into the real world. I had a small swept dirt clearing in there that I called my cubby, and from it I'd peep out to the open paddock, feeling somehow safer. I can't remember worrying about snakes, despite always being on the lookout for them on the farm itself.

I knew that when I grew up I wanted to live somewhere that had more bush, and less land shaped by people.

I found it here. Partly cleared years before, only moderately logged and grazed, although burnt many times, most of it was regenerating well. Best of all, it bordered virgin rainforest, admittedly state forest and perhaps at risk, but the house site we'd chosen faced higher mountains into whose pristine forests I knew there was not even a track.

After I moved back, just before Christmas one year a bulldozer began carving a road in towards those old-growth forests. It took six days of damage before our conservationist friend, Barrie Griffiths, could obtain an injunction to stop the work until the Forestry Commission completed a lawful environmental impact study (EIS).

The conclusions of their EIS were unsurprising: no significant ill effects would be caused by logging; rather, it would be beneficial! We submitted long objections, and went out to the old-growth forest to make a video in readiness for a publicity campaign if need be. It was awesomely different from the 50-year-old overly dense regrowth with which we were familiar. Strangely human-friendly to walk in — park-like, with well-spaced and truly massive eucalypts towering over tussock grasses, strappy clumps of dianella and lomandra, and ferns and ground orchids; no understorey except in the run-off gullies. It *felt* ancient. Some of the big trees looked vulnerable, with hollows burnt right through their bases over the years.

The EIS was rejected and, in the end, that old-growth forest was saved as a wilderness area and a new national park created to protect wherever else up here had been state forest. That ought to mean forever, but the New South Wales state government has now changed laws to better suit corporate plans, although it is of course also done 'in the best interests of the people'. Projects like coalmines are deemed to be of state significance, fast-tracked around the nuisances of hard-won protective legislation like an EIS, while also 'of course' having to meet 'strict environmental guidelines'. Why am I not comforted?

Meanwhile I could do something about my own place. The vendor reckoned it had so much tree cover because he'd left lots of 'mother trees' for seed. As these were invariably low branching, most unsuitable as saw logs, we doubted his motives, but the result was welcome. The block runs along a ridge, falling away in a series of gentle shelves to a rocky escarpment, and beyond. I hardly ever go below the escarpment, but it acts as a privacy barrier from the next valley.

There were only a few clearings where the trees hadn't grown back, and one of them is where I live — a north-facing grassy bowl, rimmed by trees, protected from bad weather from the south by the ridge above, and from the west by the tree rim. Our old bushman had warned us not to build on the ridge, but to tuck ourselves down lower, and he was right. It can be blowing a very audible gale 'up top', and the trees on my western rim will be bent near double by its force as it roars up the escarpment, but it is usually merely a breeze on my verandah.

There's a chip in the forested rim of my bowl, which gives my verandah those mountain views to the north. Each year I look up to the far-off copper flush of new growth in the Antarctic Beech forests on the mountains of the wilderness area, and I take comfort in knowing that this unique density of life is protected.

Then I look down the spring gully by my house and delight in my hundreds of pale-green tree guards, hoping that such gullies will one day again be the rainforests they were, teeming with quite a different life from that of my ridges and shelves, a life taken from them by cattle and annual burning. All that was left down there were stinging nettles and moss, the odd clump of rock orchids or staghorns, and a few spindly unknown trees with glossy leaves — rainforest remnants. They hadn't come back by themselves as the eucalypt forests were doing.

I don't know why I didn't set about helping them sooner, when I was younger and fitter. Too busy coping with life, I suppose, and too unsure of what lay ahead to commit to such a project. I know better now than to wait for guarantees.

About five years ago, I heard of grants under the *Native Vegetation Conservation Act*, via the then Department of Land and Water Conservation (DLWC). I applied, and after sixteen months of inspections and paperwork, I received a grant for fencing off my gullies and my lagoon area from the horses.

In return I'd propagate, plant and tend the appropriate indigenous plants for those areas, curtail all other activities within them and perhaps allow educational access later. This Property Agreement was registered on my deeds and remains in effect forever. Other people make Conservation Agreements with National Parks and Wildlife to achieve the same end.

Since I'm a cynic, I feel that such privately protected areas have more secure futures than state-owned ones, where conservation values can be removed simply by re-naming. After all, from a ministerial desk in Macquarie Street, if you look at an area only on paper, for example on an application from a large mining company, green areas can be greyish.

On my piece of damaged Eden, I did the lagoon area first, as it was the easiest project. These lagoons are actually 'perched', or 'hanging', swamps; they only occur at higher altitudes and their water comes from springs. Reed-filled or edged, they provide habitats for many species, especially frogs, and drinking water for all. The damp sedge-like vegetation of their associated descending chain of smaller lagoons is habitat for others, including endangered small mammals. Mine was the only one on this ridge but I'd seen several out in the old-growth forest, and each one was surrounded by a ring of tall paperbark trees, which are found nowhere else at these levels. Specific settings for precious jewels, ecologically.

My lagoon had no such paperbark trees, which wasn't surprising given the relentless burning regime of its previous owner. It did have several hugely broad and ancient *Angophora floribundas*, or Apple Gums, blackened but undamaged by bushfires. The biggest grows almost horizontally, leaning out over the water like a great dark monster, its upper branches splayed out like antennae. It has incredible presence, as does the whole lagoon area. My story 'Traces of Life', which won the Alan Marshall Award, was inspired by this strange place.

With permission, I collected seed capsules from those old-growth lagoons — Prickly Paperbarks, *Melaleuca styphelioides*. The seeds themselves were minute brown specks, hard to sow separately, and they came up in thick clumps in their pots, with the saucers beneath kept full of water to mimic the swamp. I potted them on into milk cartons and soon hundreds of them were reaching for the greenhouse roof — a paperbark forest under glass. But the fencing around the lagoon hadn't been completed and I began to worry about the delay in getting these keen little trees into the ground where they belonged.

It was a difficult fencing job, as where the terrain wasn't rocky it was boggy, but the young contractor did his best and finally I was able to plant them out. I did this nervously, as snakes like frogs, and frogs like these wet areas. Since the horses had been fenced out, the tussocks had grown tall; visibility was nil for that flash of glossy black. As it had always been rare to come here and not see a Red-bellied Black Snake, it was probably due to that lack of visibility rather than a lack of their presence that I didn't see any as I squelched my way around the edges, safe to the knees at least in my long gumboots.

Because the paperbark leaves were prickly even when young, I assumed no possum or wallaby would eat them. Nor did they for the first few months, when I was checking often. The trees were doing well, liking having their roots so wet, but I ought to have remembered the complacency factor.

Next time I went there they were all eaten to some extent. I bought extra strong wire netting and collared a male friend to cut it up for me. I made tall cylindrical lidded guards, and fixed them to the ground with spikes. Do your worst, possums!

Next visit many of these guards were squashed, by the big kangaroos, I imagined. I straightened them out, but had to wait until my son could come to bang in tomato stakes with a mallet. Do your worst, kangaroos!

The guards stayed vertical; the paperbark trees grew on, uneaten.

The second stage of my regeneration plan was for the rainforest gullies, most of which have a spring at their head, which, while not always flowing above ground, has created a deeply incised and rocky watercourse.

In the first autumn of my solo life here I collected fruit and seed and cuttings from the national park, with their permission. I didn't know what ought to be collected as I didn't know what had once been here. No advice was available from DLWC, nor could National Parks tell me anything, but they did arrange a community rainforest identification day.

We stumbled behind the botanist through a patch of rainforest, listened and looked, ooh-ed and aah-ed and asked informed questions, like 'What's that?' Back at camp we peered at our collected cuttings and pored over the ID bible, by Williams, Harden and McDonald, to learn how to use their system.

As blueprint and donor, I chose a slope in the national park that was similarly oriented to mine, and spent much time poking about in its lower brushy gullies, my eyes becoming attuned to colours and shapes denoting fruit or seed amongst the leaves, or amidst the humus of the forest floor. I was nervous going in there on my own at first, as I'm neither a 'seasoned bushwalker' nor a solitary one. Like most new things, starting was the hard part. Very soon, as my involvement grew, so did my familiarity and confidence, and the thrill of finding new plants overrode my fears.

Whenever I drove through the rainforest on my trip to town, I'd go slow, peering into the roadside brush. That's how I found the mother tree for my young Red Cedars, *Toona australis*. A tall, straight, eminently millable cedar grows right beside the road, inexplicably spared by the axe in the past. A cluster of seed pods had fallen and caught in the branches of an accessible small gum below, just waiting for me to find them, I felt. I took it as a gift, a sign of approval for what I was doing.

Not far from where that cedar grows is where I think the explorer Ludwig Leichhardt must have camped, in a hollow tree, all by himself, for three weeks in 1843. I've read his letters about what he saw then, and empathised with his raptures about solitude, the rich vegetation, the stars. In fact, I was inspired to write back, in 'Leichhardt and I — a Conversation Across Time', intended for radio. I feel differently about that part of the mountains since I have 'seen' Leichhardt there. I also see how, just a few years later, he could have lost himself and his party forever when trying to cross northern Australia; he was keen, but he was no bushman.

On my two main collecting expeditions, I had help from two young volunteer botanists, Tasman Willis and Alaina Casey, and then from my 'green' friend, Marg McLean, far more knowledgeable than I, so most of what we found was identified and given its proper name, for the record. Some they knew by sight, but many had to be put through the ID system of elimination. It was as thrilling as detective work, narrowing down the options — do the leaves grow alternate or opposite? Are they simple or compound? Lobed or not? — working our way through the many subgroups to the final decisive factor: do the leaves have oil dots or not? For me this step was the dither factor as I could rarely see oil dots.

My greenhouse was soon full of foam boxes of the prescribed light seed-raising mix, fostering hundreds of baby Sandpaper Figs, Red Cedars, Lillipillies, and many others whose common names I don't know. The greenhouse would wear its summer shadecloth coat all year round now. I installed an automatic timer on a spray watering system, which allows me to go away without worrying about their welfare. It's wonderful — cheap, easy even for me to put together, and the timer runs on two AA batteries for more than a year. I love it. So do the trees.

As they grew, I potted them into recycled milk cartons. I was using paddle-pop sticks as labels, but I can dispense with them now — which is just as well, as they turn black and illegible after about a year with all the watering — for I'm on first name terms with young *Acmena, Omalanthus, Neolitsea, Toona, Citriobatus, Pyschotria, Melicope, Pittosporum, Hedycarya, Ehretia, Ficus, Eupomatia, Pimelia, Cryptocarya, Dysoxylum* and their varied siblings.

Said aloud, many of these ring like the names of nymphs or goddesses, or the daughters of old-fashioned intelligentsia. Just imagine the scene in the manor drawing room, as young Miss Melicope Dalrymple and her friend Miss Acmena Pemberton are introduced to a newcomer to the county, Miss Eupomatia Braithwaite, whose reputation as a bluestocking has preceded her ...

Soon I ran out of space in the glasshouse. To make more room, I fashioned a rough shadehouse from star posts and shadecloth, hanging it off the western side of the greenhouse. The seedlings go out there to acclimatise before I plant them out. There are still many seedlings, overcrowded and impatient in their nursery boxes, that I haven't had room to pot on. I will, I promise them — hang in there, your turn will come. They look surprisingly healthy given their cramped conditions and inadequate nourishment.

Relatives and friends faithfully rinse and save their milk cartons for me, present me with garbage bags and boxes full when we meet at long intervals. They are the godparents to my fledgling rainforest. The cartons last about a year under the constant watering, when it's time to plant them out anyway, and instead of having to winkle the tree out of a pot, I just rip the soggy carton open.

For the last three autumns I've been planting out the little trees. I choose autumn because, while it's still warm enough for growth, the cooler weather means less evaporation, and thus more chance of their survival; rain or mist is more likely; and, very importantly, snakes are not so active.

Their new-home gullies are *really* steep and, being fenced off from the horses, are also inaccessible to my four-wheel-drive Suzuki. With my arthritic knees, it's a challenging process to get trees and gear down there. I was not expecting arthritis when I first applied for the grant; if I had, I'd have considered such a planting program to be an impossible undertaking. Being forced to do it showed me that it's not impossible, just slow.

The first problem was how to carry everything. At the op-shop I'd found a capacious and sturdy, woven and lined cloth bag, which unfortunately was of ugly brown checks. I had to choke down my distaste to buy it. Incidentally, I've noticed that many men think it's odd when my first question about, for example, a bargain car, is 'What colour is it?' They think it irrelevant!

But the homely brown bag has proved perfect for its task. In it I can wedge the seedlings, the roll of green plastic guards, three bamboo stakes each, and the rubber mallet to bang them in with. With its cloth 'handles' slung over my shoulder and the bunched stakes protruding behind, I feel like Diana with her quiver of arrows, albeit a ragtag, older version. From each hand dangles a 4-litre container of water. The spade handle is held as well, precariously, in my right hand. I really need another hand but make do with dropping the spade when my wrist begins to hurt.

I edge my way along the narrow transverse wallaby tracks, slip over rocks or grass, try not to twist my ankle on the sharp drops, narrowly avert a headlong fall … and finally reach the part of the gully where this lot are destined to grow. I try to avoid stepping on tussocks because their dense mature growth bends over and forms lovely habitats for small mammals; I can often see little tunnels beneath.

Looking back up the near-vertical slope, I sigh at the thought of the return climb. I search for a half-level spot and lower the water containers to the ground. As I unlock and massage my hands, I'm struck anew by how heavy water is. I should have known, after all the buckets I'd carted for the mudbricks, but perhaps the intervening 25 years have made it heavier.

I began planting about twelve at a time, then it dropped to eight, and now five, because I am planting so far down the gully that I'd never walk back up for more water. To get my seedlings off to a good start, I was giving them a third each of what the water containers hold, and walking back up to refill from the larger one I had in the back of the car at the closest point. So I was making two climbs each session. This autumn the soil was so dry that they needed more water each.

Most fine mornings I plant some. My progress back up the hill is urged on by a small voice telling me with each plodding step that this is good for me. 'Oh yeah,' I think, 'so's castor oil.' I make it once more, collapse over a coffee as I write down what I've planted. I keep a running tally — it's over 600 now — only thousands more to go. It doesn't sound like a lot compared to flat paddock regeneration projects, but it takes time to even find a spot where there's a spade's depth of soil amongst the loose volcanic rocks down there.

I shower off the possible leeches or ticks and let the water soothe the nettle stings. Then I start worrying over whether it will rain soon, as I have neither the energy nor the knees to go back down and water them after planting. They must survive on their own, but there were so few follow-up showers this last atypical autumn that I thought it too risky and stopped planting.

The vines — *Cissus, Dioscorea, Glycine, Eustrephus* — will go in later. I expect that birds and bats will pass on gifts of other seeds to complete the tapestry.

I hadn't expected it to be such a long-term project, but some seeds germinated quickly, some slowly; some seedlings raced towards adulthood, others remained too small to plant out. Each autumn is very busy, with far less writing time than other seasons. I've come to think of autumn as I did those first five years of my children's lives, a dedicated nurturing time when other interests take a back seat, hoping it will mean better results later.

It was suggested I get some WWOOFers (World-Wide Opportunities on Organic Farms) to help, but that would be so impersonal. These seedlings are my babies. I want to see them safely established in their new lives, not hand them over to strangers. If the patient seedlings start losing it, demanding faster progess than I can manage, I will seek help, but not yet.

And I like pottering about alone in my spring gullies; it gives me the chance to be quiet in them, to absorb their unique atmosphere. Sometimes I think about what would happen if I slipped, broke a leg or an ankle, or if I disturbed a brown snake and was bitten, but it's only a passing thought.

I choose occasional risk over constant stress — traffic, overcrowding; harassed and cranky mums with whingeing toddlers in supermarkets; neighbours' dogs barking at shadows in the middle of the night; neighbours' kids just metres from your study window, endlessly skateboarding or playing rap music … no thanks!

This fostering of growth from seed to tree to future rainforest is the most creative thing I've ever done, factual babies and fictional stories included. I only wish I'd started earlier, so I'd have more chance of seeing advanced results. I might get twenty years, but what a sight they'll be after 40!

The greenhouse that made possible the propagation and slow staging, and thus the whole regeneration project, was also the subject of an article for *Owner Builder* — 'Evolution of an OB Greenhouse'. 'Evolution' because it was built in unplanned steps over several years and was not in the end what it started out to be.

The project only began because, on a trip to Sydney, my partner and I spotted a huge pile of plain timber sash windows stacked on the footpath outside a block of flats with all new aluminium windows winking down at us. And we were towing an empty trailer. Incurable magpies we both were, but I was wavering towards leaving them for the rubbish collection when he said, 'They'd make a great glasshouse.'

We got them up here and restacked them expectantly near the chosen site. Two years later, the windows were still sitting there, flaking paint. I began to mutter about unkept promises. 'OK, OK, I'll take a week off this spring and build it.'

Nights were spent drawing up the design, the building size and shape and frame calculated to fit the window halves — a tiny glass church with turned wooden finials on the ridgepole; none of these sterile aluminium kit models for us.

The greenhouse would be level, but the site wasn't, so my partner intended to fill in below the bottom timber rail later, with rocks. By the end of the allotted week, the roof and most of the sides had windows on, but there were many gaps, including all round below. Fencing wire was used to hold it all together in the meantime. Sitting high on its skinny wooden legs, pointing its nose due north and deceptively up, it did look like a glass church about to be launched.

A year went by. I saw it suffer under all weathers, including our heaviest ever snow. I watched the wind gradually demolish my glasshouse. The fencing wire stretched and allowed a bit too much movement; the windows tried to behave like balloons and burst; the putty fell out; the frames peeled, parted company at their corners. I picked glass shards out of the grass and started muttering once more.

We sent for greenhouse brochures and began redesigning. We would use the glass out of what was left of our windows and just buy a bit extra, plus aluminium glazing bars, clips, etc. My now experienced greenhouse builder decided he'd first fill in those rock walls so the wind couldn't sneak in and burst this one. That took a long time, not only because he didn't have much to spare, but also because he preferred working in 'larger windows' of time. Since mothers always have to snatch whatever short bursts they can to get anything done, I found it hard to be patient.

Next the much-abused free windows were removed. I painted the timber frame with white enamel and it was ready for glazing, the unfree commercial way. Cute glass churches are overrated anyhow. Gravel fill made a heat sink floor and allowed drainage. It worked. On a cold windy day, inside it was sheltered and sunny, warm and peaceful, with garden and forest views; I would sit on my potting stool and contemplate moving my bed in there.

Doing it twice to get it right brought the total cost of that green-house close to $1000. Freebies can be very expensive. But had we not picked those windows up we wouldn't have started the greenhouse and I wouldn't have considered a rainforest nursery.

As inspiration for my young rainforests, just over my ridge-top boundary is the patch of virgin brush that appealed so strongly when we first bought this place. It shelters on the cool southern side, fiercely protected by a belt of tall stinging nettles and raspy wild raspberries. I venture in there rarely, and never by myself.

In there it is another world, awesome yet fragile. In there the silence commands respect as, hushed and inadequate in the dim green light, I breathe in its mushroom smell, peer at its surreal fungi and lichens, giant snail shells, bird mounds and scrapings. I tread lightly, yet still sink into the thick compost of leaves, slip over mossy fallen trunks. In there lives a Giant Stinging Tree of vast girth, hollow and ancient, but mostly it is hard to name this forest of tree roots, buttresses and trunks, laced with ropey twists of vines, their leaves but silhouettes far up in the canopy. It is only outside, from the track on the ridge above, that the cedars declare themselves with the pink–bronze of their new leaves, and unidentifiable vines flower on top of the green upper storey.

I love the absolutely independent life of this brush. I'm hoping that my rainforests will one day creep up their gullies to the ridge and link thin fingers with it. Lost generations coming home.

It's a great thought. 'Regeneration, *n.*, the process of being morally, spiritually or physically renewed or reborn.' Renewing the forests to what they once were, giving back to the land a little of what has been taken, in gratitude for what it gives me. The trees I plant might live for hundreds of years after I die.

The key, it seems to me, is in the word 'respect'. We need to 're-spect', to go back to our roots as well as those of the word — from the Latin *specere*, to look, so 'to look again'. If we can cast aside our acquired blindness, we might actually *see* the natural world to which we belong — its richness, diversity and importance beyond ourselves — and regain respect for it. Perhaps then we'd stop trashing it.

Bush matters.

Chapter 9

Hazards and Horses

NATURE IS ALWAYS DOMINANT here. Each year, I've only just accepted that it's no longer winter before I begin to worry that it's nearly summer. My enjoyment of spring is thus threaded with concern for how dry or hot it will be, because that will determine the fire danger.

The fire danger period usually begins in October and goes through until March. In bad years it's extended. I always get told if it is because it's my job to repaint the sign our rural fire brigade puts up in advance of the season each year. If it's up there in black and white, Joe Blow can't say — as his illegal fire races through his next-door neighbour's forest or through the national park — 'How was I supposed to know I needed a bloody permit? It looked like it'd burn, so I lit it, same as I've always done.'

Most past fires in these mountains have originated in such burn-offs, often from pastoral properties a long way away 'just burning off the rubbish', meaning their back bush, and they haven't worried if it kept going towards here. 'Could do with a good burn, anyway.' When we first bought this place, its previous owner would drop lit matches as he drove by, anytime he thought it would burn. It took a few years to convince him that we didn't see it as a favour.

There are new regulations, where the environment is considered in deciding what and where and how often landowners may burn off, aiming for more strategic, mosaic burning. But the old idea of 'I can do what I like on my own place' dies hard.

In this last very dry autumn, from the smoke I could see that an 'escaped' burn-off two valleys away was racing up towards the wilderness areas, driven by high winds. A day later I learnt that it had burnt the ancient paperbarks round the perched swamps, where my seeds came from. As the well-fed smoke billowed skyward I thought of those giant eucalypts in the old-growth forest just beyond, and how the fire might gain a hold inside their forked bases.

Due prior process for approvals and notifications, containment plans, etc., had apparently not been bothered with. In the night I saw the fire's hungry red progress on the slopes, and felt sick at heart at the destruction taking place out there, at all the small animals that burn with the tussocks …

Rain fell after about four days — but what if it hadn't? And was any action taken against the match-happy, responsibility-shy landowner? I'd lay bets it wasn't. Natural assets ought to be valued as highly as man-made ones. Houses and sheds can be rebuilt; endangered species and unique habitats can't.

Rather than burning off, I use horses to reduce the fuel on the ground, and thus the fire hazard. A tall, coarse grass, called blady grass, grows strongly where the forest has been cleared. Often waist-high, it burns as if it's been doused in kerosene; in a bushfire you hear a sudden great roar as it reaches and feeds on a patch of blady grass.

Not only does fire love it but it loves fire, and comes back vigorously. So it's a fire cycle: the more blady grass you have on a block, the more fire-prone it is, and the more often it's burnt, the more blady grass you get. If you plant enough trees, eventually this grass will cease to dominate, but that's a slow process. Cattle usually don't eat blady grass, but horses do.

My daughter keeps her horses on my place. They're fenced off from all but about 30 acres, as the rest is regenerating. They like blady grass so much they stick their heads through the fence to eat beyond, so they create a small firebreak outside the fence line too.

I'm not a horsey person; I think them beautiful, especially in motion, but I'm scared of their size and power — especially if I'm on them. Since they sense this, although I can ride, I mostly don't. We all took riding lessons before we first moved here, being practical, in much the same way as I did a first aid course.

My daughter was only three then, and had already been anointed a horse person by my youngest sister, who's the horse lover amongst my siblings. We still have the how-to book she gave my daughter on her second birthday, *Your First Horse Book*. So my daughter had no choice in the matter, and she's now inducting *her* daughter.

Geriatric horses put out to pasture would seem ideal hazard reducers, but there are problems. They die. And they may not do it in one hit but 'go down' and do it slowly. If we call the vet to come up and give it a mercy injection, at enormous cost, we must then bury or somehow enclose the body so other creatures can't eat it because it will be toxic. Or we must get someone to shoot it — and still we're left with what to do with the body. They're too big for hand-dug graves, and they tend to choose awkward places, too close to the house, or in a dam. Several times my daughter, a courageous young woman, has had to tie a rope around the dead horse — somehow — and tow it away — somewhere — beyond sight and smell. Years later I come across its bleached skeleton in a gully.

My daughter tends the horses on her occasional weekend visits. She's smaller than I am, but strong in the arms like me, so she can keep them standing on three legs while she rasps and trims their hooves.

People may think that so long as horses have grass, shade and water, they'll look after themselves, but they need frequent checking, often hoof trimming or cleaning, worming, maybe teeth filing, and on a bush block there's always a possibility of being caught in barbed-wire fences, or staked in the abdomen by a fallen stick trodden on the wrong way.

Both these have happened here. The latter must have been horrific for the young bay horse, Sally, and occurred while we were weekenders. My daughter's friend discovered the accident days later and phoned my then seventeen-year-old daughter, who drove up from Sydney. After the vet had put Sally down, they had to burn her body. So it was horrific for them too. If you can judge a person's character by whether or not you could depend on them in a crisis, those two country teenagers would come through with gold medals.

The other accident was only redeemed from being fatal because I was here full-time again. Jess, the oldest and wisest horse, had stood immobile all one day and night, not panicking and pulling against the barbed wire, until we'd missed her and gone looking. Always wary of being caught, moving away as soon as anyone approached, this time she remained perfectly still while we cut the wire from around her legs.

As she leapt away to join her mates, I happened to glance further down the steep fence line. A flash of reddish fur, and long white bones. Close up, it was the remains of Red, a chestnut who'd gone missing years ago.

All barbed wire was replaced after that. The rogue cattle for which it had been used were long gone, and since the national park was created, there are no cattle in the forest.

We currently have four horses: two geldings and two mares.

I'm now forced to depend on them as my primary lawn mowers as well as hazard reducers. I used to mow my entire house paddock, raking up the grass and using it for mulch. To feel less like a house-proud suburbanite, I called this 'harvesting mulch'. It was also a fire hazard reduction measure, but secretly I liked the look of the almost-lawn around the trees and shrubs.

Being hit with arthritis about five years ago made me stop that nonsense. Not only would my knees not cope with the pushing, always up- or downhill to some degree, but my wrists wouldn't let me start any of the vintage Victa toe-cutter mowers my partner had collected. Which was a pity, as they were perfect tough little slashers for these tussocky paddocks.

And for kikuyu. Thirty years ago, on the advice of the then Soil Conservation Department, I planted runners of the introduced kikuyu grass to hold the sides of the newly bulldozed track and dam. Fortunately it's too cold here in winter for it to do well outside my house fence, where the wallabies eat it right down. It now seems hard to credit our ignorance — their ignorance. I'd seen kikuyu on the coast literally drowning sheds and fences in an unstoppable high tide of viciously bright green. I knew how it could take over, yet I did what 'the experts' told me to, regardless.

My punishment for this environmental crime is that kikuyu has taken over my gardens. Now, in spring and summer, I let the horses in to graze, and what survives in my garden is what they permit. They do a good job on the kikuyu, except that they are overly thorough, and in reaching a strand of it they tramp through and flatten woody shrubs like lavender and rosemary. They back onto, tread on and break small trees, seeming to target the slow-growing, precious ones I've been nursing along for years.

You'd think they'd be content with the lush kikuyu, but no, they like variety, and what's more they are extremely flighty about it —

perverse even. For example, as they'd been driving me crazy by eating my honeysuckle vine every few weeks, I figured it'd be safe to plant some out to cover a wall on the shed. Their dependable pruning wouldn't allow it to run and sucker. I protected the base of the new plant until it was established and it grew very well. But the horses changed their minds and didn't touch it and now I have an expanding sea of honeysuckle in the grass of the orchard. They just eat around it. 'Your problem,' they imply, when they briefly interrupt their grazing to watch me straining to pull out rooting runners.

Sabbath, the chestnut gelding, has decided he likes the leaves (and fruit if it's there) of plum, cherry, nashi and mulberry, so they are stripped to the height he can reach. And he's the tallest horse. Last year he was partial to jasmine, ornamental grape and wisteria. He hasn't touched them this year, but I know he will if I get complacent about it.

Zack, the boss bay gelding, has the distinction of being the only animal here, wild or domestic, who eats the leaves of any bulbs. I have clumps of jonquils and daffodils and snowflakes and tritonia naturalised in the grass out front, thriving without any effort from me. Their annual reappearance and blooming is always a gift, gratefully accepted. But Zack likes the strappy leaves of tritonia, so they no longer get to produce their massed wands of pink bells.

He was also not averse to poking his head over my vegie garden netting fence to eat celery or cabbage or whatever he could reach. So I had to raise the height of that fence too. Fences within fences! I left its gate at the old height as raising that seemed too hard, and besides, there was only a bare path beyond it. After a few weeks, Zack found he could reach quite a few vegetables by putting his head over the gate and twisting sideways. Making a new gate was still beyond me, so I attached doubled wire netting, like a heavy curtain, across the opening. This means I have to lift the curtain to open the gate, then duck under. Which is fine for gathering vegetables for dinner, but not for carrying spadefuls of compost. A new gate has been added to my 'sometime' list.

Jess, the aged buckskin mare, likes to munch the new leaves on the citrus trees, so they remain dwarfed and unproductive. I've put netting guards around the skinnier ones — more fences within fences — but am in a quandary about the others. I'll have to do something as my knees won't stand the jarring of my angry rush across the paddock when I see she is back over there, ripping and stripping away. She does not desist until I am almost there.

I feel she is ungrateful — I never try to catch her or ride her and I always ensure she gets her share of carrots — but, because she was my daughter's very first and much beloved horse, no ill can be said of her.

However I do recall some ill being said, if fleetingly, on our weekend visits from Sydney. My daughter would spend hours coaxing the almost uncatchable Jess to come close enough to be caught, a difficult job even in a corral. She'd squat beside a feed bucket, one hand hiding the halter behind her back, speaking softly, patient for a long time, losing it as Jess yet again shied away just as the halter rope went over her neck. Storming off, giving up, quite a few angry words scorched the mountain air. But she always found replenished patience and tried again, saying it wasn't Jess' fault, since she'd obviously been frightened in the past.

Shari, the barrel-shaped miniature pony, is a skewbald, white with splashes of chestnut. She likes to straddle small trees or shrubs and scratch her tummy by rubbing back and forth, or back up to bigger shrubs and scratch her fat rump. Consequently she breaks many twigs and branches, so the shrubs are lopsided, and she snaps small trees in half. She finds my metre-high sprinklers handy to scratch her face on, and breaks their moving parts. If I put stakes around anything, she rubs against those and breaks them.

The little wretch also gets through my regeneration area fence. She puts her front feet over the bottom wire and then wriggles and pushes her fat body through, spreading the wires and loosening the posts to the point of eventually lifting them clear out of the ground.

Recently I tried to give her away to a home with better fences and less for her to damage. This family had small boys to love her and a pony her size to be her friend. They led her home on the Friday, then spent the better part of the weekend retrieving her after she escaped twice, through electric fences, and wire fences far more tightly and closely strung than mine. The last time they caught her she was halfway back here.

I returned late that Sunday night from a weekend camp, helping to survey Aboriginal artefacts near Anvil Hill, proposed site for another monster open-cut coal mine in the Hunter. We'd found tools as old as 4000–5000 years, our archaeologists estimated. Holding a stone tool where my fingers fitted perfectly, as other fingers had done so very long ago, was overwhelming.

We'd also seen that rare thing in the long-grazed Hunter: an uncleared central valley floor, rich in unique woodland vegetation. It was incredible that anyone would contemplate the total destruction of this, called the Ark of the Hunter because of its biodiversity treasures, but they were — 2000 hectares of it! In a sane world, that area would be declared 'of state significance', to be protected rather than disembowelled. The weekend had been both inspiring and depressing, and I was physically and emotionally exhausted.

Next morning I dragged myself out of bed late, and far from alert. From the verandah I could see the three horses patiently waiting at the gate. Then I literally rubbed my eyes, for I could also see a low splash of brown and white through the netting. Bloody Shari!

Then I spotted the halter and lead rope on a verandah chair. I rang. They were very sorry she hadn't stayed; the little boys had cried; they'd all fallen for her cute looks. Their mother said, 'She's the sort of animal Walt Disney would make a movie about. I kept waiting for her to say something!'

I was stuck with her. No fence could keep her in. And no amount of appeals from her big brown eyes, peeping up at me through her long lashes and thick chestnut fringe, would make me think she was anything other than a pain.

To fence off the orchard section from the horses would be a lot of work — and then I'd have to mow it. A moveable electric fence would be fine, and there are the makings of one in the shed from an early attempt by my ex-partner at keeping possums out of the house yard, only I don't know how to do it.

I remember the first night the electrified yard fence was activated. It was a last resort, as we'd tried all suggestions — chilli spray, quassia chip spray, garlic chive surrounds — and still the possums were stripping the roses and the citrus trees. That night we watched as a bevy of possums conferred just outside the bottom corner. It appeared as if they were drawing straws, after a heated discussion — 'You go!' 'No, you go!' — had proved fruitless. But none of them was game to try it and the disgruntled group broke up and waddled off into the trees.

Yet the next night, and every night after for a few years, one battered old warrior climbed the fence without visible reaction. He had tattered ears and tufts of fur missing from fights past — and an addiction to roses. Knowing what the 'Zap!' feels like, I deemed such effort heroic; the garden could cope with one possum having a well-earned rose munch.

He's gone, but the local possums must have passed on the word about the 'Zap!' because I don't see many in here, even though the fence hasn't been electrified since the last fires. Or maybe my resident carnivorous quoll deters them.

So what the horses deliver is a grazed, semi-razed garden rather than the cropped lawn I ordered. And while they do a lot of unauthorised pruning, on the other hand they don't fancy eating tussocks or weeds, so I still have to do some sporadic mowing if I want to stop the house yard regressing to a wild paddock where bush rats would tunnel and nest, and snakes lurk.

In the year after I was hit with arthritis that's how it was, since I couldn't mow it, my partner couldn't find the time, and I hadn't yet resigned myself to sacrificing my garden. The bush rats ate through the bird netting we put over the fruit trees, not to mention invading the house and shed. I want to keep my patch unappealing to them.

Now, instead of collecting lawn clippings, I shovel up horse manure for compost and for mulch around the chewed fruit trees. I've been given a wonderful self-propelled mower that even I can start, so in the warmer months, before the sun hits the orchard, I occasionally do a little bit of easy mowing, but only where needed as anti-rat precautions. I don't mow the native grasses when they're seeding, for the next season's growth, and because the Crimson Rosellas like to poke about in them, sampling the crop one-legged, one-handed, each stem bent double and nibbled along, much as we do a cob of corn.

Most mornings the horses turn up at one of the gates into the house yard. I hear them from my bed, stamping to shoo flies, maybe a bit of a scuffle as they jockey for position. To keep them domesticated

I try to give them something when they turn up. For up to an hour they'll wait to be let in or offered carrots, before Zack decides I'm not home or I'm being mean today and leads them off elsewhere.

To get them out of the house paddock is a matter of bribery. It's my last daily task and I can't relax with a glass of home-brew on the verandah until I've completed it. I wait until they're all near each other, and walk towards them bearing carrots, two each, calling 'Feedo!'

Sabbath, being the greediest, neighs eagerly and starts trotting after me as I walk briskly to the nearest gate. Once he neighs, they all take notice. I must get there first and open the gate so they can push past instead of treading on my heels. It's quite an adrenaline rush to distribute the carrots fairly for them and safely for me as they jostle and snort around me, and then to nick back through the gate and close it.

Once the whole gang refused to fall for the carrot trick, and after cajoling, and then cursing, at different gates, I gave up, though worried about what they might eat when they got bored during the night. At about 2 a.m. Zack began neighing loudly and racing round the yard at full pelt, demanding to be let out — NOW! Sabbath followed his lead, as did Shari, who has a chip on her shoulder about being so small and likes to throw in a bucking or two in her mad gallops, as if to say, 'Look at me, see, I'm a real horse!' I had no choice but to get up, take the torch and do as I was told, in nightie and gumboots, before their skidding hooves had carved trenches everywhere.

Due to the drought, for the first time ever, this past winter I've had to supplement their grazing with feed, hay one day, a special feed mix the next. I catch and tie up the two greedy males outside the fence before even showing the buckets, or there's pandemonium.

Annoying and unpredictable as they can be, the horses are company of a sort. And we've been through a few dramas together. In the 2002 fires, there was only Jess and a plump grey mare called Jasmine here. How they survived is a tale in itself, but it belongs in the bigger story of those catastrophic fires.

After the fires, since all the fences in the area were burnt, we'd sent the horses elsewhere. When our fencing was complete again, we brought all my daughter's horses over here. She didn't have Zack then, just Jasmine, Jess, Shari and Sabbath, who was thus the only male.

One day when I called the horses to the gate for carrots, Sabbath didn't come to get his share, but pranced about at a distance. This being most unlike him, I was puzzled. Later that day I saw what seemed to be two Sabbaths — two chestnut horses with white forehead stars and white socks — racing flat out across the far paddock, one chasing the other.

The chaser returned alone and joined the mares. He was not Sabbath — more robustly built, slightly different markings — and from the way he was keeping Sabbath away from the mares, I guessed he was probably a stallion. A few phone calls confirmed that an unbroken chestnut stallion had been bothering other properties; the reputed owner, whose fences were all down, wasn't interested. 'Shoot it,' I was told, by all and sundry, as if this was no big deal.

My daughter came up on the weekend. We found where the stallion had broken the newly repaired fence to get to our mares, and we fixed it in our less-than-professional fashion. He was seen mounting Jasmine, and we worried about too-small Shari and too-old Jess. Poor Sabbath was hunted and bitten whenever he appeared. We had to get this vicious intruder out. With difficulty we enticed our horses into the house yard, Sabbath first, and then the mares.

The stallion raced round and round the fence, neighing so frantically, at such a high pitch, that he was literally screaming. This state of siege continued while I tried to get various authorities to help. It appeared I had to catch this uncatchable creature first and take it to town where they would shoot it. My house yard wasn't big enough to feed four horses for long. We had to deal with him ourselves, get him off the property.

The following weekend my daughter returned, resolute. Taking a whip as protection, she caught Shari and ran with her up the track to the main gate, with the stallion following slightly higher up the hill, galloping and neighing. He was fiercely possessive, and my daughter, while scared of him, was very brave. I followed in the car. Once we, and the stallion, were outside the gate, she ran back inside with Shari and tied her to a tree, while I slammed the gate shut.

She chased the stallion along the track, cracking the whip and yelling, while I followed in the Suzuki, blowing the horn and generally trying to scare him far away. He was having none of that idea, and veered off the track at the end of my 30-acre fenced-in section. That fence comes very close to the house at one corner, where my yard fence forms part of it.

Now the stallion was galloping all round that 30 acres, wearing a deep track, crashing through my regeneration area, screaming for the mares. We weren't game to let them out of the netted house yard, in case he got at them through the plain wire fence with his teeth or hooves, and in any case Shari would go through it.

Hoping he'd give up and go find some mares elsewhere, as there were brumbies out in the national park, my daughter returned to home and work. Each night I'd be woken by his piercing calls, only 50 metres away, setting the mares whinnying and panicking. It was truly frightening, as I imagined him breaking down the fence. For days this went on. I was afraid he'd skid into the fence or down the slope and break a leg as he continually raced around the perimeter, wearing a track into the mud. So much stamping and wheeling went on in that corner closest to the house that three years later the ground is still bare.

National Parks had recommended a professional shooter who would come up here, do the deed humanely and take the body away — for dog meat. I hated the idea, but finally I rang him. He came with a large covered trailer and a winch, was extremely sensitive about where he did it, and took his time so as to be sure that his first shot would be the final one. I heard the shot; saw nothing. I felt deeply sorry for this animal that had paid for its owner's irresponsibility, but I'd had no choice.

Letting our horses out of the yard, I tried not to think of what plants I'd lost over the time it had been their intensive feedlot. Sometimes a garden seems a futile thing to persevere with, an unwinnable battle between me and the creatures, both wild and domestic, with whom I live. I am often tempted to give it up, as it's our only cause of conflict, but I'm stubborn enough to think I'll eventually win.

I am also foolish, as I keep forgetting that finding a solution to any problem here is only an invitation for my neighbours to come up with a fresh challenge.

CHAPTER 10

BITTERSWEET BIRRARUNG

In 2002 I WENT away from my mountain for an entire spring. For family reasons, my partner had been living in town that year, in a cottage we'd mortgaged this place to buy. New partners over 40 usually come with 'baggage', which can drastically re-route your shared plans, sometimes fatally. I'd been dividing my week between the two places, but his work didn't permit that.

Firewise, it was a bad time for me to go away, since there'd be nobody here to keep the yard grass short and watered green, the gutters clear of leaves. But I had to go. Opportunity was knocking loudly.

The Alan Marshall Award gave me a financial boost, but even more importantly it gave me national validation as a writer, and priceless encouragement in the praise from judge Gillian Mears, who'd won the award herself the year before. Being an admirer of Gillian's writing, I could hardly credit what I was hearing when her comments were read out at the award presentation, since they began with 'It was a rare privilege to read "Traces of Life". There was never any doubt that this was the winning story ...'

As if this wasn't enough to send me soaring, I was then offered a paid three-month artist's residency by the award funder, Nillumbik Shire, Victoria. This shire encompasses Eltham, where Alan Marshall lived, and the wonderfully faux-gothic Montsalvat, built by artists for artists.

The residency was to be taken in Birrarung, an historic mudbrick house on a bushland property now owned by Parks Victoria, who jointly sponsor the residency. The house had been designed in the 1970s by Alistair Knox, the famous architect associated with mudbricks, heavy timbers and cathedral ceilings, for Gordon Ford, equally famous landscape designer and builder, associated with 'natural' gardens of native plantings, rocks and water flows. Temptingly, its address was Laughing Waters Road, being right by the Yarra River. Montsalvat was a ten-minute drive away.

This was the first time a writer had been offered the residency; visual and installation artists had enjoyed it before. For me it meant three months of enforced break from daily duties and interruptions, apart from any copywriting work that came in by email, but otherwise with nothing to do but write. In return, only a day of workshops at the end of it. But it had to be taken that spring.

My partner having reluctantly agreed it was an opportunity not to be missed, I took the plunge, said 'Yes', packed the car with the essentials — barely started novel manuscript, computer, printer, fax, desk chair, books, juicer, warm clothes — and went, fingers crossed that my partner's spare but smoky old Peugeot would make it to Victoria and back.

Birrarung proved to be a fantastic place in the true sense of the word, and a great experience, though darkly transformed by the fatal illness of my father after I'd been there only a week. I flew back just in time to say goodbye.

The novel was never the same after that. Nor was the world.

Yet living in such a different environment *was* inspiring. Birrarung was no ordinary house; it had its own personality, and gave off emanations as mysterious as the bush that surrounded it.

The feeling of Gordon's house was older than its years. Minor manorial — with oddities. Like the glass-walled room, brick-floored, empty but for a tiny iron fireplace, scrolled and fanciful, in one corner. Inches away from the glass walls, at floor level, there was a pond, but looming just beyond it, filling the view, was a rock wall higher than the roof. One glass wall thus framed a picture of giant granite boulders, while the other two walls of glazed doors overlooked and accessed the garden and bush.

It was built onto the house as an afterthought, for up close waterfall viewing and nature watching, no matter what the weather. Only I couldn't make Gordon's waterfall work. Despite the 'natural' magic it would effect, it was man-made, dependent on machinery, with which I have a long history of bad communication. The water wouldn't pump up, so wouldn't fall for me.

Apart from rock watching, the room's other function seemed to be stunning and killing birds. The large expanses of glass in the doors fooled many, who tried to fly through them. I'd hear a 'thunk' of varying loudness from my desk, and leap up to see what had been hurt now, anxious to see how badly. I became a voyeur of the flightless, temporary or final. Small thunks: a Welcome Swallow, a Little Weebill. A big thunk — so big and so hard that tufts of soft grey underfeathers were left on the glass: a Little Cuckoo-shrike.

It was in Victoria that I saw an effective remedy for this problem: a cork with a feather stuck in it, suspended outside each window. They twirl and sway and behave like birds, and thus warn the kamikaze birds away.

For a time a Grey Shrike-thrush was nesting on an open ledge in the top of the glass-room wall. The ledge had lost its wire screen, the nest was old, but the bird appeared to take up her annual lease just weeks after I came.

Her melodious song echoed, ever oddly, in the empty room — wild birds don't live in rooms! I stayed out of there, as she would startle and fly away as soon as I opened the adjoining door. Then one day some Melbourne friends visited and, hearing of the waterfall that wouldn't, the male offered to get the pump going. I was so keen for this to happen that I forgot that he'd have to plug the extension cord into the power point in the glass room; I forgot the overly shy nesting bird. He had no more success with the pump than I did, but the songbird never returned.

Much less shy were the Welcome Swallows that had taken over the main bedroom, entering via a small round terracotta pipe vent also missing its screen wire, high under the pitch of the gable. They had built their nest on top of the pipe, inside. The babies were flying too, and I dared not enter the room for the panic it created, with half a dozen birds shrilling and flapping against the skylight and windows. The brick floor was spattered with evidence of their tenancy. They shrieked loudly, dementedly, in the daytime, which I excused because I knew what a roomful of young children sounds like, from my infant-teaching days. My bird book described it as 'high-pitched twittering', but theirs was amplified by the brick floor and high ceiling.

I welcomed the coolness of the house eventually, but until my last few weeks it was too cold. All the floors were brick, meant to be warmed by the underfloor electric heating, which nowadays was too expensive to run.

Birrarung was not solar designed. It was a dark house in most rooms, despite skylights, but much of its charm lay in the causes of its defects. The big open living room soared high to the timber-lined pitch of the roof, with stairs leading up to a mezzanine loft like a musicians' gallery, and massive square central posts of old bridge timbers. There were many windows, all set low so I could see the bush even when sitting, and many French doors, but the ochre mud walls and the dark-stained timbers swallowed the daylight as soon as it crept inside.

The main room was dominated by the very large mud-rendered fireplace, bulging and free-form, with an odd protruding lip, pouting and blackened, below the slab mantelpiece. It was a fireplace for tree trunks rather than logs, oxen rather than marshmallows. As I'd had to buy the load of wood, I was not as generous as was needed to heat very far into the empty, uncurtained room, so at night I pulled the lounge up close to the fire's maw. It was company.

Of the basic furniture in the house, only the lounge demanded I do something about it for the short time I was there. I didn't fancy curling up on its pilled synthetic brown fabric, redolent of unknown history, so I went op-shopping in nearby towns. I treated Victoria like a foreign country and relished the differences I found there. One such was a chain of commercial op-shops, with vast well-arranged premises — they even had check-out queues. A percentage of sales went to charity, and the prices were very low.

I bought a pair of heavy cotton watermelon-pink double sheets to drape over the nasty lounge, a thick slub cotton Indian rug to muffle the cold bricks under my trestle table desk, a pair of exotically patterned pillowslips, and a thick Ming blue woollen single blanket — and I paid $20 for the lot. I still have them all; one of the watermelon-pink sheets has been reborn as my 30-year-old cotton sleeping bag's new sewn-on cover, satisfying my love of finding new uses for old things. The pillowslips are my favourites, and the blanket brings colour and warmth to my spare bed in winter, but I don't have a room big enough for the Indian rug. It's biding its time for more house. All of them remind me of Birrarung — I can smell wood smoke, hear bellbirds, feel the brick floor underfoot.

'Things' matter for their nostalgic associations more than for anything else. Of my dad, I have his folding carpenter's yard ruler, much worn and handled, since he'd used it from his apprentice days. It's precious because when I pick it up and unfold its four boxwood strips, beautifully fitted with brass ends and central swivel, I see his calloused hands, usually with a blood blister under one nail from hammer blows that missed their mark; and I see a very small me, fascinated by this ruler and playing with it for as long as I was allowed; and I see his ever-indulgent smile at what an odd little creature I was. Am.

I'm sorry I didn't get to tell him about Birrarung; as a builder he'd have been interested. But he wouldn't have approved of the bush being so close.

It was a very different bush from what I was used to, as were the birds it attracted. In the remnants of Gordon's 'made' native garden immediately around the house, there were many varieties of hakea, low arching shrubs with pink and ivory, red or orange, deeply curving flowers like sea snail shells. And semi-prostrate grevilleas, with their outstretched fingers the colour of new honeysuckle blossoms. These bushes were constantly bent by honeyeaters, who also hovered in mid-air, wings beating in a blur, to sip the very end flowers of the branches.

When first I came the air was full of the scent of the Black Wattles' myriad tiny yellow balls; by the end, the wattles were drooping with great swags of light-green seed pods, long and lumpy as old beans, but daintier. There was much dead timber through this bush, mostly wattles, tall and thin and leaning, dark claws of topmost twigs curving against the sky, or snapped into jagged spars. As they died, they lost their dark-spotted bark in scrolled sections, which clung to the trunks like climbing goannas.

The other trees there were tall and erratic in shape, with patchy, flaky bark of possum-grey and beige, and large circular or heart-shaped bluish leaves. I was told they were Yellow Box, *Eucalyptus melliodora*. Mostly young, thin and straggly, but several very large and spreading, like the two around which the house was built. These had grown far beyond what nature-loving Gordon must have imagined 30-odd years ago. They were now crushing the roof with their expanding trunks, cracking the mudbrick walls and lifting the timber verandah with their roots.

One window's entire view was the overgrown tree trunk, lurking so close and scaly it looked less tree than patient monster, a creature marking time, quietly growing in strength and bulk, till it cried 'Enough!', shook off this house that had been standing on its foot for too long, and headed off down the gully.

The calls of bellbirds echoed constantly there. The Parks Vic ranger told me that they were actually a sign of a 'sick forest', which was disillusioning. At my Gosford convent school, Henry Kendall was a local hero, and we were taught to sing his poem 'Bellbirds' to the tune of 'On Top of Old Smokey'. Sounds grotesque, but it works. Try it.

By channels of coolness,
The echoes are calling,
And down the dim gorges,
I hear the creek falling.

And it certainly meant I remembered the words. I'd often heard bellbirds around Gosford, but in tall trees, so I'd never seen them. I discovered that they are honeyeaters, properly called Bell Miners, and have a vivid orange beak and legs, a bright eye and yellowish olive feathers. And they do call like bells ringing, or 'Tink! Tink!' as my bird book says.

My mountain forest has no mid-storey, so that Victorian dry bush was surprisingly splendid in the spring. I drank it all in.

There were thousands of *Bursaria spinosa*, tall, densely branching and deeply graceful small trees, rough-barked and thyme-leaved like tea-trees. Their flowers were white, minute and clustered, the effect starry in the sense of twinkling, and exceedingly pretty. They smelt like honey, and their blooming was gradual, so from a distance it was as if those elegant arching branches were slowly being touched up with delicate white pastel strokes, or lightly dusted with snow.

Another remarkable shrub or small tree — I never know where to draw the line — that was plentiful along the dusty road turned out to be the Victorian Christmas Bush, *Prostanthera lasianthos*. Its flowers were like bunches of small snapdragons, vivid, Kiwi sandshoe polish white, with maroon dots in their throats. Native cherry trees also abounded there, *Exocarpus cupressiformis*, with their fir-like bright green foliage, finely furrowed dark trunks and funny little bobble fruit — a cherry with the seed on top.

The hardy Dogwood flowered beside the road too, its long arms reaching up and out, fine, dark-green leaves drooping like terrier whiskers along their length, bearing their white flowerheads only at their very end. Nearer the narrow river flats I could see regrowth Manna Gums, clustered around the streaky trunks of the few parent trees, trailing ribbons of bark as they rose above the massed fairy white of the bursarias.

To lock the gate each evening I walked beneath a row of tall pine trees, planted by earlier settlers; their scent often dominated, as did their carpets of smothering needles, but I couldn't dislike them despite their incorrectness. A pocket of iris and crab apple, cotoneaster and hawthorn pointed to the site of the original hardwood log cabin, burnt down in the fires of the 1960s. This bush was full of dead wood and kindling, now rapidly heating up as summer approached. The house was near the end of a long, dead-end road. I began to think of fire plans — and water.

'Birrarung' is what the Aborigines called the Yarra River, which lay hidden, brown and log-ridden, just across the road. It was sullen there, so I walked to find the Laughing Waters of the road's name — only they didn't. The deeper falls boomed like distant planes, echoing against the semi-cleared hills above, while the shallower ones said 'glue-er, glue-er' over and over, very busily. Or were they saying 'birrarung, birrarung'?

People came there to swim in the wide pool, which was defined by cascades above and below, with weathered rocks reaching out into the river, full of hollows and holes and rounded ridges — and cigarette butts. The banks and edges of the river here had been much used, and many introduced plants had gone feral — blackberries, giant plantain, thistles, wandering jew, ivy, rye grass. A familiar rural story.

There was another Knox-designed mudbrick house on the property, Boomerang, although I thought it curved more like a cooked fat sausage. Never having been approved for habitation, it was only a day studio 'residency', which had been won by Leanne Mooney, a sculptor who mainly used found natural materials. Boomerang was out of sight, uphill through the dry bush. Although we didn't interrupt each other's daily work, Lee and I became friends.

My output was more intangible, but Lee's eerily telling creations gradually filled the odd house up the hill, until her final exhibition. I remember the opening primarily for the fabulous fresh cheeses her husband Ben contributed from his family's Yarra Valley Dairy — their Persian Marinated Fetta was sublime!

I wrote her an artist's statement and CV, and in return she gave me a tall triangular lamp of elegant simplicity, made of driftwood and handmade paper. It was lucky to survive the long trip back here in the laden Peugeot. One of my most cherished artworks, it softly lights a mud wall corner each evening. Lee and I stay in touch — a review of her latest exhibition recently quoted some of my words, so I am pleased that, like her lamp, they remain of use.

The eccentric house, the isolation, the silent evening presence of an empty house on the hill above, and the unfamiliar surrounding bushland, combined to create a distinctly strange atmosphere. Yet I was at ease there, even at night.

I didn't mind the spider webs — hundreds of daddy-long-legs had laced the high ceilings and skylights with dense and intricate webs to be turned silver by sun or moon. I did *not* like it when I found a dead centipede in my bed; or big black spiders of unknown venom on my mat or wall; or shredded offerings of insect origin on my pillow, fallen from the gaps in the boards above. Nor was I pleased that mice clearly dominated the swallows' end of the house, and the pantry. I left it to them, shut those doors and did not enter, kept all my food in the fridge, my crockery in plastic bags.

I don't know how a city person would have coped there, especially if alone.

Three months is a strange amount of time to live in a place. Knowing it's not permanent yet feeling it's too long for temporary. It took a week to settle in, and then there was Dad. Returning soon after, perhaps too soon, Birrarung's empty spaces echoed with my sorrow, my anger at those whom I felt had not cared enough, done enough, and the futile self-punishment of 'if only' and 'what if'. Yet its bushland peace and the fireside comforted, and the privacy allowed me to grieve unhindered by convention.

For the whole spring I rattled around that big house on my own, crossing the empty expanses of brick floor to sit each day at my laptop, drifting between the fictional world of the village I was writing about and the real world outside my window. I managed another 30,000 words on the novel while I was there. But by the end of my time I was both sad and restless.

My own place wasn't being cared for. It had been threatened by fires almost since I left. My heart was there, but part of me had bonded to Birrarung and its bushland. I knew I'd miss waking in a dim bedroom to dawn mist in the timbered gully and hill beyond the bursarias, and to the generous morning birdsong of this bush.

Being there made me more aware of the need to preserve what bushland survived close to civilisation. Even if degraded, once left alone the bush can fight back, resume dominance, as the Yellow Boxes and the swallows were clearly doing! People can experience such near places more easily, gain a taste of what their particular local world was like before it became the bright green of 'civilisation', manicured, sterile, anonymous. A rose is a rose is a rose — but a Manna Gum is not an ironbark or a boab, and a unique ecosystem thrives around each.

As Gordon Ford said, 'We must feel part of the land we walk on and love the plants that grow there ... if we are to achieve a spirit in a garden.' It's not hard to see why his gardens and his house spoke to me.

The haven of Birrarung was only five minutes from culturally vibrant Eltham. With its beautiful library and a wonderful little bookshop constantly organising literary events, it was far harder to remain a hermit there. Eltham had grown too big but still had elements of what it once was — a great 'village down the road'.

And it was close enough for me to go early each Saturday to the fabulous St Andrews markets, to buy the freshest of flowers; nuggetty breads dense with flavour; sweet treats like poppyseed strudel; organic fruit and vegies with the great tastes, varied shapes and sizes, odd clump of dirt and sneaky slug of real garden produce — and to lust after crafts and clothes much to my taste but beyond my means.

At Birrarung, I'd also written an *Owner Builder* article, 'From Knoxie to Now', about the houses, especially interesting because I met the original builder, Graham Rose, who lives locally. Gordon Ford's widow, Gwen, a fellow writer, lives at Fülling, their acre and a half of native garden in Eltham, where she runs a truly charming set of B & B mudbrick cottages. Her waterfalls work! Gwen was a good friend to me as well as a source of local information. She winkled me out of my hermitage a few times, but was not pressing.

One occasion of her successful winkling was at the atmospheric Montsalvat, for Michael Leunig's launch of his book *Sticks*. It was held in an upstairs room above the Great Hall. Backed by leadlight windows, shafts of late sunlight falling onto the table in front of him, every now and then a single swallow's feather would float down from the rafters high above, circling slowly, past his face, through the sunbeam and onto the table. It couldn't have been better orchestrated — unless it had been a duck feather.

Just before I left Victoria, I learnt that I was 'very shortlisted' in the Boroondara Literary Award, from another of the admirable Victorian Shires who support the arts. The night before my workshops was the presentation night, in Hawthorn Town Hall. I sat with clammy palms and increasing disbelief as the judge, Morris Lurie, worked backwards up the list to the main award of $2000. I'd won! As that story, 'For Beauty', was very different to 'Traces of Life', I began to believe that the Alan Marshall win might not have been a fluke.

Two national awards in one year! My life as a writer should have been beginning a steep ascendency, but it turned out to be on hold for the next eighteen months. I should have been happy, but I seemed to have lost the ability. Writing seemed a sham; how dare I think my perceptions of life were of any value to anyone when I understood its relationship with death so little?

After his mother's death, Loudon Wainwright III wrote a song, 'Homeless', that includes these lines amongst several that beautifully, painfully, summed up how desolate I felt. They made me cry when I first heard them, two years after Dad died.

When you were alive I was never alone,
Somewhere in the world there was something called 'home'.

With my father gone, there was no longer a person with uncon-ditional, non-judgemental love for me, and there never could be again. As my mother had never taken on such a role, I felt I *was* alone now, and my relationship wasn't good enough to counter that feeling.

Birrarung had given me a taste of, and for, living on my own. I decided that I would try once more to resolve the problems with my partner, but if that was unsuccessful, I'd make my way in life alone, physically as well as emotionally.

As I eventually did. That leap was only possible because my grief caused the usual priorities, like my need for security and continuity, and my concern for my future, to fall away into nothingness. What counted was being honest with myself.

I made strong decisions at a time when I felt weaker, more depressed and weepy, than I'd ever been. Decisions made under the influence of grief, yes — but I haven't regretted them.

CHAPTER 11

HOME FIRES BURNING

IN EARLY DECEMBER THE old Peugeot brought me safely back up the Hume Highway from Birrarung, to our house in town. That very night we were rung and told that a serious fire was heading towards my mountain. Smaller fires had been brought under control in the general area while I'd been away, but this one was large — and uncontrollable.

Our major neighbour, National Parks, was fully occupied with fires in other parks, threatening greater numbers of properties, and could send no help to our mountains. I said I'd be there, and drove home at first light. I was alone, as my partner had unbreakable commitments elsewhere, but my son would be going up too.

The mountain grasses were as brown as the pastoral valleys through which I'd driven. Dry leaves and fallen sticks waited like well-set kindling beneath the trees. My house yard was overgrown with long, bleached tussocks, and the usually green grass in between was dead.

Our brigade guys were already there assessing what was needed. There was no chance of turning or containing the fire; it would be a matter of trying to save each cabin or house as the fire reached it. They would send in the bulldozer to clear breaks around my house yard and my son's near-finished cabin further away, over near the lagoon. A crew from another brigade would be here later. I was to keep an eye on the fire's rate of approach, ready to call fire-fighter friends on standby to bring their ute and slide-on fire pump to help my son save his place.

I raced about trying to make up for three months' neglect. I cleared leaves from gutters and plugged them with rags only to find that they sagged forward too much to hold water. Brackets had been undone at some stage, probably to remedy the inadequate fall and drainage, but not refixed. I didn't have a riveter and there was no time now for fiddling with them. Climbing back down the ladder, I muttered anew about half-done jobs.

My son was busy at his place clearing bracken and tussocks away from the cabin, which, although clad in corrugated iron, was elevated, timber-floored, so vulnerable from below. Nor was it yet fully sealed under the eaves. We had debated the siting for his cabin. He'd wanted to build out on the point where the sunset views were grander; I'd insisted it be much, much further back from the edge, to create a flat distance in which the fire could slow down, lose heat, and allow people to safely defend the cabin from the fire front, which would invariably come up that western slope below. I'd seen fires roar up there; he hadn't. I held firm. He'd given in, though with an air of humouring rather than believing me. I had a feeling that by tonight he'd be glad he had.

I rang a friend in the next valley, whose place would be first in line of the fire. He reckoned two hours at least before it got to him. I thought how much easier this was than the fire in 1980, before we had phones, when I'd had to keep running down to the escarpment edge to check the fire's progress. From a rocky point there I'd actually watched the fire sweep over a shed, without realising that this man and another were sheltering on the lee side of that shed. They'd survived, as the fire moved so fast, but he'd had to restrain his companion from panicking and running. So he knew fires; I could trust his judgement.

I turned on the big fixed sprinklers in the orchard so at least the western end of the yard would be soaked. Had I been here those last months I'd have been using them to keep the grass green, but the whole yard was now crackling brown. I began moving smaller sprinklers about to wet other areas, like in front of my glasshouse, but with six agricultural sprinklers going there wasn't a lot of pressure left. I cursed our stupidity in having installed only one gravity delivery line, and that only 1¼-inch diameter!

Crouching, I raked out the dead leaves from under the verandah, bumping my head often on the spidery floor joists in my haste. I'd done it before I went away, but despite the fine aviary netting across the front of the verandah piers, many more small leaves from the wisteria had found their way in.

Everything loose on the verandah had to be removed so burning leaves wouldn't lodge behind or amongst them. The big gas bottle had to be disconnected and put somewhere safe — but where? For some reason I decided the toilet would do, and managed to half-roll and half-drag the bottle up there. I think my idea was that, if it blew up, no harm would be done to anything else. I barrowed the verandah things over to the power shed and stacked them in there.

Then I saw the sprinklers' shining arcs wilt … stop. Surely it wasn't possible that I'd run out of water, with 11,000 gallons in those tanks, when I knew my son had pumped very recently to fill them? He came running down the hill — the dozer had cut the buried pipe in two places; he'd turned off the tanks so we hadn't lost too much water, but did I have any joiners?

I couldn't find any the right size. This was a nightmare scenario. I rang around and found someone not too far away, much closer than town at least, who thought he had some in the shed, and my son headed off, going fast for good reason for once. Luckily we had a few hours.

At least he'd not be delayed by opening gates. They were all now wide open so that Jess and Jasmine, the two horses, wouldn't be trapped. They'd have to take their chances. The support tankers had been using my main dam to refill, so that gate needed to be left open anyway. Time was precious with such a raging fire.

To the west the sky was a vast smear of brown, with sporadic higher yellowish billows of smoke. The air was heavy with the sweetish, horribly familiar smell of a eucalypt forest burning. The day was heating up, and there was a westerly wind — the very worst kind for us. I got into my fire clothes of cotton long-sleeved shirt, jeans and boots, with a cotton scarf tied at my neck ready to pull up over my nose and mouth, and goggles hanging ready. I knew how difficult it would be to cope with the heat and smoke otherwise. I pulled my old Akubra down hard on my head to defeat the wind. I'd turn the hose on myself nearer the time.

The small crew from an outside brigade arrived. The captain took one look at my clearing and declared it a safe place from which they could defend my house. I was asked to prioritise buildings for saving, and I chose the house and the power shed as critical. They could pump from my small dam in front, and ran out their long flat hoses to reach beyond the house. I was following them around, apologising for the unprepared state of the yard, 'I've been away for three months, I only got back last night ... sorry, it wouldn't usually be this dry.' But they didn't seem interested. 'Bloody weekenders!' they were probably thinking.

The sprinklers sprang into life again. Thank heavens! The captain told me to keep the sprinklers going, and he and his crew drove off to check out my son's cabin. It was about 2.30 p.m.

The phone rang. It was from my friend on the front line. 'It's spotting on my place already,' he yelled. 'It'll be up there in under half an hour at this rate!' Something had drastically changed in the fire's route and pace. Two of our brigade members arrived and I rang our standby pair to come urgently. They did, in record time. Once they reached my son's, the main crew would return here, I presumed.

One helper and I were wetting down what we could, playing our limp hose sprays over the verandah and the plants and grass in front. I was getting anxious that the fire crew wasn't back here.

Then we saw the fire. Through the tree line on the edge of my escarpment, we could see flames. 'Where the f—k are they?' yelled my helper.

I began running to turn off the sprinklers; we were going to need all the pressure here at the house. The shed and workshop would have to be sacrificed. But just then I saw the fire crew's Toyota tearing across the paddock to us. I ran back to my station by the tap below the bottom north-eastern corner of the house. The Toyota pulled up in cloud of dust; the crew leapt out and began connecting hoses.

'About f——n' time!' said my helper.

I f——n' agreed.

There was a mighty roar as the fire came over the edge; all the rough-barked tree trunks down the hill from my house began exploding into pillars of fire, well ahead of the actual ground fire, and igniting the grass beneath them as well. This wasn't crowning, it was radiant heat at its worst. I turned the hose on myself, pulled my wet scarf up over my nose, the goggles over my eyes. Here we go!

Within a minute the fire had travelled uphill several hundred metres, leapt the bare dirt of the dozer break and was inside my house yard. The noise and heat were dreadful. I could hear helicopters somewhere above it all.

The crew were spraying the house and verandah with their big hoses and power nozzles; I was concentrating on putting out the fire in the grass as it came through the fence, but I remember thinking, 'Hope they don't aim *too* hard a jet on the mudbricks!' My face felt as if it was burning, even though I was backed right up against the house, with the hose jet as full on and as far-reaching as it would go.

Moving so fast, the fire soon leapt the track and was past the house and yard, with the wind whipping flames and sending burning leaves and sparks everywhere, including back downhill. I managed to put out the fire in the back of the bay tree next to my side fence, then ran to see what was happening in the rest of the yard. Spot fires were starting everywhere but the fire crew were racing about extinguishing them.

I saw one right near the toilet. 'The gas bottle!' I yelled. 'There's a gas bottle in there!' They were right on to it, although they must have wondered *why* I kept gas in there.

I ran back down to patrol as much of the fence perimeter as I had hoses to reach. All the trees and shrubs within 3 metres inside the fence were burnt, and the piles of horse manure I'd mulched them with were smoking and smouldering. I raked them out flat to hose them, realising they were just processed dried grass after all, so I should have thought of them as a hazard, but hadn't. Amazingly, the shadecloth-covered glasshouse seemed intact — the crew must have hosed it at the right time, as it was only about 15 metres from the fire edge. The wind was still strong. Spot fires had even started inside the sodden orchard area, although they hadn't burnt far.

The fire was well away up the hill. The captain said he thought it was OK here now and they'd better get on to the next place if I thought I could manage the mopping up. I thanked him effusively, and he said, 'You did well.' As I'd only held a hose, I wondered what he usually met with — hysteria? I didn't tell him I'd been through this before, without a hose, nor that I'd done fire crewleader training. He reminded me that if this wind kept up I'd need to keep checking throughout the night for spot fires.

One helper took off on his trailbike to protect his own place on the next ridge. The other, our deputy captain, stayed, anxious to see how my son's place and its protectors had fared. He kept trying to get across the intervening burnt area on his bike to check, but it was far too hot still. For half an hour he kept trying, as well as putting out smouldering tree trunks and tussocks at my place. I was getting really worried; the fire could have been even fiercer over there, with all that blady grass on the slope below. The slide-on tank was only small — had they run out of water? — but the fire had moved so fast that surely they were OK?

Then I heard the bike again. 'They're all right!' he called. 'So's the cabin.'

My heart settled. Through the blackened and smoking bush I saw the ute returning.

I got cold drinks for us all and we plopped onto the ground to recover our wits and our energy, realise our good fortune — this time. Aftermath smokes were lit by some. Only then did I think of my lagoon paperbarks, less than two years old. My son said the fire had roared up the gully to the lagoons even faster than it had towards his. So that would be the end of my regeneration dream.

He also said it had been easy to halt the fire at the dozer break around his place. He grinned at me and raised an eyebrow.

Our helpers moved on to aid others. Then I remembered my

spotter in the next valley. I rang, not really expecting the line to be working, but it was. He was fine except for a burnt hand when he'd tried to open the door after it was all over. A helicopter had landed soon after the fire had passed to see if he was OK.

The sudden speed of the fire had surprised everyone, including himself; it had got to his place before any brigade crew could. He'd survived inside his tin shed/cabin, crouched on the cement floor with wet blankets over himself and his dog. I knew what a perfectionist he was; his shed would have been absolutely sealed, spark and ember proof. He said the tin of the shed had become so hot it had glowed blue. Now there's a man who's been intimate with fires.

I rang to reassure my daughter, my partner. My son reconnected the gas; we ate something and began our vigils. Every two hours, we agreed, we'd get up and check. He only had a backpack of water and a rake hoe, as there was no water connected at his place.

Checking my four garden hoses, I laid them out to their furthest reach, ready. The wind had dropped a little, but not enough. The thick smoke of active fires was still rising from the valley below and, as dark fell, on the slopes around us we saw the red towers of burning trees, sending bright showers of sparks flying through the night. From the nearer ones I could see that these 'sparks' were small burning pieces of fibrous bark, and that many were still alight when they landed.

My bed gave little sense of haven. I kept opening my eyes at every crackle or thud from the forest, so close, so visible, through all my windows. I set the alarm. At 10, at 12, all was well. At 2, it wasn't. The trunk of the big white mahogany just up the hill — the one we'd set up the stove under, camped near, all those years ago — was alight at the back. So were the tussocks beneath it. I turned on the tap to full pressure, the hose jet as fierce as I could make it. I had to put the fire out before it got much higher up the trunk and set the broad canopy of leaves alight. I alternated my targets, from grass to tree. The fire's progress through the grass was halted; I stamped on the bases of the tussocks to be sure.

Although the wind was from the west, in my clearing it gets thrown into turbulence, sent off course by the tree rim over which it must first pass. That would have been how sparks had blown back downhill to set this tree alight; if its leaves caught, a similar gust could take them down onto my house and shed. I knew I could not protect both on my own. And there were other unburnt eucalypts nearby in the yard. This could start a bigger fire than I could save the house from.

White mahogany bark is rough, deeply interlaced and furrowed, so the fire in its depths was hard to extinguish. Despite my furious hosing, it was still smouldering in there. I hacked at the thick bark with the hoe, dragging it apart; flames leapt up anew as oxygen fed them, but the water soon put them out. I waited. It seemed OK. I hosed again.

But how was I to trust it, to go back to bed and sleep? I stomped about in the semi-dark for a while longer, hosing the trunk and all the ground around the tree yet again. Finally I turned off the water. The ensuing relative silence quickly became the sounds of a still-feeding fire on the move — the loud crackling, the long whooshes and brief roars. The distinctive smell of water on burnt vegetation, on charcoal and ash, filled the immediate air, but as I walked back down to the house it was overpowered by the active bushfire smell. Dry, sickly-sweet, pungent, it permeated the whole range, ridges and slopes, creeks and gullies, and far beyond. It was inescapable, even inside the house. It weighed me down with knowledge, with speculation, with fear. Only now did I remember the horses. I knew the whole block was burnt; the dam would have been their only hope. I did not sleep.

At dawn I walked to the dam with a bucket of grain, calling them. A neigh answered me as I got closer. On the small island in the middle of the two interconnected dams stood the horses. The reeds that choked the shallower dam on the western side had burnt to the water line, and had led the fire onto the short grass of the island. I don't know why it had stopped where it did, but the horses were standing on unburnt grass. Could they have stamped it out? There was also a narrow unburnt area on the flat eastern shore of the dam, where the roos and wallabies always keep the fine native grass cropped very short. That was the closest shore to the island, and quite shallow to cross as it was where the dams met.

I stood there, called, shook the bucket. Jasmine splashed into the dam and walked to me, the water only up to her shoulders. I tipped some grain out for her, patted her. She seemed fine. I called Jess. Called again, banged the bucket. She neighed, but did not move. The grass left on that tiny island was already eaten right down. She'd starve if she didn't come over.

I went back and rang my daughter, who reminded me that Jess hated water, wouldn't step through even a shallow creek if she could avoid it. Only her strong survival instincts could have made her go over there yesterday. My daughter couldn't come up to try to coax Jess off until the weekend, two days away. I'd need to get feed to her until then.

We had a very tippy old aluminium canoe. The little jetty was burnt, so were the plastic-bladed paddles, but the canoe itself was fine. I found a flat piece of wood to use as a paddle and for the next two days I ferried buckets of feed over to Jess three times a day. Nevertheless she grew visibly thinner, and the ground was covered in her manure. I couldn't understand why her good sense didn't bring her back through the water to join Jasmine on the shore. She refused to be led across by me.

I was cranky with her because there was so much else to do after the fire that I didn't need canoe trips. Luckily the wind dropped a day later and we had a storm, bringing enough rain to halt the fires and save the valley behind me. The pressure was off. And that weekend my daughter coaxed Jess back through the water. We could marvel then at the horses' intuitive flight to the island, and wonder at how even Jasmine had remained there after the fire had passed. Waiting for us to assure them it was safe?

All the house gates were left open, as my yard and around my son's cabin were the only oases of green to be seen anywhere on the ridge. Not only the horses but also any surviving wallabies or other animals would need that feed. They came, and ate just about everything down, but I was glad to have some green to offer them.

They came also to die.

After a few days, I began to smell death. I stood on the verandah, scanning the forest edge, thinking it must be coming from there. Turning to go inside, I happened to glance down, and through the gaps between the decking boards I saw greyish-brown fur. Kneeling, I peered closer. Black paws, limp head — a wallaby. I moved along the crack; more fur, grey, fluffy, pale belly — a possum? And I could see more bundles of fur. There were probably five dead animals under there. I didn't want to go closer.

By next morning the smell was bad. My son had returned to town to work. I didn't think I could cope with the task ahead of me, but I knew the smell would get worse as the bodies rotted. Then the deputy fire captain came by to see how things were, and whether I needed help. The smell was obvious so, feeling like a typical female wimp, I asked if he'd mind removing the creatures who'd chosen under my verandah as their last refuge. He said not, as men are expected to. I fetched him the shovel and the wheelbarrow and took myself well away while he did it. I was very grateful.

There were more in my yard, under my son's cabin, under my pump's tin cover — whatever had seemed like shelter. Too late. I let them desiccate where they were. Elsewhere, clusters of slender white bones became commonplace.

Since those fires I have not heard even one koala grunting or roaring for a mate in the trees of the gully below me, when I used to hear them frequently, often close by, although I saw them rarely.

All my young paperbarks were burnt to crisp sticks that snapped all the way down. Dead. Yet six months later, about a third of them sent new stems of leaves up from below the ground, where the roots had survived. Magic.

I was to discover that my Everlast cement tanks had cracked under the intense heat. They had survived several fires in their twenty years and probably would have everlasted but this had been exceptional. It turned out that my NRMA home insurance covered replacement tanks and fences. There were no dramas or delays; they were very helpful, and I will never again wonder whether it's worth paying those premiums. Unfortunately the dramas and delays came from the fencing contractor. I picked the wrong one, and afterwards wondered whether the job would have been as slackly done if their client had been a bloke.

Everywhere I looked in those black mopping-up days I saw possibilities for better fire protection and precautionary measures, despite having had better-than-average awareness previously. While the experience was fresh, I acted. Less for me to worry about in the next big fire.

For my fledgling forest's sake, I hope that's not for another twenty years, but with the warming, drying climate, that's unlikely.

CHAPTER 12

WHILE THE WOMAN'S
AWAY ...

IN 2005 I WENT away again, but only for a month.

It was early September, when the wisteria and the ornamental grape on the western verandah were still brown sticks, their leaf buds small blind nubs, barely a hint of green showing. Here in the mountains the seasons seem to become evident about six weeks after they do in the valleys.

I am rarely away for more than a few days, but this time I didn't return until mid October. Being so far from main roads anyway, every trip is a long one for me, and as petrol is so expensive, I try to combine them. Since I wanted to attend Watermark, a week-long nature writers' conference on the north coast, I found a few interesting owner-built houses up that way as article subjects for the magazine and then I went a bit further to visit family. Hence the month.

A month is too long to be away from my wildlife refuge. Too long for me and too long for the wildlife.

For a start I get too used to the company of creatures who answer with words when I talk to them, and to being able to press a button, flick a switch or turn a knob to fulfil all my needs. I welcome these comforts for a while, and then all that hard-edged man-made environment starts to get me down, as does the awareness that its inhabitants, be they dogs, cats or people, are all man-made too in a sense. I begin to miss the softer, wilder, natural world, and to hanker after my solitary hermitage back in the bush.

As for the wildlife, well, being an opportunistic lot — I suppose I should say 'adaptable' — they get too used to my territory being unmarked. They start to move in.

When I got home from my month away, before I even opened the yard gate I could see that spring had arrived with great flamboyancy. The ornamental grapevine and the wisteria had exploded into such vigorous greenery that they had twined together to completely barricade the verandah, and I had to push my way through at the top of the steps. The Crépuscule climbing rose on the eastern side had also gone into overdrive, draping the verandah posts and rafters with swags and tails of raggedy apricot blossoms.

Naturally, confronted with all this profuse growth, before I unpacked the car I just had to walk around the garden to see what other delights spring had brought. The air was full of perfume — the honeyed white cloud of the May bush, the exotic intensity of the jasmine smothering a stump nearby, the innocence of the old-fashioned pink sweetpeas in front of the verandah, and the faint almond scent of the Banksia Rose that has turned my clothesline post into a fountain of foaming white. But the Banksia Rose didn't look right. The lower parts of its drooping stems were all bare.

So, I realised, looking about in dismay, were those of all my newly leafed and very young European trees — and the rose bushes were totally denuded.

'The possums are back!' I groaned aloud.

But no twigs were broken, as possums inevitably do when they climb over them. And there remained one high topknot of leaves on the big Autumnalis old shrub rose. I noticed too that only the lower parts of the climbing roses, the Crépuscule, the Madame Carrière and the Graham Thomas, were stripped. The upper stems were fully leafed. Whatever was devastating my roses, it could not climb.

I walked round the back of the Banksia Rose, and there was a small wallaby, caught in the act. It bolted, propped a little distance away and turned to see what I was up to. Well, I was laughing, for clenched between its teeth was a stem with several tiny roses bobbing at the end — a coy marsupial Carmen.

But I stopped laughing as I spotted eight more wallabies, of varying sizes and sexes. I stared, and they stared back, in a single frozen instant of mutual shock before they took off, *through* the hingelock fence, above the lower additional chickenwire. They exited at many different spots.

I walked up closer; the hingelock netting, or pigwire, as some call it, was recycled, old and rusty, but unbroken, although some of its rectangles were bent out of shape. It had never been tested by pigs, so far as I knew, but for eight years this fence had kept wallabies out of the house yard, as it should. Why the change?

Here I admit that for months I'd known that one rogue wallaby had been breaking the rule of staying on the wild side of the house yard fence. A big male: darker and more evenly red on the back and whiter on the front than is usual, and with a distinctively kinked tuft of fur at the base of his tail. When I first spotted him in my orchard I'd gone around looking for breaks in the fence, but there were none. He must be an especially good jumper, I'd thought. Not even the kangaroos had ever jumped this fence.

Then I saw him get through it. Hingelock netting is composed of 320-millimetre-wide rectangles — that's just over a ruler length —

that gradually increase in height. Mine has 600-millimetre-high chickenwire clipped over it at the base. Above that the openings are only a large hand's span high. It had occurred to me that a joey might get through those top ones, but only if it could jump high and aim well at the same time, which would be unlikely given how scatter-brained and uncoordinated they are.

But a hefty muscular male? He had to be double-jointed!

He became a regular visitor and I saw him come and go at many different spots with ease — definitely double-jointed, I decided. I also concluded that he was a loner, out of place in the busy social scene beyond the fence. Much like me, really. And, since in those days I never saw him eating anything but grass, I didn't mind him visiting.

I began to say hello and have a bit of a chat when I saw him. Not that he contributed much, but he'd look up and acknowledge me before resuming grazing. I could use the excuse that I like to use my voice around the wild creatures so they get to know my 'call'— and that's true — but the fact is that, living in this isolated place by myself, I have started talking to my wild neighbours. Nothing too deep, just passing pleasantries. It's not talking to myself, not a sign of going crazy, although it probably is a sign of being 'too long in the bush', as I've heard it said of others.

I'd thought my rogue wallaby might be a youngish male since the time I'd caught him eating the small rose bushes on the bank and angrily reprimanded him — 'Why must you do that? Why can't you just eat grass!' The look he'd given me was very reminiscent of one my son used to bestow on me in his late teens. It clearly said, 'Settle, Gretel!'

But in between my small explosions of outrage we were quite comfortable in each other's presence. He began to take his midday nap in the shade of the trees uphill from the toilet, or under the cherry tree. He might lift his head if I appeared — 'Oh, it's only you' — then resume dozing.

Then I started to worry. What if it was genetic? A tribe of double-jointed wallabies would be quite another matter!

I watched him carefully when he was outside the fence, but he was always alone. Whatever made him an outcast, it put him off the ladies. Not once did I see him chase a female. Nor did he hang around with the males — something else we had in common at present. Perhaps he was asexual, a neuter? The reason remained a mystery, but it seemed I was safe from being overrun by his offspring.

I hadn't reckoned on him passing on his strange ability by example. I'd underestimated the wallabies. In my month-long absence the others must have figured that if he could do it, so could they; and since I wasn't here marking my territory, it was theirs for the taking.

Now I'd have to clip chickenwire to the upper section as well. That would be an expenditure of money and time that I certainly didn't need — thanks a lot, guys!

But right now rain was threatening, so I rushed to grab some dry wood and unpack a few essentials. I lit the slow combustion stove so I'd have hot water in the morning. It was growing dark, and my cabin is only lit in strategic pools by 20-watt halogen bulbs; it is mostly shadow. I like it that way, but it did mean that I couldn't be sure if the shadows seemed to be moving a bit, nor that those tiny black pellets on the far bench weren't really old toast crumbs.

Any doubts that the wildlife had extended their territory inside the house as well were dispelled at 2 a.m., when a familiar hissed 'Chee! Chee!' in the ceiling woke me, even over the continual clatter of the rain on my low tin roof. It was confirmed the next night by the mini 'mice', Brown Antechinus, that would suddenly dart onto the sink or the bench, stare at me with their big black eyes, then disappear.

I had thought I'd found and filled every crack where they could enter. They can flatten their little bodies to fit through amazingly narrow crevices, and if I'd known that when building this place I'd have made sure it was critter-proof. But I didn't, and near enough was good enough then.

Doing it afterwards was laborious and not as effective, yet patching and poking with mud and plaster and slivers of wood, and just once — never again — with that revolting and probably toxic expanding foam, had seemed to keep them out for the last two years. Until now. 'While the cat's away …' They must have been chiselling an entry with their teeth for the past month. But where?

It's not that I don't like them. In fact, the Brown Antechinus is one of the cutest of our small mammals, despite being related to the Tasmanian Devil. Similarly carnivorous, they have lots of sharp little teeth, but they have sweet rounded ears like pink flowers, a pointy pink nose and rather 'poppy' black eyes. They're great climbers.

Being meat eaters, they don't touch my fruit or vegetables — unlike the bush rats, for whom I have a strong dislike as housemates, but who, as they're bigger, are easier to keep out. My antechinus do nibble or even steal soap, and they like cheese, which is what I put in the live trap.

They may look a bit like mice, but you can't use mean mouse-traps to catch and kill them, because they're protected. Although that was clearly irrelevant to the local, who, on being told that the endangered Hastings River Mouse had been found in this area, said, 'I don't care what sort of mouse it is, if it's in my kitchen, it's a dead one!'

My live trap is an aluminium folding tunnel with a spring-loaded platform inside, which, when stepped on, snaps the door shut. The trap has relocated many an antechinus, whom I tip into the tussocks outside the fence the next morning. There it races off, no doubt annoyed, but unharmed.

The memorable fact about them — to me anyway, but perhaps it's my warped mind, or my current celibate state — is that the males not only mate themselves silly but they mate themselves to death. Before they are a year old, over a period of two weeks they race about seeking females, fighting each other for the ladies' favours and, when they win them, mating for six hours at a time. They do it with more than one female if they can.

Not one male is left alive at the end of this frenzied mating season, which is usually in early spring. Not one male makes it to his first birthday. Apparently it's the stress that does it. Talk about the pain of love!

It doesn't sound like much fun being a female either, even if they do live longer, what with males jumping them at every turn. I mean, six hours does seem overcompensation for the 'ten-minute wonder' that we human females complain about. Not surprisingly after all that effort, pregnancy, which only lasts a month, is guaranteed.

These little marsupials don't actually have a pouch; instead they have six to ten exposed nipples, which the young latch on to — and they don't let go of them for the first five weeks, so poor mum has to get about with them dragging beneath her. Ouch!

At least she knows they'll leave home by next winter, before the whole business starts again. I couldn't wait till then. With all the males dead by now, my intruders had to be female; I didn't want them raising babies in my roof.

I suppose they ate insects in the house, but they would mainly slip through their purpose-made crack to feed outside — at night when they were wide awake, for they are nocturnal. I'm not. If I didn't need sleep I wouldn't have minded sharing the house with them. But I do, and between their scrabbling and hissing, and my nervous awareness of the high possibility of them running over my pillow, and thus my head, they stopped me getting enough of it.

So you understand why I felt rather as if the wildlife was taking over my little patch. I'd given them most of the property as their refuge — I'd only claimed 1 acre for myself. I'd drawn a line between me and the wild things, plants and animals, and they'd crossed it.

It was still raining days after I'd got home. Spring is a good time to get such a lot of rain, but I couldn't enjoy it while under siege like that. From my windows I watched the many wallabies ease themselves through the fence, then lean back on their tails to balance as they stood tall and nibbled leafless the lower branches of every introduced tree and shrub. These were all deciduous, now desperately putting out new bright green leaves, which the wallabies immediately ate. They did this daintily, pulling each branch down to their mouths with their neat black forepaws, but for once I did not find their table manners a charming sight.

It was hard not to feel disappointed that, like resentful children, they'd played up when I was away. Rationally, I accepted that the garden was fair game after a month. Emotionally, I protested — it wasn't fair!

Since I was cabin-bound by the rain, reading seemed the perfect activity to take my mind off my intruders. I have lots of books, and except for the odd gift, they are all second-hand, seized upon with delight in op-shops all over the country. Having grown up in an almost bookless home, to be surrounded by walls of books that I can read again whenever I want gives me a sense of great riches. Greater riches would be more walls for more bookshelves for more books.

Most of them are on open shelves. But the pleasure of withdrawing a book from the shelves is greatly diminished by being showered with dried mud, small spiders, and sometimes fat pink grubs when I do so. Which is what happened on that particular wet, besieged day. As if wallabies and antechinus weren't enough, the wasps had really gone overboard while I'd been away.

For wasps like books too. Side-by-side books create ideal crevices for making mud nests for their eggs. They seal paralysed living spiders in with the eggs, for the larvae to eat when they hatch later on. The wasps cement the books to each other and to the shelf.

They also fill up any keyhole — in fact, *any* small or narrow hole. I have to keep a close watch on computer and printer sockets and slits, and curtain folds, and if I don't use a particular spice for a few months, I will likely find it cemented to the spice rack and its neighbouring jars.

This waspish home invasion is even more annoying because they are demolishing the home itself, little by little, to build these nests. My mudbrick walls that are still rough — the ones on my list for rubbing down — are daily getting rougher as the wasps gouge out small bits to wet and re-form between my Penguin paperbacks.

Their efforts in the past month had probably ensured a baby boom year, unless I went through my whole library committing waspicide. Only I'd need to be in a stronger state of mind, or stomach, for that.

When the rain finally stopped, I began fortifying the fence against the wallabies, slowly and erratically, depending on when I could afford another roll of chickenwire. As I clipped it on to the old hingelock netting, I was forced to get up close and personal to the past.

I'd erected this house fence ten years ago, when I came back to live here. My dream had included a large garden in the midst of the regenerating bush and its abundant — and voracious — wildlife. That required a netting fence. As my partner was already engrossed in his creative and income-earning pursuits — absolutely single-mindedly, as many men can be — I did most of it myself. I dug the holes and tamped around the wooden posts with the head of the crowbar, which isn't easy to do on your own and still have the heavy posts end up roughly vertical. A fair bit of boomps-a-daisy balancing was needed.

In between the wooden posts I banged in the steel star posts with my wonderful 'putter-inner', a heavy iron cylinder, closed at one end, that a friend had welded up for me. The shop ones, called post-drivers, have handles, and I suppose they are all bought by weak women — Real Men use iron mallets that I can barely lift off the ground, let alone above my head.

And I'm no weakling, despite being small. But some jobs don't only depend on strength. They're just bloody impossible without the right tool — like my 'puller-outer', a shop-bought manual post-lifter, which makes removing star posts and tomato stakes amazingly easy, and which, I suspect, even Real Men might use.

These are the sort of tools I love: dead simple and very effective, requiring neither mechanical knowledge nor great strength, needing no manual, using no fuel, hiding no spark plugs, able to be forgotten and left out in the rain without damage, enabling little me to do heavy work. In fact they're the sort of old-fashioned items that are usually discontinued nowadays — too simple, too enduring, a one-off purchase that brings no economic and ongoing joy to anyone but the buyer. What a useless thing to keep manufacturing!

Posts all in, my partner strained up several strands of plain wire for me to attach the hingelock to, as I can't seem to get into my head how to set the chains and teeth of my fence strainer so it works. Or perhaps I'm just scared of the way it bites and snaps and strains almost to breaking point.

Then I unrolled the old hingelock netting, relic of my first dream of a bush life seventeen years previously. My then husband and I had fenced in several large areas for vegetable gardens, since we thought we'd grow fancy foods like globe artichokes and asparagus — and back in the 1970s these *were* fancy, rarely seen in shops. After the marriage broke up, so did the fences, only more slowly.

The artichokes quickly died, but nothing could kill the asparagus; nothing eats it once it's past the tender shoot stage. I'd have thought they'd be delicate plants, but they're so hardy that, unfenced, unfed and untended, each year since they have come back up through the grass. The problem is that when I haven't been around to stop those succulent shoots continuing to grow into ferny leaves and produce red berries, these have been eaten by birds and the seeds thus spread over the mountain, forming my main crime against the flora — after the kikuyu, that is.

Having demolished the falling down garden fences, I'd saved the hingelock netting in great rolls, with dead tussocks and bracken still entangled.

So, fencing the second time round, I'd recycled it, much as I did with my bush lifestyle dream. For ten years the fence had worked. The second relationship had lasted about the same length of time. The rusty and fire-brittle hingelock probably should have been discarded along with youth and optimism; it certainly wasn't doing the job anymore. But I come from thrifty Scottish stock; I throw nothing away. Except perhaps my men?

Eventually I finished adding the higher chickenwire, leaving the top of it flopping outwards, which is supposed to deter possums. The wallabies gave up their acrobatic feats of invasion. Except for one, and guess who? Yep, the rogue wallaby.

But surely not even a double-jointed wallaby could get through chickenwire. He looked at me most boldly when I threw up my hands and asked 'HOW?', before resuming his nibbling of rose leaves. I'd hoped the latter might get ahead of him and survive his indiscriminate pruning. But he is so conscientious that I think not.

He must eat the grass and roses close by my house at night, because in the morning there are so many droppings that they need raking out of the way. It seems to be a greater amount than elsewhere — as if emphasising that my territory ends at the steps, the rest is his.

I have now seen him make one exit and one entrance — by climbing up the netting, not by pushing through or jumping over. What on earth has he been genetically crossed with? Wallabies aren't supposed to climb; it isn't natural for wallabies to climb. But then neither is it natural for humans to walk on tightropes. I guess he's just clever and keen — and weird.

Actually I'm not sure if he ever leaves anymore. He's so relaxed that I've seen him drinking at the horse trough/bathtub near my clothesline. It was an incongruously domesticated scene, because he *is* a wild animal.

We may grow old together. I wish I didn't like my heritage roses so much.

The irony is that his favourite is the Autumnalis, an 1812 shrub rose that was the only rose the possums didn't eat. So I propagated dozens of cuttings and planted them in various parts of the yard, in rows like hedges and in corners so they could spread. They should be metres-high and -wide, bearing masses of bright green leaves and clusters of little pink buds and creamy-white roses. Perversely, he strips them all, thorns notwithstanding.

Country blokes look at me as if I'm dense when I complain about him, since for them the solution is obvious: 'Shoot it!'

No, I've given up, resigned myself to sharing the house garden with him and his unorthodox topiary, much as I became resigned to my post-arthritis horse-grazed garden.

But if I do go away for a long time again, I'll get a caretaker in, to maintain my claim and water the yard. When I get back from the next writer's retreat with a village down the road, I want no unwelcome surprises.

As if it's in my control …

CHAPTER 13

WET AND WILD

DOROTHEA MACKELLAR'S ICONIC POEM, 'My Country', describes hers as one 'of droughts and flooding rains'. As is mine, although it's no 'wide brown land', but steeply crumpled green, more vertical than horizontal. Yet rain dictates the fortunes of my country just the same.

The years of the big fires have also been the years of little rain, of relative drought. Our 'little' may be twice what outback areas ever get, but here it means that, beneath the trees, the long lush growth from normal wetter years is drying out, turning from green to brown to blonde — and waiting.

On the steeper slopes where the topsoil is thin, so is the grass, but the eucalypts droop their leaves, avoiding as much evaporation from the sun as they can, and shed many, which join the fallen twigs and strips of bark to form an incendiary carpet below. Waiting. All it needs is a spark from an old trailbike as it revs up an overgrown track, or a lucky strike from a fork of lightning.

For summer brings many dramatic electrical storms to these mountains, and this last summer was notable for the ongoing frequency of such storms — climate chaos at work? They may be my equivalent of the worldwide hurricanes, floods, earthquakes and landslides, increasing in both scale and frequency. Disasters that I no longer call 'natural'.

So far Australia's been lucky, just a longer drought and a stronger than usual cyclone or two. Rural stuff. Public awareness is rising at last, but it will probably take a tsunami at Bondi to get the voting majorities to look up from their shopping mall worlds to the bigger picture, and demand *real* action on climate change from the powers-that-be.

If people were given the choice, rather than have the climate become even more chaotic, I'm sure they'd prefer to endure infinitely smaller hardships, like turning off lights. Industry and commerce may have to be legislated out of their profligate power use.

Then the government couldn't claim that demand was forcing them to allow more coal-fired power stations, major, major producers of the rising CO_2 levels, the 'greenhouse gases' that cause the global warming that cause the climate chaos. That'd be a start.

Then a mix of renewable energy sources could meet our needs.

The logical next step is not to mine and sell the coal to other countries' power stations — there are no atmospheric borders. If that sounds economically subversive, I mean it to be. We *must* think of other ways of economically progressing. Every new coalmine will add nails to the global coffin. I find downright immoral the view taken by the federal MP responsible for the area where the huge Anvil Hill mine is proposed — that if we don't sell them the coal to burn, someone else will. You could say the same about nuclear weapons.

It used to be said that Australia rode on the sheep's back. Do we really want to be now riding on the back of global warming, from coal; or nuclear danger, from uranium? We're rich in coal and uranium, but we're also rich in sunshine and wind. We could be proud of our economy riding on those instead, famous for our technological and manufacturing skills in these energy industries that have a safe and proven record, and a future.

Since his last trip to the US, Mr Howard has been talking about nuclear as 'inevitable', his solution to global warming, a term that has now become politically useful to him. If coal is now dodo technology because it's turned out to be globally self-destructive, nuclear is already proven to be dangerous: in process, in possible uses and in by-products.

'Safe nuclear' is as much a myth as 'clean coal'.

Who's keeping the blinkers on our 'leaders'? They see black, they see red, but they can't or won't see green, let along *go* for it. This cynical little old solar-powered lady dares to wonder why.

My mountain will be safe from tsunamis, but the storms here don't need to get any wilder. They are already a spectacularly powerful reminder of human vulnerability and insignificance in the face of nature. From my open 'skybowl' clearing I have front row seats — and what the sky delivers, the trees amplify.

From the edge of the escarpment below, many ranks of trees stand between me and the full force of the winds. Silvery smooth blue gums, rough brown mahoganies and stringy-barks, flanked by skinny she-oaks — wind-curved at the back of the troops and ramrod straight in front — are laced with rising branches to form the sides of my bowl, their upraised arms ending in thin fingertips dangling fans of gumleaves to fringe its rim.

These fans are rarely absolutely still, and are constantly creating different patterns. Often they are part of a more energetic dance, being shaken about like cheerleaders' pompoms as the upper branches sway from side to side in what can be a very lively routine.

I accept this fluid nature of the top half of the sides of my bowl; it allows me to see all the different colours of the leaves as they bounce and turn and shimmer, to hear them gently humming the tune to which they dance, to keep me aware that they are very alive. It doesn't make me feel nervous about the safety of my bowl at all.

What *does* is when the dance passes into frenzy, when the humming becomes screaming and roaring, when fans are thrown from one side of the bowl to the other, when their very arms are broken off and dashed to the ground.

Sometimes the dancers whip their bodies back and forward so violently that they break in half, or forget the first rule of this dance, which is that their upper halves perform all the actions — their feet absolutely *must* stay on the ground. They fall headlong, crashing heavily to the earth, their toes turned up in fatal exposure and their fans still quivering in shock.

During such extreme storms I admit to anxiety, occasionally verging on fear, here in my little cabin. I hope none of the closer trees above me fall downhill, in defiance of the wind's direction. Even though I built in a clearing, and thought I had left enough space in front, in 30 years the trees have grown taller and I am no longer sure of safety there either.

The aftermath is always shocking to behold: splintered shafts like pitiful amputees, shredded leaves and smashed branches strewn every-where. Worst of all are the living dead — the great trees prostrate when they ought to be upright, their huge root masses still holding soil, exposed to air and light instead of safe in their own dark under-world. Behind them gape the matching holes, lined with severed rootlets. The trees die slowly, the leaves turning brown and falling, the bark cracking, the broken limbs splitting, the trunks drying until they are no longer registered as trees, living things, but as logs, usable commodities to be sawn up and split for posts or firewood.

A tree on the outer edge that falls like this may bring others down too, creating a tangle of three or four, uprooted and smashed to the floor of my bowl. Such a major collapse leaves that part of my tree rim very thin and weak. All of a sudden I can see through it in patches to the distant light-green hills of the valley, and the wind finds its way in when before it was forced to blow over the top. I plant new trees at that spot, erect a temporary fence around them, and hope it will recover. So far it has.

For nearly two years after the last bad fires the tree rim didn't look like mop heads at all, for there were none left. Instead, the silhouettes on my horizon were of upraised skeletal arms and claws that gradually grew furry as the interim leaves shot all along the branches until the trees could recover. Cleverly designed things, our eucalypts. Then strange post-fire colonising shrubs appeared, adding to this alien landscape — some native, like the purple-flowered Kangaroo Apples and Nightshades of the *Solanum* family; and some exotic, like Inkweed, *Phytolacca octandra*, that grew everywhere, 2 or 3 metres high, with red stems, purplish-black spires of berries and reddish autumn leaves. I was assured these would not be residents for more than a couple of years, and so it proved.

One uncommonly wild storm came over when the extended front verandah was not quite completed. It was over 3 metres wide, so its tin and polycarbonate roof presented a large area of uplift. My partner had only put in half the amount of roof screws needed before he ran out of the time he could spare. At least the roof was on, and had been in this half-fixed state for some time — but how firmly was it on?

Late one afternoon, we heard what sounded like jet engines revving flat out, fast approaching from the west. We looked around, saw that the sky there was an ominous pale leaden colour, and within seconds the tree cover on the western rim turned thin as leaves were whipped flat, trunks lashed into that dance to be feared. Then it was upon us.

The chairs on the verandah suddenly flew to the far eastern end and piled up against the rail, their cushions sailing up and over and beyond. Doors and windows slammed, loose objects in the yard became airborne. I thought of Dorothy and the hurricane that took her to Oz. The verandah roof creaked and groaned, lifting, straining to leave the battens and cut loose, but, miraculously, it held. Torrential rain followed the big wind, sounding like a continuous barrage of nails on the roof over our heads.

Next day, the remaining roof screws were added while I searched for and retrieved the far-flung items from their strange landing places.

Yet being close and exposed to the sky does offers compensatory pleasures.

As a child, I would lie on my back in the warm ploughed dirt between the rows of orange trees in our orchard and watch the clouds for as long as I thought safe from detection by my mother, who was always on the lookout for time-wasting. She'd have thought cloud-dreaming even worse than reading.

There I was below the clouds, Gosford being almost at sea level. Here I'm high enough to look side-on at the cloud masses as they glide silently past like grand ocean liners, and close enough to see their slow explosions from within, their metamorphosis from one shape to another.

Often they descend, surround me with the most gentle moisture, fill my bowl with cottonwool so finely spun as to be translucent, transform the familiar to the mysterious, vague shapes and elusive silhouettes seen through sheer white curtains. Sometimes the cloud which encloses me is suffused with sunlight. It's such an ethereal ambience that my spirit soars into what I have to call bliss — and I don't do bliss lightly or often. And I'm moved to say, 'Thank you!' —

though to whom or what I don't know — for my good fortune to be here. On a more practical level, on days like this I know it will be sunny way out there in the unseen valleys and above my cloud, and my solar panels do collect a little power.

The cloud might visit me for a morning, a day or a week. Much as I love it, after a week, when my solar panels are in need of genuine undiluted sunshine to recharge the batteries, aesthetic considerations fade if I am about to need to use high-wattage items. I could run the generator, but usually patience wins; the cloud lifts, the sun returns, and the batteries bubble again.

As the cloud rises, its leave-taking has occasionally coincided with the sun setting through the tree rim on the western edge, creating some breathtaking special effects of refracted fiery light, fanning out like rays of revelation. If the gods had anything to say to us mortals they'd say it then, or if there were a mythmaker about, she'd make one.

My neighbours have better wet weather intuition than I do. The frogs go crazy, vying with each other in volume, in the lead-up to thunderstorms; the black cockatoos appear, wheeling about, doing astonishingly agile aerial runs between the trees with their big wing spans, squawking loudly — I am told that if they fly up the creek (or is it down the creek?) rain is coming; and the ants build high circular walls of dirt around their holes on the track.

At the first rumbles of thunder, I unplug the telephone and the computer; it only took one phone sizzled by lightning to get me into that habit. If I am on the line when it starts to crackle, I say goodbye hurriedly. Often after a bad storm, my phone line will buzz, hum, whine … or die. It can be out for days, sometimes weeks, as it's tough terrain for repair teams, and 18 kilometres over hill and dale and creeks from the exchange.

To report a fault, I walk up the hill with my CDMA mobile until one bar flickers on it — if I face a certain way. Digital doesn't work at all. The old analogue system worked fine at the house but when did the powers-that-be care about us bushies? Now they're phasing out CDMA. Why am I sceptical about the resulting effect on me?

When I get through to the centralised computerised fault report centre, the person assures me it will be fixed in two days. 'No it won't,' I yell down the poor line, trying to explain the remoteness and the reality of time and distance. They merely repeat what their screen tells them. I give up; reality can't compete with virtuality.

The intrepid repairmen travel by four-wheel drive for over two hours by a back route through private property to get here, as there's no road from my exchange to me. They have to come in pairs because it's remote, and the same blokes have been coming for twenty years because a rookie could get lost en route. So we're old mates, although I doubt I'll be seeing them once Telstra is fully privatised. Because of the high cost of servicing this line I've remained loyal to Telstra, reasoning that they should get the profits too.

On this sorry landline my dial-up modem sent and received emails at snail's.pace. As it was increasingly assumed that everyone had broadband, half an hour would go by as an unnecessarily image-laden email creaked its way through the line to me. Trying to access an Internet site for my work could mean waiting fifteen minutes for a page to load.

Poor communications are the main disadvantage of living here; I can't get broadband without a satellite dish, can't use a wireless modem because of the bad CDMA reception, and couldn't afford them anyway. Telstra ran out of government grants for satellite broadband in 2005. I'd put my name down, waited, enquired twice, waited six months more to hear when the next grants would be available, and never did.

Now I've gone with another company who have grants and good prices and who rang me. I'll have to maintain a server for dial-up access when away from home, and I'll still have an erratic phone service, but I recently had my free satellite dish installed and, although it looks incongruously high tech on my cabin roof, it seems to work fine so far. Yet rumour has it that reception is susceptible to storms, which would be just dandy if these are on the increase.

People tell me that 'Voice over Internet Protocol' (VoIP) is the coming thing to replace my landline. I will investigate this, although it's bound to require additional gear or service payments, meaning money that I don't have.

Just in case things get worse, do they still make carrier pigeons?

While my place can't actually flood, after heavy rain the hillsides are moving sheets of water, all drainage is inadequate, fountains cascade over banks and steps, slight dirt furrows quickly form ravines for rivers, and the spring gullies become white water rushes, roaring like express trains, pouring over rocks, scouring out holes and banks all the way down to the creek in the valley far below. It's exciting and worrying at the same time. Will I be able to repair the damage to the track, the drains? Why is the roof suddenly leaking in that spot? Will my telephone junction boxes be flooded? Have my little rainforest trees been smashed by the force of the run-off waters?

The worst storm damage I've had was recent, from a really furious hailstorm that arrived accompanied by sharp wind gusts. The greenhouse was wearing its shadecloth cover, but over the years the supporting plastic pipes for that had sagged, so the cloth hung too close to the glass instead of being tautly suspended above. Eight sheets of glass were smashed. One casement window in the house was blown off its catch and back against the wall. Frame as well as glass was broken.

Replacing the glass in the slotted tracks of the greenhouse fixing system was a nightmare, especially on the sloping high roof. A friend helped, poised on a ladder outside, precariously leaning out over glass, while I was inside on a ladder, sliding the sheets in from the ridge, working blind, under tense instructions like, 'One more millimetre — careful! No, too far!' and trying not to let go. We had very frayed tempers by the end, but no broken glass or cut fingers.

Not that our rain only comes in storms; like anywhere else it can be heavy, light, constant, intermittent, welcome or unwelcome. The creatures that like it most, no matter what form it takes, are the leeches. Damp forest litter with a warm-blooded creature like me walking slowly about on it — or, better still, stopping — is what constitutes bliss to them. And dinner.

It's another reason I wear gumboots everywhere, but I have to keep glancing down to see if any are on the move, inching up to go over the top and down into the socks, and thus between the toes. Ugh! The height of the gumboots at least buys me time. National Parks rangers wear short work boots, but rub or spray the tops of the boots, bottoms of trousers, and boyangs, if worn, with insect repellent, as they reckon leeches don't like it.

Boyangs, by the way, are loose cloth cylinders, elasticised at one end, pulled on over boots, socks and cuffs to keep burrs and grass seeds out. I have made some from old shirtsleeves, so, unlike the sober khaki shop ones, mine are in unlikely colours and patterns.

Leeches aren't a worry in the garden, but down in my gullies they are plentiful. I know leeches are part of the natural world, but I will never like them, and I am not offering them refuge — or sustenance — in my boots. Possibly my narrow view is a result of childhood trauma.

The year was 1955, a wet one statewide, and our first year on the farm. I'd been mucking about in a clay irrigation ditch, making miniature dams and weirs, releasing and stopping the flows of rainwater. Going across to the house for lunch, I sat down on the top step, on the folded-hessian-bag doormat, to pull off my gumboots. As I did so, I saw something black — and alive — stuck to my leg.

I stamped, screamed in real terror. 'Mum! Mum! There's a baby snake biting my leg! It won't let go!' Mum came running, but she was no wiser. She tried poking at it with a stick, but it held on fast. I was hysterical. 'Get it off! Get it off!'

Fortunately a neighbour was visiting. 'Hold still,' he said, and to my even greater terror, took a box of matches from his pocket, struck a match and held the flame to the tail of the creature! Within seconds it shrivelled and fell away, leaving a small hole which soon began to trickle blood. Our nonchalant source of country wisdom said that you could use salt to make them let go too.

'But what are they?' we panicked still.

'Just leeches,' he said contemptuously, 'there's millions of 'em round here in the wet. *They* won't hurt yer!'

But they did as, apart from the shuddering reality of having some creature clamped onto my flesh and sucking my blood, on me at least they cause large red lumps that itch for weeks afterwards.

In every likely work pocket or bag, I have stashed ex-film-roll containers filled with salt. Sprinkling salt on leeches does make them drop off. It also kills them. Which is wicked for a so-called conservationist, I know, but I consider it a matter of survival. If they broach the barriers, I want to be able to get them off, and quickly, with as little blood loss as possible! So after planting out trees in damp bush, I strip off for a search and a shower. From experience I know it is necessary to search *every*where.

Surprisingly, I wrote a short story about leeches, called 'B-grade Reality'. Not so surprisingly, it turned out to be a horror story, the only one I have ever written.

Perhaps my original trauma was reinforced by a leech being the cause of my most embarrassing school memory. By the time I was thirteen I was used to our farm creek flooding, when I had to wade barefoot through knee- to thigh-deep water that covered the lower parts of our track and the road to the bus stop, half a mile away. My school shoes and stockings and a little towel were in my Globite school case, balanced on my head with one hand, the other keeping my tunic tucked up into my navy bloomers.

There was first the hurdle of our rickety wooden bridge, which lost at least one of its round logs each flood, the gap hidden beneath milky brown rushing water. It was a matter of inching forward, feeling with my toes for the gap that might drop me through to certain drowning, as the creek was full of bobbing and whirling branches and logs — more than a match for my feeble dogpaddle.

The farmer's wife at the house next to the bus stop always let me get dressed on her verandah. I'd dry my cold legs and red feet, still tingling from walking on the sharp gravel of the road, and put on my black cotton stockings. Later in this particular flood school morning, I was commanded to the blackboard by the formidable Sister Augustine. I had passed up the aisle between the desks and was halfway across the open space of lino before the blackboard, when Sister's sharp Irish voice rang out in the slow-rising-then-fast-falling rhythm she used for my name when I was about to get into trouble: 'Sha-a-a…ryn *Mun*ro!

What on earth is that?' pointing at the floor near my feet.

Everybody stared at a trail of dark red spots that led from my desk to where I stood and where the spots were forming a small pool of what appeared to be blood. This blood was coming from somewhere up under my tunic, and given that menstruation was in the offing for all of us, she could have been more tactful. I was so ignorant it didn't occur to me, or I'd have been even more embarrassed.

I was publicly commanded to go and find out what the trouble was. As I slunk out the door, she called, 'Well at least there's nothing the matter with your blood; it's a *lovely* rich red!' (She also taught biology — and geography, as it was a very small school.) In the toilets I rushed to unclip my suspenders and pull down my stockings. Out rolled a fat, gorged leech, its puncture mark on my thigh, just above where the stockings ended, still steadily oozing blood. It must have been there for hours, as it was now nearly eleven o'clock.

On my return I explained what the cause was, which drew not much more than a general 'Ugh!' from the class and a 'Really!' from my teacher, who gave me a bandaid and sent me to fetch a mop and bucket to clean up the blood. I had the distinct feeling that I had displayed something too basic, peasant-like, for my superior town classmates.

If they could see me now!

CHAPTER 14

THE SIMPLE LIFE

EVEN THOUGH I'M NEARING 60, and there are many signs of old age — hair greying, sight and memory failing, joints creaking, flesh drooping and wrinkles deepening — I'm not *old*. I'm still the same me, it's just that, sometime in the last ten years when I wasn't looking, my smooth outer shell was exchanged for this cracked and saggy one.

I think that living here keeps me young. I don't know how long I can stay here as I really do get old, for if I were physically feeble daily life wouldn't be possible. Contrary to popular mythology, the simple life is not found in the country but in the city, where you simply pay your bills and press a button for everything you need, and you don't have to know how any of it works or be able to fix it yourself.

Since I live far from the madding crowd — or mechanics — this life is only idyllic so long as nothing goes wrong with my self-sufficiency survival mechanisms. These range from complicated ones like solar power, to water pumping and delivery, cooking, space and water heating, right down to the very basics like sanitation, drains and garbage. All daily involve time, effort, forethought, energy and strength, to varying degrees.

I'll begin with the least complicated system: garbage disposal. I keep only a small lidded compost bin inside. Out on the verandah I have two larger open containers: one for recyclables like those glass and plastic items for which I can't think of a use; and one for burnables, for my incinerator. Actual garbage is very little, and it goes in the suspended plastic bag bin that the quoll likes — though she checks out the burnables too. She does this in case food has stuck to a sheet of newspaper.

Family save local papers for me, and a friend saves me the 'Review' literature section of the Saturday *Australian*, giving them to me in bundles every few months, when I binge on reviews and catch up on cultural news that I missed on Radio National. Occasionally I am also given Sunday tabloids, which contain a lot of … paper.

I keep an opened-out pile of newspapers on my kitchen bench to catch the scraps from my cutting board. This Handy Household Hint came from my ex-mother-in-law, who'd roll up the scraps in the top sheet and put the parcel in the bin. I tip the scraps into the compost bin and shove the paper into the firebox to start that night's fire. I always lay these papers right way up so I can read while peeling and chopping, which is how I find out what celebrities and socialites were up to six months ago.

Now and then I take a bag of garbage or recyclables to town to my daughter's wheelie bins.

My next self-sufficient system is sanitation. I have what is called a 'long drop', a big hole in the ground with my old jail's lidded seat over it and a shelter shed over that. It was originally a metre-cubed hole, dug into bedrock with pick and crowbar in 1978. I'd assumed it would last a few years, but it's still going. Beside the seat is a lidded enamel canister which officially says SUGAR, but as nobody takes tea there I think it's safe from confusion with my Texta-scrawled LIME. A sprinkle of the latter now and then is enough to keep the material breaking down, while an evaporation pipe dries it out and reduces the volume.

I always thought I'd build a dry composting toilet one day, but the only real difference from my current one would be that I'd get to use the resulting compost.

A few overly civilised visitors have had difficulty using my sanitation arrangements. I've never asked whether this was from the dark pit yawning beneath them or the idea of communal storage, but the ensuing psychosomatic constipation was real. They couldn't wait — or rather, they could — to get back to a proper flushing loo. I feel sorry for them, so unable to accept that they're part of the animal world, with the same basic processes necessary for survival. They were possibly also uncomfortable without a door to shut, but the toilet faces away from the house, and they wouldn't see the birds and trees otherwise.

Having grown up with a pan toilet — a far-too-short drop — I consider mine quite manageably distant and salubrious. That toilet, complete with harsh and unabsorbent newspaper squares impaled on a large nail, was dark and spider-scary because it wasn't done to leave the door open; and smelly, often maggoty, because it was never emptied soon enough. When Dad worked away from home for a month once, Mum and I had to do it, and I understood why he'd kept putting it off. But that first row of orange trees, in the burial range, had the glossiest, greenest leaves, and the biggest, juiciest fruit, of all the trees in the orchard.

The disadvantage of my toilet is that it's a fair hike up the hill when you're in a hurry or it's raining. If the pit ever does fill up, I'll build the new toilet on the flat, still outdoors, perhaps reached by a covered walkway. And I'll plant an orange tree on the old site.

My drainage system? That barely exists, and is an ongoing digging effort, an especially frustrating use of time and knee-power. In our sudden storms, leaves and silt and sticks quickly fill up my too-shallow manually dug drains that are meant to protect my buildings and outdoor access spaces. They're on the 'hard' list for improvements, as is my temporary grey-water system, which is awaiting the permanent bathroom, which is awaiting money, machinery, man-type plumbing knowledge …

Wood-fired systems: how quaintly rustic, and what could be simpler? I have a slow-combustion heater and a slow-combustion stove, for cooking and hot water. To keep these going requires daily housekeeping, the degree based on a gamble on the weather.

I forget to keep up the supply of dry kindling at my peril, but picking up sticks from under the trees is easy. It's the bigger wood that's my problem, as it not only involves time and physical effort, but courage — and a chainsaw, which is machinery, and thus mysterious. I couldn't even start our original 1970s Stihl chainsaw. Still perfectly serviceable, it's all metal, therefore back-breakingly heavy, and has no chain brake for safety. I'd yank on its pull cord until I was exhausted or my wrist screamed 'Stop!' but that Beast never started for me.

Once I was on my own, I was dependent on visitors to cut wood for me. My son having moved north for work, he was rarely able to return to the mountain, and then only for brief visits. So the woodcutting fell mainly to my diminutive daughter. This was fine in summer, but in winter the amount of wood needed was beyond occasional help, and my daughter's back didn't like the Beast at all. Too often I reverted to rugging up and gritting my teeth, to 'top and tail' warm washes rather than hot showers, to save firewood.

Then I had a small financial windfall about the same time that Stihl brought out a new 'easy start' chainsaw, with a gentle double recoil. No yanking needed. Mechanical magic! And nearly half the weight of the Beast. For the first dozen times I used it, I had the manual open beside me as I went through the steps. To remember their sequence is like learning nonsense syllables, lacking any understanding of their connection. Except for turning on the fuel — I get that bit.

I am religious about checking the chain oil and the fuel, and cleaning it, just like a man. But, unlike a man, once it's going I'm scared of it as a lethal tool given to unpredictable behaviour, like kicking and pinching, grabbing and seizing, or so says the manual.

Although I am extremely careful, each time I use it away from the house I make sure I have my mobile with me, to call the ambulance. Even at the woodheap I have vivid flashes of sudden slips, of gashes, slashes, slices, gushes, of red blood and white bone. I think about how I would find, pick up and pack the cut-off bits, of dragging myself to the phone, of which I should do first; I try to recall my first aid — but did we do bleeding stumps of limbs? I'm a nervous wreck by the time I have a wheelbarrow full, every time. Phew! Survived one more load.

My little old Suzuki Sierra and I head out now and then to find an accessible log: old, dry, and hopefully splittable later. Woodcutting's not as easy as you might think from watching blokes, who nonchalantly stop the log from rolling with one foot and cut right beside it — they clearly have no imagination. I must keep propping and restraining the log so I can saw it up without blunting the chain on the ground, and without abbreviating my gumboots.

When my arms begin to ache, I stop. I load the wood into the back of the Suzi, being wary of scorpions, spiders, ants or ticks. When I get home, I unload, being similarly watchful. Any bits too long for the firebox, but too short to be cut safely by anyone but a mad steel-toed male, I place in a sort of wedge made from two pairs of star posts, banged crisscross into the ground. This neat idea for sawing up smaller pieces came from a friend, but because he's a bloke he banks up and cuts through about ten times the amount that I do in one go.

Then I have a shower to wash off general sawdust and dirt plus any ticks that have hitched a ride, or leeches that have got into my boots.

When my arms have recovered, I can take the splitter, a sort of axe with a heavy fat head, and forestall some of that incipient upper-arm flab by breaking the cut logs into burnable slabs. When I'm missing the log more often than I'm hitting it, and liable to hit my boot instead, I know it's time to give up for this session. Some logs have interlocked grain that won't let go and require ten times the effort to split. Others are not splittable — or not by me; the splitter just bounces off, jarring my wrists and threatening to knock me out on the recoil. Such logs have to be left for the heater, which has a bigger firebox than the stove.

One of Nanna's most enduring sources of pleasure and pride, before failing eyesight forced her to give it up in her eighties, was being able to 'splitta bitta deal' for kindling for her fuel stove. While my hardwood is far more obstinate than the packing case 'deal' or pine she used, the activity itself always reminds me of her. Perhaps there's a 'tough old lady' gene? I'd be proud to have hers.

If I have visitors who can back a trailer, which I can't despite many attempts to learn, we might take the Suzi and my small trailer to get a bigger load. Not too big, as she might strain something. Backing a trailer is something I admire, but I see it as a gift rather than a skill. Otherwise I'd be able to do it, wouldn't I?

Like everything here, the wood provisioning can involve unforeseen complications. Take the other week when, busy on a writing job, I'd let my indoor woodpile run very low. I thought I'd better split a wheelbarrow full, since rain was forecast. It should only take ten minutes.

But my 25-year-old wheelbarrow chose that moment to snap the last rusty threads of its axle bolt. I knocked the broken bolt out with difficulty, and went poking about in the shed for the right length, right diameter bolt. After much to-ing and fro-ing, which intensely annoyed my quoll, I admitted I didn't have one. I'd need to file the metal hole bigger. That took quite a while.

The wheelbarrow and I rattled up to the woodheap. There were really only the unsplittable rejects left. To save time, I decided to drive over to my son's cabin and pick up the last of his building off-cuts. I found the pile overgrown with tall bracken and interlaced with rotting chipboard sheets. Sorting through it, with an eye out for snakes, took quite a while.

Loading the wood into the back of the Suzi took quite a while too. With wood that's been on the ground like that I have to turn over each piece in case some small creature has already claimed it as habitat, in which case I put it back.

I did beat the rain, but when I finally stumbled inside with my armfuls of wood, I realised it had taken nearly three hours to fill that wheelbarrow.

Yet wood gathering is only part of the wood system. Despite avoiding damp or green wood where possible, I have to clean the flues regularly — a filthy job, but creosoted flues and blocked dampers catch fire, usually when it's dark and raining, and climbing on the roof in a panic, dragging a running hose, slipping and cursing, is no fun. In fact, it's another way in which I could maim or kill myself here.

And then there's the actual wood-burning units, composed of loose bits of metal and firebrick that occasionally fall out and won't say where from. The stove is particularly good at this, and appears to be held together with screws of an infinite variety of sizes that don't fit any of the increasing number of visible holes. Without taking the whole heavy cast-iron unit apart, I can't access the parts that are supposed to move to see why they no longer do. It also has nastily disintegrating asbestos seals that will have to be replaced at some stage. Clearly neither the stove nor the heater was designed by women.

They both do a great job. I am warm, my water gets hot, my bread tastes great, I can slow simmer soups and stews beautifully — but simple, they are not.

And I'm not even going to talk about the highly esoteric hot-water system, devised and built by my ex-partner. I can see that the 44-gallon drum that kneels quaintly askew on my roof is rusting through, and I try not to think about what's going on in there around the copper inner tank, nor what I will do when it needs replacing.

Hot water comes from cold water and that cold water comes from my big dam a few gullies away. For over 25 years a faithful duo — my Lister diesel engine and its Ajax pump — have been squatting there, ready to pump water 60 metres up, but longer in actual distance, to the cement tanks on top of the ridge. Even when I was 30, I couldn't crank that pump engine fast enough to start it. To do so demands a ridiculously ferocious burst of effort for a short time — the perfect heart-stopper. I have seen all but the biggest of males just about 'bust their boilers' in trying, but they manage in the end.

It remains impossible for myself and my daughter, and we are both strong. It is not a human-friendly pump, let alone a female-friendly one. A small drinking water tank on the house means I'm never actually waterless, but pressured water is factored into all systems and is essential in the fire season. Having to count on my rare male visitors for this was hardly self-sufficiency.

Invariably the shanghai-ed male would give it one rapid burst of cranking and away she'd go — puff, puff, chugga, chugga — and slowly but surely the water would rise up the pipeline. I would leave it doing this overnight, as I had to make the most of that male's effort; who knew when the next one might turn up? I had fleeting fantasies of Sirens on the island in the dam, drawing passing men to me and my pump. Only I can't sing, and it might be months before anyone at all passed.

It infuriated me to be so helpless.

After I'd been on my own for about twelve months, and my ex-partner was re-matched via Internet Dating, I weakened and tried this techno matchmaking myself — and not for the pump's sake. With hindsight, it was/is a hopelessly unrealistic and over-optimistic, back-to-front matchmaking method, and I don't recommend it. But through it I met someone with whom I thought I was in love. Well, I was, briefly. His emails were long and articulate, and he could spell — you'd be surprised how rare that is; he claimed to be a Radio National listener, from which I assumed too much; from photos he looked just my type; at the next stage of progression from virtual to real, I found he had a deep and melting telephone voice. Who could blame me?

I am mortified to recall how besotted I became, raving about him to all who would listen. I was even going to marry him. You may gain an inkling of how badly I was smitten if I confess that I played John Denver love songs — and wept. What happened to cynical me? Please understand that the CD wasn't mine. I mean, I didn't buy it; it was an old one of my mother's, kept by me solely for the country song 'Grandma's Feather Bed', to play to my granddaughter. Honestly. Cross my heart.

But what does this pathetic hormonal behaviour have to do with the pump? Coincidentally, the object of my affection was very clever with things mechanical. He devised a way to replace the Herculean cranking system by connecting the big diesel engine, via a rubber belt and a pulley, to a smaller engine that theoretically I could start. Each time he set the system up, I watched, then had a go. It worked every time. I was happy — mechanical independence loomed. The down side was that I had one more machine with its attendant mysteries.

My rose-coloured glasses having begun to slip after only a few months of the real relationship, John Denver sounded soppy once more and was relegated to a dark drawer. After six months, I dropped the romantic dream in there too and stomped on those silly glasses for good. My generous Internet ex insisted I kept the small engine, amongst other items for which he had no use — like the lawn mower — and which I could never have afforded to buy. He'd been a big spender on men's toys.

A pity I'd found him and his world too narrow and uncommitted. He was a nice man, but then so was my ex-partner and, once upon a time, my ex-husband. At least I was now cured of looking. I could share my life, enrich it further, with an equal, or I'd live it contentedly by myself. I'd finally understood that this didn't mean carrying a vacant space around beside me. Nor a sign saying 'To Let'.

The first time my daughter and I tried to start the pump this way, we thought we were doing well in getting the new system all connected up. We took turns in revving the little engine flat out, the vibrations shaking our teeth and every bone in our heads, the noise deafening, the pump engine going 'puff, puff, puff'. 'Throw the pressure switch!' I'd yell, but when we did, nothing further would happen; it could not get past 'puff, puff, puff'. We gave up, unbolted the engine, but left the pulley screwed on for another try when our strength and faith had returned.

A few weeks later, a most atypical female friend who understands motorbikes, and therefore 'small engines', came to visit. I showed her the pump engine and its manual. This genius worked out that my daughter and I had run the pulley backwards, and therefore the pump engine was not at 'top dead centre' or some similarly esoteric term, which it apparently had to be for starting. The pressure switch was not connecting with anything. What we had to do now was use the crank handle to turn the engine over to the right spot.

Only we couldn't get the pulley off the crank handle shaft. Running it backwards had wedged it and its grub screw on too tightly for feminine bashing and pullings, no matter what unidentified heavy metal tool we applied to it. But at least I knew what was required. A male.

I called a relatively nearby local (half an hour away by trailbike) who'd previously agreed to accept money for his time if I needed help. He came a few days later. With much bashing and tapping, he got the pulley off. He fitted the crank handle and went for it with a fury, and the monster started up. I rejoiced. But he refused to accept any money, so I knew I wouldn't feel comfortable calling on him again.

Since I only need to run the pump every few months, it's a while between battles. But I was confident I had it sorted now. I knew which way to run the pulley, for I'd drawn Texta diagrams on it and the small engine, as I had on the bolt to undo for priming. Since the universal undo direction of anti-clockwise has exceptions, grunting in a red-faced and futile effort to undo, when I am actually over-tightening, is something I can live without.

After two victorious pump runs I had a right to faith and hope.

But then the next battle left me defeated. What on earth could be wrong now? I'd checked and re-checked everything I knew about. I was due to go away for a week and it was summer; I could not leave with the tanks nearly empty.

I walked home and had a coffee to calm down and consider the matter. Then I remembered the oil being rather black when I'd checked the level. I had no idea if it would help, but I could change the oil, because I'd bought the right diesel oil months ago. The job had been on my list of things that I'd never done before, so kept putting off. This must be a punishment for my procrastination.

My diesel engine is very close to the ground. Even more so, it turned out, was the plug I had to undo to empty out the old oil. I had a slim tray with me to catch it, but even that couldn't be wedged under the plug. Since surely no one would design a drain hole that couldn't be drained into anything, I assumed that when the plug came out, so would an extension tube or something. I'd forgotten that engines are designed by men. As soon as the little plug was halfway unscrewed, thick black oil rushed everywhere.

Catching what I could with the tray, downhill of the engine, I daubed the excess over every bit of cast iron in sight. Rust protection, I told myself. As I did this with my hands, and as I'd been kneeling as I scrabbled to channel the flow, I was a mess.

I emptied the oil into a patch of thistles that needed exterminating, found a rag in the car — leaving oily black marks as evidence of search for same — and wiped the plug clean and my hands at least a little less dirty. I poured in the new oil.

To do all this I'd had to disconnect the system, so I now reconnected it, took a deep breath, said 'Please!' and started up the little engine. 'REV-VVVV — puff, puff, puff, puff' — flick the pressure switch — 'chugga chugga'! 'Yay!' I yelled above the welcome noise of the diesel engine and, more quietly, 'Thanks!' as I danced over to the gate valves to let the precious water start uphill. Never having mastered cartwheels, I did a few pirouettes over the grass instead. Several wallabies on the dam wall sat back on their tails and queried my unseemly behaviour.

I couldn't stop smiling and was so proud of solving the problem that, as soon as I'd showered the worst of the oil off myself and put my clothes to soak, I rang a male friend, to share my advance in mechanical competence.

'Well,' he said, 'I doubt if that would've been the reason it didn't start. New oil'd make it run better, but that's all.'

Confidence quashed; mysteries of machines and male understanding of same reasserted.

Six weeks later, I set it all up again, expecting no problem with the diesel engine this time. I didn't get the chance to find out because I couldn't even start the small engine! Not a peep. I walked back to fetch the manual. Over-cockiness, I thought. I must have forgotten the sequence of pushing buttons and squeezing levers. But doing it by the book, still no peep. I must have flooded it, I reassured myself — which was what I'd heard men say about reluctant car engines.

I waited, and tried again. Nope. I unbolted it all. I took the little engine to town when next I went, two weeks later. There my son-in-law started it first go, pronounced it OK and gave it back to me.

Feeling foolish and female, I brought it back here and went through the whole process once more. Same result — nil. I rang for help. He said that was surprising, but perhaps it was the spark plug on the way out then, and I should remove the plug and buy another.

Easier said than done. I vaguely knew that spark plugs require special spanners, but since I didn't know what one looked like, finding the latter amongst the metal things in my shed was an IQ test that I failed. I gave up and took the engine down to him once more. The special spanner turned out not to look like any spanner I knew. Plus I discovered that spark plugs can be in awkward positions, so that even had I found the special tool, I couldn't have used it. I was initiated into a piece of assumed knowledge: you often need extra levers.

Are males born with this stuff?

But, once I get the water into the tanks, it simply runs downhill in the buried pipeline, gravity feeding to my taps. Except that the pipe can be unburied by animals and broken by horse hoofs and leak and I won't know until no water comes out of the tap and it's a long uphill walk to find where and I may not have the right diameter joiner to fix the leak nor the wrist power to work the two wrenches to tighten it enough even if I find a joiner and I have to keep walking up and down the hill to turn the tanks off and on to test if my join leaks and even when it's fixed there'll be an airlock so I'm still not getting water in the taps and I can't light the stove without water in the tank up top or I'll blow it up …

Simple, eh?

CHAPTER 15

OVER MY HEAD

I OFTEN ENVY THE lifestyles of my neighbours, which they seem to have down to an effortlessly fine and simple art. Of course I've only been working at mine for decades, but I'm also disadvantaged by being hopelessly grounded, for much of the social activity in my world goes on above me. I can't always see what's doing up there, but I can certainly hear it.

From one side of the tree rim to the other, birds constantly dart, swoop or lazily flap, in following, chasing two or threes, in panicky, chattery flocks, or determinedly single. They fly over my clearing, an aerial intersection, and always make it across, but not always without incident or alteration of course. That's because the upper reaches of it are patrolled by a group of dapper and daring magpies, who choose, apparently at random, to keep the others on their wingtiptoes by hurtling out of nowhere like turbo-charged sheep dogs, deflecting them offside into the nearest tree edge. They continue this pursuit between the trees at the same speed, unerring and unrelenting, only to abruptly veer off on other business as soon as their point is made.

They allow the lesser birds to visit the base of my bowl just often enough to become complacent before they strike. For days the kookaburras are permitted to decorate my fence posts and stumps, the rosellas to waddle about in my grass or sit on my verandah rail, and the currawongs to direct their beady yellow eyes and quick black beaks to the reddest strawberry for their morning snack. Then one of the bosses decides it's time they were reminded of the order of things and in a black-and-white second he's scattered them all. He never bothers about me.

The inhabitants of the forest seem to have very active social lives, with much tree swapping, violent bursts of cackling, squawking and shrieking accompanied by great shaking commotions of leaves and branches, interspersed with brief solos and duets before the gang arrives.

My small dam in front of the house is a great meeting place — hanging out at the local pool. As always when different gangs meet, there's a lot of showing off, like the wattlebirds daredevil-diving from a high branch to skim the water and up to a tree on the other side. I sometimes see strangers, such as a lone cormorant or heron, stop by for a drink or a swim. Wood ducks from my big dam try too, but the magpies hustle them on their way, protesting, quacking and flapping.

Some of the get-togethers down there sound like unsupervised group therapy. The weird friar-birds, with their bald black heads and knobby beaks, have a scale of maniacal cackles straight out of bedlam, and over the top of them loudly boast the wattlebirds, 'I got the lot, the lot, the lot!' The racket goes on and on, up and down, back and forth, apparently reaching no satisfactory conclusion — a bit like parliament on one of its less than statesman-like days.

If I was going to apologise for perceived anthropomorphism I should probably have done so long ago in these pages, except I don't see it as that. Living alone, with animal and birds as my only daily companions, it's an affectionate way of relating to them, differentiating them, that comes naturally to me.

Birdcalls do begin to interpret themselves as speech, and I can't hear them any other way once that happens. Even bird books, when trying to approximate the calls, sometimes use actual words, the choice of which can only be subjective. In my book the Red Wattlebird is credited with saying 'chock a lock'. Now why would anybody hear a bird say that? At least 'I got the lot!' makes sense.

I suppose I only pick up on the choruses of the birdcalls, as they are the parts most often repeated. So what seems to be their very limited conversational range may be my very limited auditory discrimination, or due to my very considerable ignorance. I have tried listening to birdcall tapes to educate myself, but I drift off after a while.

Certainly repetitive is the call of the Willy Wagtail, who unceasingly compliments everybody and everything, or perhaps it's himself he's talking about — a treetop Narcissus? 'Pretty pretty, pretty! Pretty, pretty, pretty!' Others, who repeat their calls so unvaryingly that I find myself wishing they'd get an answer and shut up, are treetop dwellers that I haven't been able to see, and thus haven't identified.

One is the sociable bird who greets all comers with 'Hello mate! Hello mate!' A bit of a stutterer, he sometimes has trouble getting past the 'Hello ... hello ... hello ...', but he's very persevering for, if I listen long enough, a few minutes later he triumphantly gets out the final '... mate!' I can't tell if it's him or a sympathetic mate who often lets out a long, relieved 'Whe-e-e-w!' after such feats.

Then there's the bird who's a contemplative type, doesn't like to give too hasty an opinion, so he goes to the other extreme, 'I think ... I think ... I think it can!' He varies this with a more positive judgement, delivered in a W.C. Fields descending tone, 'I like it ... I like it ... I like it w-e-ell.'

Many of the little birds speak far too softly and quickly for me to catch any of it. The blue Fairy Wrens and their brown consorts are often in the wisteria vine on my verandah, a few metres beyond my computer, but they're never still for long. Little birds mostly get about in big groups, fussing, fluttering, never sitting still for more than a second, always chattering and twittering and tinkling. Like the various Thornbills and Weebills, who mimic a handful of yellow-turning leaves being perpetually tossed up in the air to flutter quickly down, or the Grey Fantails, who dart about to land here and there for a quick, proud spin-on-the-spot to display their pretty tails.

Most voluble of all are the kookaburras, but they laugh too much to actually *say* anything. They start the day off with a rousing dawn chorus of belly laughs and cackles, tailing off into small half-suppressed chuckles; they sit around all day watching for, catching and scoffing worms, meet a few of their mates now and then for a quick snigger and then as the twilight is about to fade one of them decides IT'S TIME and begins the big event: the evening chorus. He never gets past one solitary bar before his mates start to join in, pointing their big beaks to the sky, throats vibrating, the volume swelling as they all get in on the act, till suddenly the hidden conductor gives the 'Cut!' signal and they drop into silence. But whether someone asks for an encore, or the keener ones just feel like it, sometimes they'll have a second, less substantial, go. There appears to be a few irrepressible ones amongst them who will not take direction and find it hard to make that final note *final*, who just have to give one more salutary chuckle to the last of the light.

Farthest down the line when the singing talents were handed out were the Yellow-tailed Black Cockatoos. They don't come often, but they are very big and very raucous, so when they fly over or sit in my nearby trees for a spell, usually when it's wet and misty, all else gets drowned out. They sound like something mechanical that badly needs oiling. Yet they were at the head of the queue when the magnificence rations were being doled out, for they're impressively beautiful — oversized for the branches they perch on, regally deliberate in their movements, glossy black feathers stiffly sculptured.

I once came across two of them sitting in a low branch of an old forest she-oak, neatly cracking open the woody 'nuts'. They took no notice of me standing not 6 metres away, but continued calmly with their feast, each with one claw clamped to the branch, the other claw manipulating one nut after another up to the hooked beak to break the hard seed pod compartments open and prise out the seeds. Low squawks every now and then expressed approval of the quality of this year's crop.

The Sulphur-crested White Cockatoo is a little less grating of voice, but there's only one who passes over here, and when he does, it's early morning, flying from east to west, and back again around sunset, uttering no more then one or two screeches. He's been doing the same for nearly 30 years — at least I assume it's the same bird, as they are very long-lived. The mundane theory is that he's a scout, checking crops for readiness to call in the flock for a feast. My dad had so many of them round his last farm that he used to plant a third more corn that he needed, factoring in what the cockatoos would eat. But I think my cocky's a tragic figure, not content to join the great white flocks eating farmers' corn and decorating dead gum trees, condemned to wing his lonely way. Shades of Jonathon Livingstone Seagull — is he another fellow weirdo?

I'm glad I have flocks of Crimson Rosellas instead. Gorgeous enough visually as they flash past, rich red with blue and black, they are also near the top of the musical scale, with several sweet and lyrical passages as part of their wide repertoire. They are a delight to hear as they call to each other back and forth across the bowl and around the rim. They also make less delightful squawks, especially when they have a barney over whose turn it is at the bird feeder on the verandah.

From my desk I can see them now, in the 'window' that I keep clipped back amongst the vines near the feeder. This is a large upturned black plastic pot plant saucer, with holes drilled in it, which I've screwed to a protruding crosspiece that I screwed to the railing. Another of those male projects that didn't get done until I was male-less, it's rough, a little wobbly, but it works. I toss a handful of parrot seed in there now and then, or a sunflower head from the garden, just to keep the birds interested, not dependent.

The rosellas sometimes fly the length of my verandah, under its roof, shooting out the far end 'doorway' amongst the vines; or perch on the guttering, tails hanging below it, now and then twisting upside-down, so a beak and two bright eyes come into my view instead.

When a currawong lands in the bird feeder, it fixes the rosellas with a yellow eye and they vacate but don't move far, just to the backs of the chairs at the nearby table. If a magpie arrives, red eye fixes on yellow eye, they both fluff up and look mean, and the currawong backs off, to another chair.

Alfresco dining thus requires removal of bird shit first; it's strong stuff, and since I recently sanded and repainted those yellow chairs, I'm not happy to see paint come off along with the black-and-white drips and drops. Still, it's worth it for times such as when we are sitting at the table and several brilliant jewels of rosellas land beside us to feed, only a few feet away. Welcome!

'Aren't they tame!' a visitor might exclaim. The rosella cocks an eye at him. 'Aren't you!' it might be thinking. They aren't tame at all, merely unafraid, under our established rules of live and let be. If I were to approach the feeder while they were there, instead of going about my own business, they'd fly off at once.

Because I spend so much time at my desk, I am intimate with this view through the window in front. It's an old window, with coloured bubble glass side panels of amber and green and three small coloured panes at the bottom of the lower sash — green, rose and amber — the very same colours as were in my courthouse windows. I can see two yellow chair backs and a crescent of round table, a weathered timber post and railings, layers of wisteria and grape leaves in sunlit patterns and depths of green, the birdfeeder, and birds feeding.

As autumn advances, the wisteria leaves turn from green to butter yellow, but not all together, so echoing my green and yellow window-panes, and the yellow chairs. The ornamental grape leaves go through a riot of shades of pink, red, burgundy and copper. When pink predominates I often place a faded-to-rose lace tablecloth on the oak table, purely for the visual pleasure of the synchronicity of colours. Dyed years ago to hide a claret stain, its usual role is to cover my little TV set, since high-tech black does not suit my rustic cabin.

By winter all the leaves are gone. My view is more open, an intricate pattern of twisted and arching brown stems framing wider views of my tree rim. Its leafy summer cover gone, the translucent sheet in the roof lets in the sun once more; as the sun angle lowers, sunlight reaches my window and my desk. The verandah is used less, the yellow chairs soldier on, often mist-drenched, until they're needed in spring.

I'm fond of these plain wooden chairs, bought some years ago for $2 each in an op-shop. The cheery paint protects them — and renders the table even more reproachful. Of sturdy oak construction, it's been with me for over 35 years. Sealed and oiled long ago, it's now slowly turning black from the elements; it needs, and deserves, better protection from my mountain mists and sunshine. That job is on a list, the 'hard' one, as sanding it will be slow — gripping a sanding block tightly is not possible for long without protest from my thumbs.

When the verandah is free of greenery, kookaburras frequently use the railings as vantage points for spotting the minute activity in the grass that signifies a worm, so I can admire their intricate feather patterns up close. Like the rosellas, they don't move if I walk past on the verandah. Compared to a worm, what am I after all?

Nor are the magpies bothered by my passing, but then, as the bosses, they wouldn't be. The kookaburras don't actually sing while on my verandah, but the maggies do. Magpies seem to have 'got the lot': good looks, great flying skills, and top singing talent. And they really do sing, aiming their voices skywards, warbling in unison. They seem to enjoy it as much as I do. Unlike the rosellas' whistled tunes, I can't imitate the magpie song to talk back to them. I've tried, but it was like gargling while making the French uvular 'r'. I think I'd need a different throat.

Another songbird, heard only occasionally, is the Grey Shrike-thrush. Her rich, pure melody catches the ear immediately and I go looking for her. As at Birrarung, she is shy. Soft-grey toned, she has a large head and a large dark eye, less 'birdlike' in the gimlet sense, so she gives an appearance of gentleness.

The blue-black Satin Bowerbird used to only bring his large harem of olive-green females here in summer, the stone fruit season, until a few years ago. It was spring, and I was on the verandah with my then three-year-old granddaughter, when we heard a creaking whirring call. 'That's an odd one,' I said. 'Could it be a rosella?' My grand-daughter shook her head in pity at my ignorance. 'No, Grandma, that's a bowerbird!' As of course it was, instantly recognisable as soon as she said it but, out of season, out of context, my brain hadn't computed it while hers, less rigid, had.

Far more loftily removed from all the noise and squabble down here — mostly — are the three Wedge-tailed Eagles who lord it over these mountains. Elegantly, lazily, they circle over us on the air currents, barely moving a wing. At times so high as to be mere specks, at others low enough for me to see the colours under their mighty curved wings.

For years I didn't, or couldn't, hear their plaintive calls, so didn't know they spoke, but perhaps it took me a few years to rid my ears and head of the ingrained city-noise and city-ness. Their call doesn't fit the image of the fierce and mighty hunter. My bird book describes it as 'pseet-you, pseet-you'; it is a very thin piping. When I first connected it to them I thought one must have been hurt, somewhere in the trees below me, and the other was fretting. Perhaps when I hear it a lot it is actually a young one? Unbecoming as it is, toddler eagles might be whingers too.

If the eagles are kings of the upper reaches of the sky, the magpies have a clear opinion of where their dominion ends, and 6 metres above the treetops is far too close to the border. They are harried noisily and fearlessly away by the magpies, like yapping fox terriers shooing a lumbering bull. Eagles aren't good at quick evasive action and must manipulate their large wings with unaccustomed frequency to move up and out of this enemy airspace and back into their own thinner air.

I have surprised eagles on the track with their prey. So close, the immense size of their legs is a shock, bringing with it the reality of how much weight they can carry. One day when my daughter was small, her hair blonde like the tussocks and she about the same height, an eagle came so low to investigate that I worried it might think her a plump rabbit, swoop down and pick her up. It easily could have.

But there is an intruder into the airspace of both eagle and magpie before which they are powerless, and so am I — military jets in training, F-111s. I was assured by the military that they only allow this intrusion eight times a year, but that's still too much.

Living on a mountain, you often find yourself looking down on things that would be more usually looked up to. Like the white sea of mist in the valley, or the moon skulking along behind the downhill trees. But to see these jets zoom past down there is another matter. My bowl feels very frail under the impact as they break the sound barrier. I have to be quick to catch a glimpse of the small dark shapes, usually two of them, one after the other, their lights quick-winking dots as they flash past.

It's shocking enough when they appear so violently over the top, across the sky's edge, but it's worse when I see them so low, often tilted sideways, through the V-shaped chip in the tree rim of my bowl, because then they are against a backdrop of mountainside. I know that out there they are hurtling amongst convoluted peaks and ridges and valleys, trusting their computerised instruments, their remote pilots, their radar, to think and react and steer and veer! They must assume nothing could ever go wrong, yet this year it was on the news that a wheel fell off one just after take-off. High tech, huh?

The military say this area was chosen for training because it is remote and only sparsely populated. Having chosen it myself partly for those reasons, I am not happy to be dismissed as an irrelevant sparse population. Like the indigenous people around Maralinga, where they did the nuclear tests?

But by 'population' they only mean people, and therefore don't take into account how the other inhabitants handle being terrorised by these sudden blasts of unnaturally loud noise. My heart lurches every time, my hands fly to my ears, my face winces, my body involuntarily huddles — even though I know what the noise is. Wallabies scare easily; I've heard of them dropping dead from panic and fear. And 15 or 20 metres closer, what must it do to a small bird, or her nestlings?

However, 'not happy' is inadequate to describe my feelings when the jets have flown *towards* me. I stood and watched incredulously as the first jet came, nose scooping hard as it appeared from between a fold in the ridge opposite my bowl, heading up the slope towards my V-gap, pointing directly at me, then belly exposed as it sped in, up and over my astonished house and me. It is impossible not to be unnerved as such heavy, fallible metal things zoom *at* me, so low I could see the pilot's face if the thing was going at a fraction of the speed.

But that leaves 357 days a year of mostly uncivilised and undisturbed sky.

I look up as much as I look down. The highest mountain opposite me, to the north, is over 1600 metres. As much part of the sky as the land, it has a great affinity with clouds, so I am treated to a perpetually changing visual feast. Clouds may keep passing by over all the rest of the sky, but one will often hook on this high peak and slew sideways, so that it billows anew on the eastern flank, streaming out and airbrushed smooth by the currents flowing over the top, sculpted into a white extension of the mountain itself.

If I'm lucky there'll be a pile-up of clouds there at sunset, so high that it reflects the glow from the 'real' western sunset opposite, even though the land below has already lost the light of day. Then I get a double spectacular. The clouds transmute the bold west's reds and oranges, yellows and purples, hot pinks and bright bronzes, into a subtler beauty, of puffs and streaks of pale gold, soft pinks and lilacs like the insides of shells, and rare blues of intense purity, like those in the background skies of early Italian paintings.

I look from one to the other, not wanting to miss the fleeting variations in either effect.

When the higher northern show has faded to dusky grey, I can turn undistracted to the west to see the last act of the drama, the darker stages of deeply bruised purple flags of clouds, brilliantly lit and edged with gold from below, streaming out across a sky that shades in colour from apricot to vermilion at the world's edge, behind the black filigree of my gum-tree edging.

Talk about food for the soul.

So far from artificial lights, my night sky is unsullied, the moving lights of distant planes less common than falling stars. I literally reel from the starry dome above on moonless nights, and it's one reason why I'd never want an indoor toilet. Blokes get to stargaze when they wander outside to water the grass. They do this naturally, but ladies need encouragement — like no choice!

Even indoors, from my bedside windows, stars rule. After I turn out my reading light, I don't close my eyes until they have adjusted to the darkness and the stars become visible. When I see so many that there is no blackness in between, only degrees of more distant, fainter stars, I can sleep, heart-eased with the renewed knowledge that wonders still exist that are unspoilt by man. I ignore the niggling pessimism of the voice in my head that says, 'Give him time.'

Yet I'm equally taken with the mystery of my bowl under the pale bright beauty of a full moon. It's hard to close my eyes then for, as the night progresses, the moon and its shadows transform every shrub and tree, call to brilliance each white flower, and strike silver from any pool or bowl of water. I wake at intervals to see what magic is going on out there, and I'd never be surprised at strange shapes slipping by.

I prefer to close my curtains only in winter, to keep the night's cold out and the fire's heat in.

Starlight or moonlight? I can't choose, but the horses seem to prefer the nights around the full moon, when they stand in the open and moonbathe, silently soaking it up, statue-still for hours. Or have they been bewitched?

Once I thought I'd seen a sort of magic. My partner and I were sitting on the verandah after dinner, sipping port. Far down in the steep gully below, we saw a bobbing light approaching, like someone running uphill with a torch. As it got closer it clearly wasn't a person, since we couldn't see anything but the light, which was quite big and bright, flashing on and off. Despite our pursuing torch beams, its source remained elusive as it danced all around the garden. We didn't *really* believe we had a fairy at the bottom of the garden, but were unable to come up with a rational explanation.

We thought of a firefly, but dismissed it as too small. Neither of us had ever seen one, and imagined a tiny dot of light, the size of a fly. Thinking ours might be a giant phosphorescent moth, whose light fluctuated with the pumping of its wings, we passed on the query to an entomologist friend. The dry reply came back: 'If it wasn't fireflies, I don't know what caused the light they saw, but whatever it was, it needs diluting!'

Slightly offended — we didn't drink all *that* much — we accepted it must have been a firefly. I've since seen small groups of them come up from that gully and it's always a treat, although never quite the same wonder of that first solitary visit. I have still never seen the actual insect in whose tiny body this magic resides.

I watch the moon and the stars on our arching nightly passing, but can name only a few. I bought a star chart, but it's one of those things

I may not get around to doing more than feeling mildly guilty about. I can't read by starlight, and the thought of juggling a torch and the book, perhaps binoculars or a telescope, taking my reading glasses off and on, always seems too hard. Slack, I know. But the book's there for me to study if ever I undergo a long convalescence or similar period of immobility. Perhaps I'm thinking of old age as a time for guiltless lolling about and reading, when the knees have given up, the trees are all planted, and the lists all crossed off — my last chapter.

CHAPTER 16

LET THE SUN SHINE

BY DAY MY NORTH-FACING skybowl is full of sunshine — when it's not full of cloud, that is. Summer is over-the-top solar power time, but I get sun nearly all day in winter too, ideal for my vegetables and my comfort as well as my power generation. And I much prefer that winter sun.

Summer once meant glorious, golden sunshine, for outdoor playing and swimming, from sunup to sundown if we could wangle it. Painful sunburn and peeling skin was inevitable, every year, for everyone except those with foreign — that is, not English, Irish or Scottish — skin. We soothed the burns by dabbing with vinegar or cut tomatoes, picked at the dry skin as it peeled, and drew satisfaction from extra long strips removed. Noses and shoulders were always the worst and most frequently burnt. As new freckles appeared we joked about 'sunkisses'. I could count mine then.

By my fifteenth year it was all about sunbaking in bikinis, a race to 'get a tan' quickest, grilling our bodies like skinny sausages, assisted by a coconut oil baste. This ritual was interrupted only by an occasional stroll to the water, mainly to see and be seen by the unattainable golden boys with their goods on show in Speedos. As our costumes shrank to four brief triangles, soft and virginal bands of flesh burnt so badly the pink turned livid, yellowish, and school uniforms and seats could hardly be borne on Mondays. But we persevered, for white skin had the connotation of slugs, not porcelain. Not that I'd ever have the choice again, having by now acquired a permanent shawl of sunkisses.

Fifteen years later, summer meant the annual angst in front of unfriendly mirrors and lying saleswomen over whether we could still get away with wearing a two-piece costume. It was spent supervising sandcastles and shell collections, soggy towels and gritty kids, with hardly a minute to ourselves for sunbaking. As we still did, with suntan lotion overall, zinc cream or sunscreen only applied to acknowledged vulnerable bits. We did wear hats.

These days summer brings danger. Sunbaking, suntanning, sunkisses — such antiquated words, such tragic innocence. Forget sunscreen; with the hole we've made in the ozone layer, we need sunblock. Slip, slop, slap. Kids are growing up with sunblock as their second skin; they swim in neck-to-knee Lycra and aren't allowed to play outside at school without a hat. They are taught to be as afraid of our once-beneficent sun as of strangers. It's like science fiction come horribly true. I dread the announcement that constant exposure to sunscreen has been found to be carcinogenic, but I won't be surprised.

My swimsuit mostly functions as a relic of my past, to be found scrunched in the back of a drawer along with lace handkerchiefs, suspender belts, French knickers and tired g-strings. Summer glare and heat are too savage for me to want to be outdoors at all. Instead of exposing winter flesh, I cover up more, never leaving my verandah without throwing on my sun-faded Akubra hat and the long-sleeved cotton shirt, usually a man's work shirt, second-hand, that will be hanging there.

Too many threatening spots and lumps have already been removed, after hiding amongst the thousands of freckles of my inappropriate Celtic skin. I go to my skin cancer clinic every six months for a check-up.

The doctor, genetically brown-skinned and unfreckle-able, shakes his head at the mottled map of my youth each time I take off my shirt.

I am in awe of the powers of the sun in more positive ways too, for without its electricity generation I could not work from here, and living would be much less convenient. I could manage, since I am not dependent on as many electrical aids as some people must be, judging by the range offered in the glossy catalogues that fall from my donated newspapers. Bread maker, sandwich maker, pie maker, pizza maker, coffee maker, rice cooker, slow cooker … of course I do have all those things, but it's a sort of combination machine — me!

Before I was on my own I treated the solar power shed, like all the sheds, as exclusively male. It held an array of machines and metal boxes with coloured lights and LED displays and dials and switches and buttons and leads and plugs and dangerous substances that blurped behind my back when I thought I was alone. I only ever went in there because that's also where I store my out-of-season clothes and my fabric pieces, in four waist-high, lidded and critter-proof cardboard drums that declare they once held bulk powdered milk.

My partner had understood it all; he could talk the language with Dave from Sunrise Solar, who designed and set it up for us. It was pure magic to me. The sun shone on the solar panels, which were patterned with circles in squares like giant board games, and in doing so, somehow became something that could run down thin wires and be turned into something that lurked in the dark liquid depths of the linked rows of batteries and then ran through thicker wires, partly to the house as 24 volt for our small bar fridge and the halogen lights, and partly to the invertor which turned it into 240 volt for all the power points in house and workshop. I knew 24 volt wouldn't kill me, but 240 volt would, just like in any suburban house.

How or why any of this was possible, I could not fathom, despite reading about it, any more than reading about radio waves made me see how and why radios worked.

There was also a battery charger and a back-up generator in this shed — *more* machines and manuals to deal with by myself, and tasks to be done … or else! I cannot afford to replace any of this ageing equipment; it must be looked after to last as long as possible.

If I had a problem I could ring Dave, as his after-sale service seems to last forever, but I'd exhaust all my own resources first. As men tell me the magic spells for the starting and maintenance of any machine, I write them down in a little indexed notebook, left over from one of my Sydney jobs. So under 'B' I find Basins, Bidets, Bath materials, and Brass, to which I have added Brushcutter, and Batteries.

BATTERIES:
- *I must keep the battery terminals clean and free of that green stuff and every now and then I must disconnect them and do a proper housekeeping job with warm soapy water and then Vaseline.*
- *I must keep them topped up with distilled water.*
- *I must be careful not to splash battery acid on myself.*
- *I must check the batteries with the hydrometer after a few days of cloud cover.*
- *If it reads less than full (1.25) but more than 1.18, I must keep an eye on power use and maybe run the generator and battery charger if I really must use power-hungry gadgets like the iron; 1.18 is also a good time to defrost the fridge.*
- *I must not let the batteries get down to 1.16 [which I never do, cross my heart!], but if so, I must turn the fridge off, as my main power user. And start charging!*

I follow these rules rather as I used to follow the Ten Commandments. I don't know why I must obey except that I believe the consequences will be terrible if I don't. I hate blind obedience and I hate my own ignorance in these matters.

It may have something to do with my inability to relate to numbers; I don't remember them and I can't manipulate them. Sister Augustine, exasperated at my continued B's in maths despite A's in everything else, verbally exploded one day. 'Sha-a-a...ryn *Mun*ro! You are de-*lib*erately being obtuse about maths! There is no *need* for this blind spot in your intelligence!' But it wasn't in my control, and the blind spot remains for both mathematics and machines.

And then there's the generator. It's supposed to be able to be started and stopped by pressing a button in the house or by a key on the generator — electric start. Unfortunately the electric start works off a little battery of the generator's own. I discovered that this battery goes flat if I don't run the generator much. With my ample sunlight and moderate power use, I rarely *need* to use the generator. So I have a ludicrous system where I must run the generator for no other reason than to keep the generator battery charged so it can start the generator if I do need it. Talk about unsustainable design!

A friend has recently suggested a trickle charge set-up from the invertor to solve this, so the solar would be keeping the generator going, which is a funny concept. I've put that on the 'fairly urgent but daunting' list.

For six months I faithfully marked on the calendar each time I went through this idiotic, noisy, wasteful, but apparently necessary, ritual every fortnight for twenty minutes or more. Not once did I actually need the generator for power. Then we had a week of rain and

I *did* need to use the generator. Perversely, it wouldn't start, yet it had started straight off the week before.

I got out the manual and checked what I could find, although as usual the models in the diagrams were just different enough from my machine to confuse me. I ruled out the battery, given my diligence. Remembering my success with the pump engine, I thought I'd change the oil — but I couldn't undo the drain plug. A male friend was coming to stay in a few days; it would have to wait till then.

My friend and I changed the oil; it made no difference. 'Never mind,' I said, 'the sun's out now.'

After he'd gone, the generator being too big to take to town, I rang my son-in-law for advice. The spark plug was once more named as the likely culprit. I couldn't find it.

So a few more weeks went by until he came up and showed me its hiding place under a black cover at the back. How clever of them to make it both invisible and inaccessible. He had to use a screwdriver to turn the spark plug spanner in there. Next time I was in town I bought a new plug.

I got it in. Still no response. It had to be the ungrateful bloody battery.

It was raining again and looked as if it was set in, so I might well need to run the generator. I decided to try the pull cord start, which had rarely been used. In doing so, because of the location of the generator, pegged to the ground close by the wall where the exhaust pipe goes out, I bashed my elbow into the wall frame — Ow-ww! — and knocked the good (and expensive) hydrometer off, which shattered on the cement floor. I swept up the glass shards.

Then I inched the very heavy generator around slightly, turning it on the peg to gain a little more room, and tried again, with my throbbing elbow pleading for mercy. No go.

'It's no use,' I snivelled pitifully as I backed away, nursing my elbow, 'I could never start these things, not with my wrists.' Leaning against the doorway, I cursed the generator — 'And as for you, you stupid battery! — and then I noticed that the key switch on the generator was turned to OFF, not ON. Having switched it to ON, I yanked the pull cord twice, and the generator leapt into life. Oh, you stupid woman!

I haven't admitted that episode to anyone before; it's so typically what males expect of women that I cringe at fitting the bill so well. How many times have I seen red, when, after describing my problem with a domestic machine to a technician, he says, 'Have you checked if it's turned on at the wall, luv?'

I'm claiming a deteriorating mental condition called old age.

I must be learning a little from the disasters I keep having, but it doesn't feel like it. The brushcutter is the current machine that won't work. I couldn't even bear to look for its spark plug — if it has one; I wasn't feeling strong enough. Instead I put it back in the shed, gnashed my teeth and did its intended job by hand. One day another male will visit and be only too pleased to start it. First go, I expect. It'll be something simple that I've overlooked.

But recently I was given a precious piece of knowledge that men have been withholding from me for decades. I had bought a connection for using a smaller LPG gas bottle with my old camping stove. It fitted at the stove end, but not at the bottle end. It would not screw on; was it a metric/imperial problem?

Not wanting to strip the thread — which, like ripping pool table felt, is another of those things men think women are likely to do — I took it back to the shop, with the bottle this time, when next I went to town. He had clearly sold me the wrong fitting.

The man heard me out, smiled, and took the items from me. He gave me *that* look — pitying, knowing — and screwed the fitting on with no trouble. 'Reverse thread, luv.'

I threw up my hands and went into a rave about why weren't they all standardised and how was anyone supposed to know which way was on or off if they kept changing it … but his raised eyebrows halted me. He jabbed his finger at the brass top piece.

'See that nick?' he said.

I saw it.

'That means it's reverse.'

I could have kissed him, I was so grateful for being let in on the secret.

I wonder, if I'd been a boy, would my dad have taught me about things mechanical? Only once did he ask me to help with a machine, when I was about twelve. The little Austin panel van had broken down in an awkward spot on the track and he'd got the tractor into position to tow the van out backwards. I can't remember why I was to drive the tractor instead of steering the van.

We went through the procedure a dozen times — 'Take it slowly, ease off the clutch, slowly, slowly …' — until I thought I had it right.

Feet balanced on the pedals, palms sweating, I waited for the signal.

'Right!' he yelled. The tractor and I lurched forward down the track, pulling the back doors clean off the Austin like the wings off a fly. We stalled shortly after. Dad was such a gentle man that he didn't even swear, or not so I heard. But he never let me near anything more mechanical than a hoe after that.

Not that he was especially gifted that way himself. I mean, why had he tied the towrope to the doors? The one time he tried to use a more-than-manual farming method, it was a disaster; in fact, a tragedy of epic proportions to nine-year-old me. Going broke fast with the oranges and vegetables, Dad had a go at raising chickens. Built a small shed, strewed sawdust on the ground, and installed a special kerosene contraption in the centre, that from memory was supposed to not only keep the hundreds of cheeping yellow balls of fluff warm, but feed and water them. It blew up, burnt the shed down and fried the chickens to small crispy debts.

No, Dad and I had a simpler, outdoor relationship. Next to trees, I like growing vegetables best, and I got that from him.

For market, Dad grew mainly beans. Brown Beauty. I can still remember my sense of importance the first time I was allowed to plant the smooth seeds, like dried kidney beans, walking alongside the furrow, dropping them carefully and evenly. He'd be following behind, walking backwards, hoeing dirt over the seeds.

They grew into neat rows of fragile green bushes bearing vegetables that I loved eating raw, but dreaded once Mum had cooked them according to the practice of the day — long boiled to a greyish green, with salt and bicarbonate of soda added, till even burying them in forkfuls of mashed potato could not disguise their slimy yet sharp texture and horribly familiar taste. She wouldn't let me eat them raw in a meal; it wasn't a proper tea without cooked vegetables.

Dad also grew Swede turnips, which I scrubbed clean in the cement laundry tubs before he bagged them, and tomatoes that I picked and sorted, my fingers stained greenish-brown, into green, semi and coloured, and packed into shallow boxes. Making them fit was very satisfying, like a 3D jigsaw.

Summer was bean-picking time. I'd always helped Dad pick and bag, and from the age of twelve, I picked beans in the holidays and on weekends for a neighbouring farmer as well, but for money. I became a fairly fast picker and could put in a full day's work without too much backache, although I finished some days on my bare knees because I could no longer bend. Then I'd have to decide which was more painful — back or knees — as the latter became too red and tender to shuffle along on the gritty dirt, pushing my square kero tin of beans in front of me.

All the female pickers wore shorts or skirts. Jeans were then only seen in American films, but Mum wouldn't have let me kneel in them, or slacks, as we called ladies' trousers, since they'd get dirty. Almost none of us wore hats, but I suppose we had our heads down most of the time.

For me, apart from the delight and pride of receiving a cheque, there was the new experience of talking with grown-ups as an equal. We chatted as we picked along our rows and we chatted at smoko, over strong tea and slabs of fruitcake supplied by the farmer's wife.

It wasn't always hot in summer; sometimes it would be raining, but beans don't wait and nor do markets, so we'd still have to pick. Cold, wet and muddy, with water dripping down my raincoat neck, my nose dripping of its own accord, running a high risk of leech attack, and thoroughly miserable — I can smell wet hessian right now.

Hot or cold, bean-picking was a sobering taste of what being grown-up meant — that some things had to be persevered with, no matter how unpleasant. Most people then seemed to apply the same rule to marriage.

Later, when I was in my senior years at school, I swapped bean-picking for working in a small fruit and vegetable stall cum petrol station, up on the main road. It was more regular money, but I was embarrassed to be seen in daggy work clothes, complete with apron, pumping petrol for carloads of kids my own age who were heading for the beach and a good time.

I learnt how to use a petrol pump, pre-automatic shut-off, pre-self-serve, and only drenched myself with petrol once, face-first, when filling a jerry can; how to operate a cash till, pre-metric, despite my anxiety at the perpetual mental arithmetic required; and how to panic customers, by cutting up a huge pumpkin on the counter in front of them. To stop it sliding about, I'd enfold the convoluted Queensland Blue with one arm, holding a massive knife in the other; I'd make an initial violent central stab, then I'd have to thump the knife handle from behind to force the blade through the tough flesh — towards my stomach.

I also learnt that wooden crates of bananas were my weight-carrying limit over any distance. In fact, like full hessian bags of potatoes, they were probably over my limit, and I wonder I didn't damage the 'something' inside that people always warn about straining. It infuriated me that I had limited strength, when the bantam-sized male owner could carry such things apparently effortlessly.

But it set a high benchmark for my lifting capacity, which came in handy on the many occasions I had to move house in Sydney. It would also have influenced what I was willing to tackle here in my pioneer days, and now. This time round I know the bar's been considerably lowered, and the strainable 'something' may not even be there any longer.

This body is definitely fifteen no more.

CHAPTER 17

MAINTENANCE AND MUNG BEANS

SOMEWHERE IN *WAR AND Peace* Tolstoy called the body 'a machine for living'. If I think of it that way I oughtn't to have been surprised when, six years ago, my body let me down. Seized up, wouldn't run.

Although I still had a partner, I did the outdoor work except for getting firewood. Suddenly I could do nothing. Because of my afflicted knees, I couldn't bend, kneel or dig; and because of my similarly afflicted thumb joints, I couldn't use a trowel or secateurs or grasp weeds to pull them out. Nor could I knead bread or manage my heavy cast-iron pans, or work the computer mouse and keyboard for long, or even hold a book open to read in bed.

The thumb joints had been bothering me for some time, but I'd put that down to RSI from the computer. It was more of a shock when my knees became so swollen and sore that I couldn't bend them to climb steps — I could barely walk.

My GP eventually sent me to a knee specialist, who surprised me by first looking at my fingers, which had a few bumpy joints but were not at all sore. 'Aha!' he said, 'Heberden's nodes!' and diagnosed osteoarthritis of an inherited sort. He offered anti-inflammatories, which I declined, thinking of the ulcerous side-effects, and predicted such a rapid decline that I'd be looking at knee replacements well before I was out of my fifties.

I was utterly depressed. Arthritis. A death sentence for my mountain life. Spare parts already!

The usual 'Why me?' My father had only developed slight arthritis in his late seventies; my mother's reiteration that *she* had none clearly implied some fault on my part. It must have skipped a generation.

I turned for rescue to herbalist Pat Collins, of the Total Health & Education Centre in Muswellbrook, whom I'd first seen about my early menopause. This had followed a hysterectomy at 45, after a cancer scare, and because of massive uterine fibroids and endometriosis. I'd been a literal bloody mess before, and quickly became a figurative one after. As I'd never had noticeable PMT, I was unprepared for the hormone takeover that ensued.

This was like being force fed a drug; I was not myself in mind or body. I'd heard about hot flushes, but not about chilli-footed ants crawling all over my face, nor about senses being heightened to unbearable levels, so an everyday noise, like shutting a cupboard door, actually hurt my ears. It took months for me to realise that the noise was at a normal level — it was me who wasn't. My partner was very patient, but often his only option was to stay out of my way, spend longer hours in the workshop.

What biological purpose such disruption serves I cannot imagine.

He convinced me to seek help, and for two years I was very successfully treated with Chinese herbs, by Anna at Balmain Chinese Herbal Centre, seeing her almost every month, but then I developed an inexplicable, ongoing and apparently unique reaction to that treatment. Just my luck.

At the same time I was hit by a barrage of illnesses that turned my life upside-down. My body began malfunctioning like the most obstinately mysterious machine of all.

I started to have what turned out to be anxiety attacks, including several acute ones where my limbs stiffened as if they were filling with ice and I thought I was dying, would die when the ice reached my heart. All the casualty doctor could advise was to avoid stress, and when I said that was impossible at present, he asked me if I wanted Valium, adding that females were prone to this sort of thing!

These attacks continued in various frightening degrees for months, until I sought help from my much-missed Sydney GP. On enquiring after my family, and hearing just a brief summary of my worries about them, she suggested that, unwittingly, perhaps I was sighing a lot, getting too much oxygen. She told me how to redress the CO_2 imbalance with the first aid trick of either holding my breath, or breathing into a paper bag, for 30 seconds. It may take a few goes, she said, but it works. It did, it does — bless her. Shouldn't all doctors know this?

I also became unpredictably subject to prolonged bouts of heart palpitations, thumping my whole body about, or so it felt, and leaving me so exhausted I would crumple wherever I was, even in the dust. Tests could not tell me why.

To top it off, I had a severe recurrence of irritable bowel syndrome, which, having been linked to the endometriosis, I'd assumed had been solved by the hysterectomy, and so it had seemed for the two years since. Because my body couldn't get the benefit of the food I was eating, I became extremely debilitated.

These three all hit me together, only months after I'd taken on new and public responsibilities, which I had no choice but to abrogate, despite feeling pathetic about doing so. But my body was no longer a reliable carrier. I was terribly weak, and the palpitations would occur at any time. The mind cannot function when the body is overwhelmed. My partner was as supportive as possible, but I was getting worse.

Only later did I fully understand that this physical breakdown was stress-induced as well as stress-exacerbated. The stress was from several family sources, including death and dying and related emotional manipulation, but the worst involved my best-loved ones defiantly heading for pain and destruction, while I tried unsuccessfully to stop them — sighing.

So I dragged myself to Pat. She helped me back to running order, thereafter manageable through my diet, breathing tactics, and awareness of causes. When symptoms recur, I can keep them at low levels. Maintenance works.

Never since have I underestimated the power of stress, nor the reality of the physical illnesses it causes, and the wreck it can make of a life if ongoing.

This crisis time, to ease the acute inflammation in my joints, Pat immediately took me off all members of the nightshade family, the *Solanums*, which included some of my most frequently used ingredients: tomatoes, eggplants, capsicums, chillies and potatoes. My heart sank — goodbye to my beloved Mediterranean dishes. But she said that once the pain and swelling had gone I could re-introduce those foods one at a time, for a fortnight, and if there was no reaction I could keep them in my diet.

She also gave me a list of beneficial foods and herbs to include in a fresh daily juice to be based on celery and carrots, to which I add a large spoonful of flaxseed oil, the vegetarian's Omega 3 source. All we needed to find was a plant equivalent to the undeniably effective anti-inflammatory natural treatment, Glucosamine, since that was derived from fish. Pat sourced a plant called *Boswellia serrata*, an Indian herb whose bark resin had been well tested and proven in clinical trials in Germany and India.

Under this regime, within weeks I was walking without pain. I then found out, from X-rays taken by Chris, the chiropractor to whom I had gone for a sore neck, that I also had arthritis in my spine and neck and shoulders — spurs everywhere. Chris helped with the immediate problem and prescribed a permanent set of daily exercises.

In a few months I had no pain anywhere and could see that my physical life would be possible here, although limited. The depression flew off to await the next setback; the sun shone once more. It wasn't time for me to be forced off my mountain yet, but I had to become a different sort of mountain woman. No more over-revving of this machine and no skipping on its regular services. Or else!

So I can't do long bursts of any knee-demanding activity or keep them in one position too long, but I can do fairly lengthy bushwalks, so long as any steep sections are short, and I can stand from a squatting position — no hands — and that would have been unimaginable before! For my thumb joints, I bought a different computer mouse and worked out alternative ways of kneading bread and carrying heavy pans and performing many other manual tasks; and where finer grasps, such as in holding even a large needle, are required, I do it only for short spells.

I've never been game to go back to eating those nightshade foods as daily items; the memory of my incapacity and pain is too strong. And whenever I've thought of doing a 'scientific' trial, there are too many activity variables in my life for the results to be trustworthy. It's not as if I'm allergic to them — I eat any of the 'bad' items without fuss if there's no choice when dining out or at people's places. After all, it's hard enough on most people to cater for a vegetarian, let alone a restricted diet as well.

And that's the other question I'm often asked, apart from why I live way out here: why are you a vegetarian? In essence, my answer is the same: 'Why not?'

After my first child was born, I followed my lifelong inclination — I 'went vegetarian'. Growing up, I'd always preferred rissoles or thin sausages to chops or roasts because the origins were less recognisable. I'd quelled that squeamishness at uni, in my desperate search for peer approval. My ex-husband later complained that I became too 'cocky' after having our children; if that means I gained confidence it may be why I was finally game to 'come out' of my fake carnivore shell.

In 1973 vegetarianism was for weirdos, who were sentenced to the side salad and chips at restaurants, and macaroni cheese at private dinner tables.

The initial critical moment came one morning after I'd bathed my new baby in his inflated plastic bath. As I lay him on the towel-covered kitchen bench beside it, stretching out his arms and legs to dry those creases and hollows, his little pink body suddenly strongly reminded me of the skinned rabbit I had bought and cut up, right here, just months ago, for a Robert Carrier ragôut. The two images merged and I felt sick that I could ever have done that. Never again, I vowed.

'Aha!' I hear you say, 'Clearly a case of post-natal something or other.'

Well, if so, 33 years is a long 'post'.

From then on, if I looked at a piece of steak I saw it as the bloody slice missing on the living cow — it was that vivid. Still is.

For a year longer I was comfortable eating 'white meat' — fillets of fish and chicken — and then it struck me how hypocritical that was. Just because those creatures didn't have voices to cry out when killed, or didn't bleed like cows or sheep or pigs. Just because they were less like us.

No. No more slices of dead bodies for me — red or white.

I admit I found it difficult to give up tinned anchovies. A small casuistic voice kept tempting me to that irreplaceable salty flavour: 'But they're hardly big enough to count as bodies!'

'Tell that to the anchovies!' I'd force myself to reply.

While I've never tried to convert others, some seem to need me to defend my 'position', starting arguments about carrots silently screaming when pulled from the ground, or pointing accusingly at my leather shoes, etc., etc. No use, because I act from a totally personal 'gut feeling', not a rational position. It's what *feels* right to me.

As these 'debates' are usually initiated during meals, I use more abstract terms than 'slices of dead bodies'. I explain that I can't kill an animal, and I could no longer allow others to do it for me, out of sight and mind; that I know it's unnecessary for any animal to die for me to live well, eat well, for health, taste and variety. I might condone killing for defence, for survival, but not just because I 'like the taste'. I daresay cannibals would say they like the taste!

Recently I met a vegan, who assured me that I'd inevitably progress from vegetarianism and stop eating *any* animal products. I didn't admit that I haven't progressed for a long time, but I'm very aware that there are worse things than killing done under the practices of modern 'factory farming'. One day I may well get a 'gut feeling' strong enough to take me to veganism.

Eggs will go before cheese does, as I've often wavered about them.

I once innocently took my courthouse playgroup on an excursion to a battery hen egg farm, and was so shocked at the appalling conditions that I've never bought any eggs other than free range since.

Unfortunately most people haven't seen inside such a place, so buy their eggs unaware.

Let me just briefly describe the accommodation set-up. Don't worry, I'll omit the gruesome details of what the stress and frustration does to the birds. I trust your imagination.

Picture a 440-square-millimetre cage made of steel mesh, including the floor, and in this cage are squashed four or five chooks. The cage is so cramped that each chook has the space of less than an A4 sheet of paper in which to 'live' its whole life, unable even to spread its wings or move about. Now picture five-storey stacks of such cages. Food and water in, shit and eggs out.

Imagine keeping a pet like that and not being prosecuted for animal cruelty.

There's a big fuss in the Australian industry at present because laws are being introduced to increase the cage size. To 550 square millimetres. How kind. More civilised countries, like those in the European Union, are phasing cages out altogether.

They cage the hens like this because it saves labour costs and increases profits, so they can charge less for the eggs, capture the main market and keep the whole vicious cycle turning.

When I see people standing in front of the egg section in super-markets, looking understandably confused, I have to bite my tongue, for I want to say, 'Ignore all the blurbs about what they feed the hens — multi-grain, organic; look for how the hens are kept!'

'Caged' or 'Battery' is bad. Unbelievably cruel.

'Barn laid' is better, much less cruel, because it means the hens are uncaged, can move around, and have nests, perches, and litter to scratch about in. But they still spend their lives indoors.

'Free range' is best, because it includes all that barn hens get, plus they spend a certain number of hours a day outside. It's more natural, and a nicer connotation — warm sunshine, rich yellow egg yolks for that breakfast dip-in egg.

Still not much of a life compared to that enjoyed by smaller farmyard flocks, which lucky people may be able to support at farmers' markets, but for most of us paying more to buy free range is the best we can do. Well, actually it's the *least* we can do.

I recall the punch line of an old advertising campaign — perhaps for Carnation tinned milk? – 'From contented cows'. Whether it was true or not, we'd all rather think of our food as coming from contented animals. Happier hens would be a start!

However, one result of modern food production systems is that people don't see, so rarely think about, where their food comes from. Consequently decent people who'd be up in arms if a cat or a canary was mistreated simply don't know about the cruelty of factory farming or 'intensive farming'. Denied any semblance of a life, 'tortured' is not too strong a word for what animals like chooks and pigs endure as they are forced into becoming the products that will bring the most profits at least cost — hey, boneless would be good!

The ABC's *Australian Story* television program introduced me to the committed and generous Sherman family, who've formed a group called Voiceless. It's trying to redress that gap in people's knowledge, to spread the message that animals deserve to be treated with compassion and respect, and that commercial animal husbandry can be — is being — done this way. All it takes is for more of us to demand that our meat, milk and eggs be provided from humane animal farming, so the major companies will see it as profitable to do so. As consumers we have all the power — dollars talk louder, get heard, where campaigns against animal cruelty don't. Take a look at the

Voiceless website (www.voiceless.org.au). It's revelationary, offering information and hope and ways to help, as well as the terrible truth.

Do as you would be done by?

It was in my childrearing/gone vego time at the old jail that I really learnt to cook. I'd done a sporadic apprenticeship for dinners and for the gourmet weekends we had there, when friends like Tony came to stay. I'd gone to ridiculous lengths, like mutton marinated for twelve days 'to taste like venison', complicated terrines and breathless soufflés.

Being a full-time mum gave me the chance to practise cooking so much that it became instinctive. One morning each week, during the kids' nap time, I'd leaf through my cookbooks and plan a week's menu of dishes I hadn't tried, making a list of ingredients to be bought on the weekly shopping trip.

'Vegetarian cooking' was then disgustingly bland, promoted for health, not taste, and the recipes were derived from British-type meat dishes deprived of the meat, rather than being inspired by the vegetables themselves. So from my books I chose traditional ethnic meatless dishes — Indian, Middle Eastern, Mediterranean, Indonesian — with which I'd already been experimenting because they were cheap.

I also read books on vegetarian nutrition, on what food combinations provided complete protein, especially important because of the children. My mother-in-law muttered about iron and blood and anaemia for years, and every time she did I got a mental vision of Mia Farrow guzzling raw liver in the film *Rosemary's Baby*. Meanwhile my children grew on — healthy, strong, bright and beautiful.

In Newcastle then there were hardly any ethnic restaurants, apart from glutinous Australianised 'Chinese' and the great saving grace of Hamilton's Italian community. Few foreign foods could be bought. I was making ingredients like tofu or pesto, and dishes like samosas or falafel, before I'd ever seen or tasted them. I learnt to have a go at anything; I learnt to love cooking, and still do. Nor has cooking for one diminished the pleasure or driven me to baked beans on toast.

Despite great advances — even pub counter lunches will now toss a token vego dish on the menu — vegetarians are still a misunderstood minority in many places. For example, if I double-check with a waiter whether a dish has any meat in it, the reply could be, 'No, just a bit of ham.' When I therefore politely decline it, I often spot a rolling of eyes, a raising of eyebrows, an implied 'as if that'd matter!' — as if I am being so-o-o difficult.

On hearing I was a vegetarian, one woman exclaimed, 'Oh, I could never do that. I love food too much!' As if I don't? Perhaps it's a muddling of clichés, where vegetarian = trippy hippies eating nothing but steamed vegetables and brown rice. Peace, love and mung beans? Not me — I love food too much.

When my father retired, his main interest was his backyard vegetable garden, especially his few annually cherished tomato plants. The progress and welfare of our respective plants was a primary topic in our phone conversations. I missed a few tomato summers, but now that I am more confident about how to manage my arthritis, I do grow just a few heritage tomato plants — for the taste, for keeping the varieties going, and for Dad. Nothing like the amounts I used to grow, for Vacola bottling, making tomato sauce and paste and chutneys.

I let most of my vegetables go to seed, both to self-sow and be saved. I belong to the Seed Savers Network, a good way to swap non-hybrid and heritage seeds. Like Good Evans, a plum-sized, thin-skinned, sweet and juicy tomato, seedlings of which I was first given by my Uncle Brian. My uncle is gone and so, I expect, is Mr Evans, but their tomatoes are a constantly renewed memorial.

My dad and his younger brother Brian had a lot in common: both had been carpenters, union men and Labor voters, both liked growing vegetables, and both ended up with prostate cancer. They used to compare symptoms. When John Howard's Liberal government was re-elected for a second term, my uncle rang Dad in distress and disbelief.

'Frank,' he said, 'do you realise this means we could die under a Liberal government!'

As they did. They'd be wondering what they'd fought for if they'd lived to see the recent Industrial Relations changes. At least my tomatoes are still up to their standard.

Dad is responsible for two of our family's breakfast habits that strangers consider odd. The first is to slice tomatoes onto toast spread with peanut butter. Salted and peppered as a matter of routine for him, it was — is — a delicious combination of tastes and textures. My contribution is to add a thick layer of chopped parsley, or basil in season, under the tomato slices.

Over this tomato season I have eaten very few compared to what I used to; my knees are aching a little, but is that because the ground was so dry in autumn, and I had to jab my foot harder on the spade when planting my trees? You can see what I mean about the difficulty of a scientific experiment. But the lovely tomatoes are finished and I'll be off them again until next year.

Later, when Dad discovered avocadoes, his alternative breakfast became avocado on toast which he'd spread with Vegemite. I am addicted to this, again adding parsley under the avocado topping and I tend to layer, rather than spread, my Vegemite. People have had to leave the room at the sight. A squeeze of lemon, a quick grind of fresh black pepper, and my day starts well. Thanks, Dad.

The toppings are especially delicious on real bread. I like crunchy, flavourful bread, so to my basic spelt wholemeal I'll add sunflower and sesame seeds, cracked rye or millet, as well as rolled oats or maize or rye flours. A treat — being healthy is a bonus.

There's a John Updike story in which a man is on a long drive to his father's deathbed and trying to think of some life lesson for which he can thank his father. The only thing he comes up with is that his father taught him how to butter bread, all over, right to the corners and not just in the middle, without breaking it.

Our fathers. Daily bread. Sharing it even when absent.

Vegetarianism led me to a new world from the 'meat and three veg' of my childhood, where meat was as basic as bread. Doing without my basic tomatoes and potatoes made me even more innovative, with reluctant farewells to many favourite recipes, especially those of my first cooking teacher, Elizabeth David, while making substitutions in others.

My use of sweet potatoes expanded and my beloved chips were of sweet potato instead; pasta sauces were more inventive, as less tomato-based; oranges and grated fresh beetroot added colour instead of tomato, leading to new salads, new directions in taste; miso pastes were experimented with to avoid tomato paste; fresh ginger and lemons seemed to more often demand a place in my cooking; inspiration flourished in the spaces left by those basics — such as slicing cumquats into a stir-fry.

The change was liberating, and for special occasions I can always include a forbidden fruit if I want. There are dishes where nothing but a finely sliced fresh chilli will do the trick.

It's natural for me to see food as a creative and sensory delight, as well as fuel and oil for maintaining this 'machine for living' — and to choose food that does not cost the lives of other creatures. I can, therefore I do.

If I were a Laplander, and there was no choice, I guess I wouldn't!

CHAPTER 18

SNAKES ALIVE ...
AND DEAD

APART FROM BUSHFIRES, AND skin cancer, summer also means snakes. I accept that I can't live in the bush and expect to avoid snakes, but I'm afraid of them. In the warmer months I walk less through the bush, and when I do, I always wear gumboots and try to stick to the narrow wallaby tracks.

Most people never have to face snakes in their daily lives and yet are still haunted by a vague fear of their possible presence when anywhere less civilised than a well-kept lawn. In the West at least, our feelings seem to be dominated by fear, motivated by our instinct for self-preservation. That fear is tempered with a token acceptance of the snake's place in the ecological balance, and underlaid with an almost genetic revulsion for it as the Devil incarnate. After all, there was that business in the Garden of Eden.

When my dad removed our family from the man-made safety zones of suburban Sydney, he committed us to confrontations with snakes.

As a schoolgirl, my route to the bus stop included a solitary walk of about a quarter of a mile down our track, which was occasionally mowed, but nevertheless ran like a treacherously narrow alley between the tall grass and weeds — paspalum and kikuyu, Stinking Roger, Farmer's Friends and Paterson's Curse — that towered over my head. Beyond these on one side ran our neighbour's irrigation ditch, providing a cool, moist, well-camouflaged snake haven. I'd walk nervously in the middle of the track, eyes darting from side to side.

Sometimes I saw a heart-stopping black tail-tip disappear into the jungle just ahead, or the whole sinuous shape cross the track further on. They were menacingly silent; everything depended on my eyes — a slight wavering of the grasses, an unsticklike black shininess. Dad assured me that these Red-bellied Blacks were not aggressive, except in the mating season, or if you were between them and their young. How was I to know what I was unwittingly in the way of?

'Make a lot of noise,' he said, 'and you'll be right.'

So spring and summer saw me stamping my way along the track, chanting bold and brave things to myself, and silently pleading to them, 'Please let me pass!'

Over the years the track became a minefield, with my heart constricting as I approached every spot where I'd seen a snake, followed by involuntary dashes past. In my teens, when I sometimes had to catch the late bus home from school, it was one long gauntlet of terror, as twilight made it hard to distinguish shape from shadow. I leapt along in a series of *grand jetés*, figuring that the less I touched the ground, the less likely I was to tread on any possible snake. To make it safely inside the door, to the comforting teatime smell of rissoles and gravy, was always a miracle — Thank you God! I'll even eat my beans!

Once, when I was about nine, Dad and I and the leech-burning neighbour were in the bean paddock when we noticed a really big black snake sunning itself on a log beside the track. The practice then was to kill any snake one saw. The neighbour told Dad to throw his hat on the ground in front of the snake, and then run home for the hoe. He reckoned the snake wouldn't move until the hat did.

I didn't believe the snake would be so stupid, while the neighbour and I were standing — living, breathing, and so vulnerable — nearby. But he was right. That powerful, brilliant black creature was mesmerised by the hat and ignored us completely. Dad arrived, panting, and before I could think about it, swung the hoe high above his head and down, with all his strength, onto the motionless enemy. He chopped through the thick body once, twice, seemingly many times, in a turmoil now of thrashing black and red, and pink, until it lay still.

I think Dad felt as sick as I did.

Years later, when the first set of traffic lights went in at Gosford, my parents sold up and moved north before the town became 'like Parramatta'. Dad wanted to have a go at cattle, so bought a property at Terrace Creek near the Queensland border: humid, lush, and even more snakey. It was an old house, with an overgrown garden, and there my mother was to have more to do with snakes than in her worst nightmares.

I was a mother myself by then. We visited there each Christmas, and whenever we went down to the pebbly creek for a swim we saw at least one black snake slither off into the maidenhair ferns, but my mother didn't swim, so she missed them. Nor was she involved in the farm, so she missed out too on the opportunities for snake panic presented by the old dairy, where Dad stored the corn beloved by mice beloved by snakes, or the paddocks, where death adders awaited the tread of the unwary walker.

But she didn't need them, for the snakes came to her ... in the house. Each Christmas there was a new snake story.

The first occurred when Dad was in town, so she was on her own. Entering her bedroom, she caught a swift movement out of the corner of her eye — unbelievably, a snake! At her gasp, the creature slid up over the sill of her open built-in wardrobe. And there it stayed, its curves gracefully arranged over her good shoes. She ran to the phone and called a neighbour for help. He rushed to her aid and despatched the intruder; a tiger snake, he said. She was so grateful she didn't even complain about the mess.

Mum convinced herself that this was an aberration, a lone wanderer that had somehow got inside, until one evening when she and my youngest sister were watching television. Before their incredulous eyes, a tiger snake made its way from under a couch, unhurriedly slithered across the rug in front of the television, and disappeared from sight, never to be found. Every nook and cranny was stuffed and sealed after that, and Dad was made to check under every piece of furniture. No wonder Mum hated the country.

But the worst was yet to come. Late one spring afternoon, the family was congregated on the glassed-in front verandah. This was a post-shower, pre-tea ritual, beginning at 5 p.m. when Dad would open a bottle of his home-brew. Mum and my sister were sitting on a lumpy couch left behind by the previous owners. It was covered in faded cretonne and had a long bolster at the back, lumpy like the seat, probably stuffed with kapok.

Mum felt a movement at her back and, thinking my sister had her arm there, wriggled impatiently to let her know she found the movement annoying. The movements continued. Then my sister felt the bolster distinctly heave, and turned round to see what was going on.

The bolster on which they'd been leaning was coming alive! They jumped up, to see a long, languid python emerge from one end. It had probably spent the winter in there, which didn't bear thinking about even though it wasn't a venomous type.

Mum appears to have found refuge from them now, in a hostel. But here in my refuge there are my childhood bogeys, the Red-bellied Blacks, plus the aggressive Eastern Browns, and Eastern Tigers. There are also Diamond Pythons, but they're harmless apart from the possibility of giving me a heart attack when I see one in the garden. Here I live behind the enemy lines.

When my husband and I set up camp here all those years ago, we agreed not to kill black snakes when we saw them, as we often did, moving logs and rocks for garden and house, fencing, laying water pipelines. Digging out a rotten log plumb in the middle of the house site, we found a nest of tiny baby black snakes that writhed half-heartedly at us. There was no sign of the mother, so we lifted them on spades into a bucket and carried the wriggling nursery at arm's length up into the forest. Tipping them out to survive as best they could, we felt much as I imagine Hansel and Gretel's father did.

I felt I could cope with the familiar black snakes. The National Parks ranger came to inspect the property after we'd applied for it to become a wildlife refuge. He casually remarked what perfect terrain it was for browns. They were, he said, extremely territorial, and aggressive with it. Despite them being protected, if we saw one near the house we'd need to shoot it, since we had young children. I don't know what the advice would be now. 'Don't even think about trying to kill it with a hoe,' he added.

We didn't own a gun, and didn't want to, so I was glad as the months went by and we didn't see any. One hot day, the kids at school, my husband in town, I was in my vegetable garden, tilling up rows for potatoes. I'd been doing so for ages, lost in heat-drowsed thought as I worked backwards in the warm dust. There being no grass for snakes to hide in, and because of the heat, I was wearing thongs instead of my usual gumboots.

I don't know what made me look around as I neared the fence edge, and it took a few seconds to register what I saw, but there, sunbaking in a furrow a foot or two away, perfectly camouflaged in the brown dust, was a *huge* brown snake. If ever I thought it possible to die from fright, I learnt then that it's not — or I would have. Sweating, shaking, I backed away slowly until I reached the garden gate, when I ran to the verandah. From there I watched it undulate through the fence and across the grass, and into our timber pile.

We felt obliged to do as the ranger suggested and buy a gun. Much as we both hated guns, we loved our children more. We chose a shotgun that made it easier to hit a narrow target, and taught ourselves to use it, but we never saw a brown again.

Yet I am ashamed to admit that, in the weekender post-divorce years, on two occasions I did dispose of black snakes. The first was when we found that the picturesque, gnarled old log embedded in the ground right near the cabin's front steps was home to a big black. I don't know if it had lived there for years and we'd just not seen it, or if it was a new resident.

Having to go outside to the toilet at night, when it would be out and about hunting, we didn't want to run the risk of sleepily stepping on it, which would evoke a possibly lethal reaction. We reluctantly agreed that it had to be shot. The log being only feet away from the verandah, we took turns watching from there until it appeared at the hole again. As the best shot in target practice, my son was to do the shooting.

But this was for real, and I felt for him as the snake slowly emerged and he took aim. He fired twice, and with a final flurry of dust and coils and nerves, it subsided into a pulped mass. We all felt ill, physically and morally, at this crime.

Then we had to draw straws as to who would get rid of the body. I 'won', but after a long time trying to work up the nerve to put a shovel under the mess, I realised I couldn't. I don't think I ever missed having a husband so much; being Mum and Dad has some very nasty sides to it. In the end, I cheated, and shovelled dirt on top it, burying it where it lay. This left a mound, a reproachful reminder to be gingerly skirted for a year or so until time and weather levelled it.

The other occasion, again dealt with by my son, with hindsight was a totally wrong decision. We'd gone up to our big dam where, before the reeds had taken over, we liked to swim across to the small central island. From the little jetty that allowed us to launch ourselves or our canoe without sinking into the clay, we spotted a black snake lazing on the island. At the noise of our approach it roused itself and slipped into the water, gliding effortlessly and rapidly to the far bank, its head up and the rest just a swirl in the water behind. It was clear that we'd never outswim one, and none of us wanted to use the dam or the island while it was in the vicinity, so after much discussion and conscience searching on my part, but possibly concealed eagerness on the part of my then teenage son, we agreed it should be shot. Given what I now know about the shyness of Red-bellied Blacks, that death was unnecessary, and I have regretted it ever since. I think being responsible for the children affected my judgement. I have now sold the gun, and will take my chances with snakes, on equal terms.

Do as you would be done by.

Coming back to live here second time around, my first snake encounter was of course when my partner was away for a few days. I'd found snakeskins, but that afternoon I spotted the first snake of the summer. I'd just moved the sprinkler, and as I turned the water back on, a black snake slid into visibility and under a very small ring of grass-clipping mulch around a Native Frangipani tree, where it became immediately invisible. It hadn't liked the water. I had dozens of small mulch piles like that and was often plunging my hands in to weed them. Now they would all harbour possible snakes.

I seized the hose and turned a full jet onto the mulch. Nothing emerged. I watched for an hour, wanting to know where it went, as my shower was outdoors then and on that side of the house. No sign of it. I gave up, went to bed unshowered and, despite the heat, slept with all the low windows shut.

Next day there was still no sign of it and hosing again flushed out nothing from the mulch. It must have gone. After lunch, as a reward to myself for completing two copywriting jobs plus having a story read on Newcastle ABC radio that day, I lay down on my cool bed for the indulgence of a daytime read. All the casement windows were wide open, as it was 35 degrees.

I heard a rustle just outside my bedroom windows and, curious, I peeped over the sill. There was a long black snake, just below me, in the dry leaves on the gravel, edging against the rock base of the tank, less than a metre away — and heading for my low, low windows. Banging the immediate windows shut, I raced around both bedrooms, shutting all low windows before the snake could slither in. Then I ran to the verandah and looked back along the wall. The snake was moving downhill. I began clapping and throwing odd items in its wake — thongs, gumboots, a candle, a dustpan, lumps of wood — to keep it moving, out, out through the fence. Please just be visiting!

I was stamping on the verandah, thumping on the railing, calling, 'Go, go, go!' The snake went though the fence and headed for the tussocks with me yelling louder and keener than any racegoer to help it keep up the pace. Noise was the trick, I decided, feeling victorious, and hoarse, but nevertheless I wasn't game to collect the thrown items until the next day.

It had been a handsome young Red-bellied Black, neat small head, glossy skin. So long as I knew where it was I was unafraid, I told myself, but as I couldn't watch the fence lines all day, my imagination had slender black shapes gliding gracefully up and over the windowsills whenever I turned my back.

Since then I have often seen black snakes in the garden or heading uphill across the 'lawn' and either clap them along from a safe distance or, if they are in my vegetable garden, encourage them out with the hose. They do seem to be just visiting. And I have at last made a few mesh screens to clip on the inside of the awkward casements for summer nights, to permit the entry of breezes but not wildlife — I don't like to sleep with my neighbours. The screens can only be attached with the windows at the narrowest opening, as otherwise the casement stays would poke through the mesh.

I take them off in the daytime as my theory is that flies are best given through passage in and out of the house. I don't know why I no longer fear snakes entering that way by day, but it's more convenient if I don't, so I'd best not think about it! Rationality is overrated.

The only brown snake I have seen since the gun days was far from the house, in the bush, when walking the regeneration area fence line with my would-be fencers. I was striding down the mountain, trying to measure in metres as I stepped, which is quite difficult on rocky, steep and tussocky slopes without going head over heels. As my right boot extended for the next stride downhill, I saw a brown snake coiled in the ring of tussocks beneath it. Fear sent the message to my right foot to remain airborne, and I landed a few levels down instead, not even twisting an ankle, and not stopping to look back.

Re-reading Miles Franklin's *Childhood at Brindabella*, I was struck by a passage about a childhood experience of hers, when she'd seen a black snake lying by the creek, perfectly at home in its surroundings. Its majesty and beauty so impressed her that she did not, as she was supposed to, report the sighting to her uncles so they could shoot it. Then many years later she saw a black snake at the same spot, occupying that same role, and felt pleased that perhaps she had made this continuity, this rightness, possible.

Now I try to take the same approach to snakes here as I do to all the animals. I only want the house yard; they can have the rest. To that end — and to deter the bush rats — I keep the yard fairly clear at ground level.

I look long and hard at magazine pictures of charming cottage gardens surrounding Australian rural homesteads. I scour the text beside them, but nowhere, ever, have I found reference to how they manage to tend these prettily prolific gardens without coming across dozens of snakes. Don't they realise yet that Australia's not really England downunder?

Their garden paths are narrow and overgrown, the beds of tall plants tumble over one another above dense ground covers, the iris-edged dams almost writhe before my eyes, and as for the knee-high wildflower meadows — snake heaven! How do these chatelaines/gardeners, pictured in elegant hats and spotless gardening gloves as they cut roses for the dining table, avoid the snakes?

Perhaps, like dogs only attacking people who are scared of dogs, it is only the snake-nervous like my mother and I who see snakes?

Chapter 19

Casual Relationships

IT'S NOT ONLY SNAKES who pass through my yard. Other wild neighbours invite themselves in, and some of these camp for a week or two, always without notice. When I haven't seen them for a while, I invariably get a shock when I come upon them.

Like a few months ago, when I went to pick some lemon balm to spice up my breakfast herbal tea, which is basically a digestive mix of peppermint, sage and meadowsweet, all of which I grow, although not yet in the quantities I consume. My lemon balm grows in the rockery herb garden just in front of the house. On this particular morning I had to go without, for that bed was occupied by an echidna, startling me with the sudden glimpse of wrongness of texture, of bristling brown quills instead of leaves and flowers.

I tiptoed away to get the camera; when I returned, the echidna was still busily snuffling amongst the herbs. Crouching about a metre away, I clicked. It lifted its pointed, hairless snout at once, turning its head towards the sound, its small dark eyes apparently not seeing me. The snout was covered with dirt, as you'd expect, given what it does with it, but I could see the two nostrils on top. Echidnas don't have a mouth, just a hole at the end of the snout, from which they shoot a long sticky tongue to catch ants or termites. They must catch a lot of dirt at the same time.

While their vision is poor, their sense of smell is excellent, and their hearing very sensitive. So I froze until it went back to ant-hunting. I inched closer, hoping to get a shot when it looked up again. Which I did, but the click was too close for comfort and it immediately became an immobile ball of spines without a visible head. From past experience I knew its cautious nature would keep it like that for a long time, so I went back to my breakfast, *sans* lemon balm.

When I came out half an hour later, I saw from the verandah that it had unrolled and was heading in my direction, with its funny sideways rocking gait. I grabbed the camera and knelt on the verandah steps. When it was sniffing at the bottom step, its small face blindly uplifted, I clicked. It vanished under the steps at once.

My five-year-old granddaughter came later that day and I told her about the echidna being right here near the house; she'd never seen one, she said. A few hours later, as if to order, the echidna re-appeared, waddling downhill across the short grass towards the bottom gate. We hurried ahead and crouched, waiting for it to emerge underneath the gate. As it did, she got a close-up look at the snout, eyes, fur and spines, and the short, clawed feet, the hind legs looking like they'd been stuck on backwards.

Echidnas were now *real* to my granddaughter. At her age, from books, I'd known porcupines and hedgehogs, but not echidnas. Feral grandmas have their uses.

Once an echidna stayed in the yard long enough to get used to me being near as it went about its business, scratching itself, digging, sniffing. Echidnas stay on the move except when a female makes a burrow for the post-natal stage. In case mine decided it was safe to do that here, I kept an eye on her. An echidna lays a rubbery-shelled egg, like a reptile's, but she lays it into her own pouch. The echidna isn't related to the porcupine or the hedgehog at all, but to the platypus, the world's only other egg-laying mammal, or monotreme.

Like the rest of us mammals, the echidna is warm-blooded and suckles her young, but she doesn't have teats or nipples. She just sort of oozes milk through the pores of her belly skin for the baby to suck. If you find that odd, wait till you hear what she does with the baby!

The echidna still holds mystery for zoologists, and I've read varying opinions about the weaning and childrearing process. One said that at some stage, when it's still a naked, grey–blue, blind, earless, helpless little thing, perhaps only 75 millimetres long, the mother evicts it from her pouch and buries it in a hole or under a log or debris. Apparently it emits a dreadful smell, which is its only protection, and may be how the mother finds it again, for she is said to return every few days to feed it until it has grown quills and can head out to fend for itself. If that's so, not much of a childhood, is it? But whatever it does, given that it's one of the oldest mammal species, it's clearly successful.

That echidna left the yard, but I know one is visiting now, because of the snout-shaped holes in the leaf litter and exposed dirt, and the bark pushed off posts as it forages for termites. I've only recently read that an echidna's sex can be determined from the rear legs; while both males and females have enlarged second claws for scratching amongst their own spines — rather like those pointy 'teasing combs' used for 1960s bouffant hairdos — the male's claw is *greatly* enlarged and very obvious.

If I see this current visiting echidna I'll put my sexing skills to the test, but what I'd really like is to see is their mating. No one seems to know much about this, but it must be an awkward and prickly process. Like the wallabies, the lead-up can involve six males following one female, but for one to six weeks, in a 'courtship train', which is a sight in itself. I saw a photo of one online, in an issue of *The Puggle Post*, the

Echidna Care newsletter from the Pelican Lagoon Research Centre on Kangaroo Island, where Dr Peggy Rismiller is working to dispel some of that mystery about echidnas.

Only last week I saw another gang of wallaby males, five of them, grunting along in pursuit of a female, those thin pink crescent dicks pathetically out and eager. Later a large splash made me look to the little dam. I was surprised to see a wallaby waist-high in the water, since I didn't realise they did anything more than put their toes in when drinking at the edge. I grabbed the binoculars in case something was amiss. There were actually two females in the dam, and they seemed fine.

I heard the grunting before I saw the randy wave of males come over the top of the dam wall. No wonder the girls had gone in. They clearly preferred being wet to being wooed. It made me think that teenage girls have it easy — most adolescent human males just hang about outside milk bars or out of the windows of cruising cars and do their grunting. And they keep their dicks in their trousers.

In the house at present I have more mysterious visitors. I had been using cotton buds — those plastic sticks with cotton wool on the ends — for dabbing Hypericum oil (St John's Wort) on itchy hives. As I was only using one end at a time, I would lay the cotton bud in the saucer beside the little brown bottle of oil. This sat on my high chest of drawers in the bedroom. For about a week I kept going to use the other end of the half-used cotton bud that I thought I'd left in the saucer, but since none was there I clearly hadn't. Senility was approaching faster than I'd expected. Then I began saying to myself, 'But I'm sure … well, almost sure … I left one there!' Had it been bumped off, blown off? But to where? I began to suspect theft, but by what, for what purpose?

Agatha Christie's Poirot would have been proud of me: I moved the saucer and bottle to the kitchen, to a lower, more watchable bench; I made a note whenever I left a half-used cotton bud there. They kept disappearing. Whew! I was no more senile than I'd been a few weeks ago.

I placed an unused cotton bud there instead. It was still there in the morning. So it was the oil that was the attraction, but why not just suck it or eat the cotton wool off the stick? Why take the stick away, and to where?

Thinking of the tooth fairy's palace of baby teeth, I began imagining a delicate white edifice of crisscrossed plastic sticks, a summerhouse for some small creature. But what was it and where did it live? Surely my cabin had no cracks big enough for a creature lugging cotton buds to squeeze through?

Nothing was being caught in the live trap, although the cheese was taken every night, so it must be something so small, so light, that it didn't set off the spring under the cheese platform. Antechinus are heavy enough to spring the trap. The other odd thing was that something was also dragging my little yellow pear tomatoes from their dish, and eating them. Antechinus are carnivores.

Then one night I heard the trapdoor snap shut, but none of the usual noisy scrabblings followed. In the morning I carried the trap down to the forest to release whatever it was. I turned it up towards me, so my captive could slip to the bottom, and opened the door for a peek first. There were two very small critters in there; two slim, sleek grey animals with pale tummies, pointy noses, pink ears and delicate legs that seemed longer than those on any antechinus I'd seen. They leapt up at me — or freedom — which was not antechinus behaviour either. I quickly tipped them into the tussocks and they disappeared.

Were these my cotton bud thieves? Or were the two events unrelated? Poirot, where are you when I need you?

Despite looking through my books and asking friends at another wildlife refuge, I still don't know what they were, nor if they took the cotton buds, or where to. A Dunnart? A New Holland Mouse? Or a House Mouse, at which I should go 'E-eek!'? But I am still hoping to find that fanciful white structure; after all, if a bowerbird has an aesthetic sense, why can't a mini marsupial?

There are unexplained visits as well as unexplained visitors. The strangest was the frog in the food processer. You may have heard that awful joke, beloved by little boys:

Q: What's red and green and goes round and round?

A: A frog in a blender.

This story is not so gory, but it's definitely weird. I lifted the food processor from its home on top of my little fridge to use it on the bench; I was going to chop parsley and mint for tabbouli. The pusher part was hollow, quite deep, and beige, not transparent like the container itself. I don't even know why I looked into the pusher as I removed it to put the parsley in the chute; I don't think I usually did. But sitting cramped down there at the bottom of the pusher was what looked like a large, fat cream-coloured blob, looking up at me with two big dark eyes.

I didn't have my glasses on, but squealed anyway. Whatever it was shouldn't be in this indoor thing, this clean, kitchen-type non-animal-habitat plastic thing! Rushing it out to the brighter light of the verandah, I tipped it up. Nothing emerged. I tapped the base firmly and out plopped the occupant — a frog. A big one for here, sort of putty-coloured, with two fine black stripes running backwards from its eyes.

'How the hell did you get in there?' I asked. 'And why?'

Possibly a little shaken by its experience, the frog said nothing, took a few plops to the verandah edge and disappeared into the greenery.

From the photos and known distributions in my frog book, I think it may have been a Whistling Tree Frog. The description said that the call is 'a loud whirring'. The fanciful idea occurred to me that my frog was a female who'd heard my food processor whirring and, thinking it was a *very* virile male, hopped in one day to see. She waited until all was quiet again, hopped up, sought her ideal mate in the now-dormant food processor — and got stuck.

It seems nowhere is out of bounds for wildlife here.

These casual wildlife interactions are at much the same frequency as my human ones. It can be months between visitors, and it's usually weeks between my trips out, so weeks without seeing another human face. Will I be branded as misanthropic if I say I don't miss that?

Once I managed to stay up here for three months, but my then partner was going to Sydney for business occasionally, so he could top up supplies — cheese and red wine being the main consumables we'd run short of. They still are. If I got my act together to make them, as the youthful I had intended, I'd be able to stay here for six months. If petrol gets much dearer I may have to.

Even going to my rural town doesn't stop me losing touch, since it's a world apart from Sydney, which I visit once a year at most. The last time was for my second ever demonstration. It was against the Anvil Hill coalmine I mentioned previously, and so against yet more climate chaos. We waited outside a city building for Mr Beazley, the then head of the Labor Party, to arrive to launch the Opposition's Climate Change policy, and then we waited for him to leave, to maximise our press opportunities.

While waiting, I stood in my sensible shoes, black jeans and Anvil Hill T-shirt, and from behind my pleading placard, 'Stop Climate Change — Stop Anvil Hill Coal Mine', I goggled at the well-dressed business women coming and going from the building. Not a pair of trackpants or a 'peasant' skirt in sight; no bare flesh bulging over hipsters; no slides or thongs. It seemed to me that they *all* wore simple and smart dresses or suits, and elegant high-heeled proper shoes.

I was in city culture shock, but snapped out of it when Mr Beazley and his entourage re-emerged. I managed to hand him a 'Save Anvil Hill' T-shirt — extra large. He was very polite in accepting it, but I suppose grey-haired little old ladies look non-threatening, especially from his elevated position. I hope it fitted. I hope he got the message.

Here on the mountain, time slips by without formal shape. I have rung friends to ask what day it was. One suggested I look at the calendar. I had to explain that this doesn't help unless you know the date and if I knew that I'd know the day! But my current laptop puts it infallibly (I assume) in front of my face, so I have no excuse.

However it does *not* tell me when daylight saving changes, and I have thrice arrived an hour late or early to appointments, only to cause disbelief followed by hilarity at my Rip Van Winkle blink when told it changed a week ago. It's particularly embarrassing if this happens in a crowded waiting room. My daughter now takes it on herself to ring and remind me to keep up with the world. She has also promised to inform me when my age gets ahead of my dress sense — jeans too tight for a grandma, that sort of thing.

I never receive casual human visitors, as getting here is rather an expedition. I have an arrangement that expected visitors ring me from town, as I may need them to bring a few supplies and so I know when to go searching if they're overdue. This is in case they get lost or into trouble on the rough tracks or creek crossings. Over the years I've had three visiting vehicles lost, two bogged and two damaged — sumps and axles being the main worry.

I drive down to the tar road to collect two-wheel-drive visitors, leaving their car at a friend's, and take them back to it at the end of the visit. This makes three hours' driving in total, but I choose to live way out here, so it's up to me to make visiting possible for those friends who want to share it with me, to give me the stimulus of their conversation and company and a good excuse for trying new and special dishes, mountain vego style.

The drive in is always a reverse culture shock for such visitors, as well as a bodily one. I assume my fifteen-year-old Suzuki Sierra has some sort of suspension left, but she seems to have none of the cushioning effect I've experienced in newer ones. The dirt roads used to be dreadful, so bad as to be impassable at times, but most have recently been improved to 'safe and trafficable' level, after my ten years of begging and battles with various levels of government for emergency vehicle access. To reach home I still must travel over about 5 kilometres of bone-shaking, teeth-chattering, boob-bouncing, rocky dirt track, including my own. It's a crawl in first or second gear, 2 to 20 kilometres per hour, and often steep, but never smooth.

From the depths of my ignorance I try to look after my Suzi, in that I check the oil and water, but if anything went wrong there'd be no point in me putting up the bonnet and looking at her engine. We can never be intimate friends, for I simply don't understand her. I depend on Charlie, my trusty mechanic in town, to keep her happy, replace the parts I wear out and check for any bits shaken and rattled almost to breaking or falling-off point. Charlie thinks I ask too much of my old Suzi, but I don't have a choice.

I like my Suzi because she's reliable, she's basic — no carpet, no fancy lining — and she's light, more like a grasshopper than a tank, which may be why she bounces so, but she hops over humps and logs and banks and tussocks and doesn't slide much on wet clay slopes. And she's little, so doesn't use more fuel than necessary. Even so, a return trip to town currently costs close to $20, depending on the route I have to take. My petrol tank is small, so I always fill up before I leave town, just in case I need to do some visitor-ferrying, although I keep jerry cans here. A full jerry can is not only getting dearer, but heavier, harder to lift and balance for pouring, I notice.

I don't like gambling on fuel, and try never to go below a quarter-full tank, but in my experience most blokes hate to pull in to a petrol station if the tank isn't empty. How many times have I gritted my teeth as the male driver played Aussie roulette on a long highway drive? He pulls the trigger, but we'd both suffer if he lost the game, which begins when the dial on the petrol gauge is flicking E for Empty.

Click! Another garage passed. 'Nah, there's always a bit in reserve.'

Click! Another garage passed. 'I was in the wrong lane. She'll be right.'

Click! Next garage almost reached. 'Oh hell. Thought for sure we'd make it to that little place over the hill. I'll just walk over and get a can full.'

Click! 'Um, they were shut.'

My daughter has a modern four-wheel drive, so has no trouble getting here, although she dislikes the mud or dust that inevitably accompanies her home. When she and her little family visited lately, she set about rasping the horses' hooves, while my granddaughter mixed mud pies and cakes on the verandah where she maintains a well-equipped kitchen, and my son-in-law obliged by taking a look at the latest machine that wouldn't — the brushcutter.

He first asked had I checked the spark plug; I confessed I hadn't been able to bring myself to face looking for its location yet. He headed for the shed. I was delayed in following as my granddaughter was taking orders for mud morning tea. Then I heard the sound of the brushcutter engine. Damn! Another machine that went first go for the first male that tried, when it had refused for me!

He stumbled from the shed doorway, coughing, carrying the offending brushcutter — going, but spewing white smoke from its rear; surely that wasn't normal? I glanced beyond; the shed was full of smoke.

'You couldn't possibly have put two stroke in it, could you?' he asked politely.

'Well, I could have,' I replied, 'Anything's possible, especially since I don't know what that means. Is that petrol with the oil mixed in, like the chainsaw?'

He nodded.

'I keep getting mixed up; but it's a tiny engine — how can it be it a four, why isn't it a two?'

'You'd better write 2S or 4S on them with Texta,' he suggested.

'But how would that help? It'd still be a cryptic symbol. I'll have to write proper words like Unleaded or Mixed with Oil or something. I mean, I used to think all mowers took the oily stuff but the one I've got now doesn't. Why on earth can't they all be the same!'

I know why, but I'm not game to say it for fear of being accused of harbouring conspiracy theories.

A mind that can confidently remember that 2S relates to one thing and 4S to another, without any reason or clue, is beyond my comprehension. At school, even as a teacher, I was never sure which playground bin was for what. They were blue and yellow at my last school, one for papers and one for scraps. But which? I'd have to lift the lid and look inside every time. Why didn't they paint the paper bins pink, or purple? Then I'd have known the other bin must be for scraps!

It's a matter of me understanding the way my mind works, or doesn't, and accommodating that.

I'm gradually emptying the shed of any object whose function I don't know or can't make use of, not even 'one day'. My ex-partner has now taken most of his stored gear, which included many jars of rusting nails and screws and bits of metal that were parts of larger metal things that only he would recognise should they ever turn up again, and containers of magic substances to keep old cars running, or at least get them through registration.

He seemed to spend half his life under the bonnets of cars that had cost very little — if you didn't count the time they demanded. My one stipulation when we moved up here was that the yard wasn't to become a car graveyard, knowing his fondness for keeping wrecks to cannibalise for spares.

My dad didn't throw anything out, and as I'd done the final clean-up in his garage after he died, and I couldn't throw out anything of his, I have a great deal of potentially useful items in the shed. Bits of twine, short lengths of wire, off-cuts of wood, handle-less rasps and chisels, tool-less handles that don't fit any tools I have, and rusty but solid and strangely shaped pieces of iron that may be just what I need for something some day.

When you're this far from a shop, the farm shed is a priceless repository of possibilities, so I haven't been too ruthless in my clean-up, although two trailer-loads of things with no imaginable use despite my good imagination, like tins of dried paint, have been taken to the tip. Of course I've had the mandatory post-clean-up realisation that something in one of those tip loads was exactly what I now need.

I tidied up because I had to know for myself what the shed held in its dim depths, and also need to be able to see where I'm walking on the earth floor — snake-free spaces — which was not the case for the first year I was on my own. I rarely entered, left it to the quoll. The shed held its male mystique long after the male had gone; I needed to reclaim it, to de-mystify it.

My relationship with machines will never be more than casual, but at least we won't be strangers. I'm getting there.

Chapter 20

And the Future?

I'm not sure what lies ahead for me, here on my mountain, what with me and the wildlife being so unpredictable. Nor out there in the world of people, often sadly all too predictable, but sometimes gloriously atypical.

I do know that taking any step leads to another, and often not along the path envisaged. But a first step in some direction must be taken or we're only marking time. And time's too precious to waste. Ask any cancer victim.

One small step with unforeseen consequences was my first unpaid *Owner Builder* contribution, which led to an ongoing income. Another was when I decided to send in a 'Country Viewpoint' to ABC Radio National's *Bush Telegraph*. I'd often written down funny, interesting or frustrating events in my life on the mountain, but for myself, not thinking of an audience. One day it struck me that listeners to that program might like them. They did, they do; I'm a regular contributor now.

What grew out of that was my idea of making a collection that might be publishable; then a friend suggested I write a whole book about living here. *Et voilà!*

Taking the difficult personal step of going solo had freed me to concentrate on writing like this. After that one final and aberrant hiccup, my Internet romance, I was also freed from a lifelong delusion that had often distracted me from creative paths: Romantic Love.

Just as in childhood I wrote bad derivative poems about Trees or Spring, in late adolescence I wrote equally bad ones about Love. Fortunately few survive to embarrass me, but those that do reveal a pathetically unrealistic Romantic. Like the last line of this one:

There has to be a love supreme for my faith in life to persist.

Oh dear, 'supreme', no less — *la grande passion*. Like pizza, love with the lot. No wonder I kept being disappointed, and dismissive.

It only took me 30 years to get back to my creative path, so that my days are now illumined by Real Life instead of Romantic Love. Each day dawns for me with an undercurrent of excited anticipation. I hurry to do my planting or potting; attend to any pressing survival or maintenance matters, like the vegetable garden, firewood or fencing; then check emails and deal with any paid writing jobs or unpaid 'green' networking, write any letters needed … and at last settle down to the treat of writing.

Now, I'm too busy to look for Love. If it finds me, well, I'll see what happens. One step at a time, close no doors, work hard to create opportunities for my own destiny, which may cross another's, or not. And keep trying to do as I would be done by.

Many small things I do here are with the future in mind, but a bigger future than my own. Apart from the tree regeneration program, whenever I eradicate a potentially feral garden plant — like the dratted honeysuckle — I feel as if I'm making a will, bequeathing a better place to my descendants, and the world.

My refuge exists to protect native animals. We human animals seem to need protection too — from our own progress. Since we're not quite ready to set up a refuge for humans on Mars, I think we need to look seriously at this 'progress'. The word implies an advance towards something better, but it's been misused as an excuse for anything to be imposed on the populace, and endowed with such sanctity and national pride that protestors are labelled mad, bad — or worse, green.

'Standing in the way of Progress' is a Sin.

Yet much Progress is not advancing towards anything except Profits for the few and side-benefits for the governments who allow it to happen. For the little people and the environment it is often Regress — 'a going backwards' to a worse state than they already had.

As our primary aim we'd do better to replace Progress with Sustainability if we want to leave our grandchildren a viable planet. I'm not advocating that everyone go and live in a tent to re-learn what is essential and work up from there, as I did. We can't all be weird, or at least not in the same way. But we can't go on guzzling power and water and resources without a thought for the future, destroying our own world. We knew no better for a long time, but we do now.

Global warming is a fact. Rapidly increasing CO_2 levels are the reason.

Burning coal for energy emits vast quantities of CO_2 — it has to stop.

Trees absorb CO_2 — land-clearing has to stop.

Here's the biggest 'weapon of mass destruction' the modern world has faced and this time we not only know where it is but it's in our power to put an end to it. How come the President of the World has shown no interest in tackling this one? Someone should enlighten him: 'P-s-s-t! No planet, no profits.'

The polar ice caps *are* melting, as are the glaciers, right now threatening whole countries like Bhutan. They knew it wasn't just a green conspiracy myth.

Low islands are already being evacuated as the ocean level rises; the 680 inhabitants of the Carteret Atolls off Papua New Guinea were the first official permanent evacuation due to climate change. They knew it wasn't just a green conspiracy myth.

Our already 'sunburnt country' is drying up. The farmers knew it wasn't just a green conspiracy myth.

The world's climate *is* in chaos — 'natural' disasters of massive extent are hardly news anymore.

It would be nice if the government could work towards a future beyond the next election.

It would be nice if they genuinely got behind renewable energy industries.

It would be nice if they stopped saying coal is necessary for the economy, and admitted how much the industry *costs* us in economic terms, which they should understand.

For I was shocked to learn recently that the government gives a 38 cents per litre diesel fuel rebate to these hugely profitable mining companies. Why? It's not as if they need an incentive, or as if they're struggling. BHP Billiton reported a $13.7 billion profit in 2006.

This is the same fuel rebate that farmers get, but *their* profit margins are hardly in the same league as the resource giants. Nor is their fuel consumption.

Just one of those monster mine dump trucks consumes 2800 litres of crude diesel every 24 hours. As an example, take one particular open-cut mine in my region, the Hunter Valley in New South Wales. This mine uses around 70 million litres of diesel annually for its machines, and so receives about $26 million in subsidy per year!

Don't you think that's shocking?

And yet politicians keep saying that coal is cheap energy and renewables are too expensive. In fact, the New South Wales government *pays* the Hunter coal industry *more* in subsidies than it receives from it in royalties. Hunter coalmines were given $300 million in diesel subsidies in 2005. Imagine that much money going into developing renewable energy industries. For example, $26 million would buy solar hot-water systems for an *awful* lot of houses. Imagine what $300 million could do!

With the Howard government's recent sudden leap into awareness that climate change has reached the status of a political issue — and they need to be perceived as doing something about it — they announced a fund of $500 million over fifteen years to develop low greenhouse gas emission technology. Gee. Wow.

Let's get that in perspective. It's just over $33 million a year. Why, this same government spent over $200 million on advertising last financial year!

It shows how seriously lacking they are in genuine intent to solve this critical problem. For one thing we can't wait fifteen years; for another we already have 'low greenhouse gas emission technology' in renewables — but they don't involve coal; and then consider that in those fifteen years the coal giants will have received $4500 million in my area alone! Imagine what the national mining subsidies figure will be.

Now that you know about this, I bet you'll think of it whenever you fill up your tank, as I do. Mentally subtract 38 cents per litre from your fuel bill. Then write to your MP asking why these huge companies making huge profits should be offered it at all, while we keep paying more and more. And write to the PM, who assures us he *feels* for us, but can't possibly drop the excise, which is 38 cents a litre.

It would be nice if they all stopped speaking with forked tongues.

Now I've admitted I'm bad at maths, but isn't $300 million a lot of *our* money to be giving to the mining giants, most of which are foreign-owned, when the government says it can't afford funding for essential social services — for *us*. If you're on a public hospital waiting list, say for a new hip, or your keen children can't get university places, and you'd have to mortgage the house to send them if they did, you might like to see those millions of dollars spent differently.

Sometimes it seems that those big money makers and takers live in a different world from us little people, and superficially, they do. But there's only one earth, and they can't buy immunity from climate chaos any more than we can.

We all need to take steps to stop it. Small steps and big steps, and not just token green-glazed steps. The keys are energy efficiency and renewable energy.

Business has to treat power as we are beginning to treat water. Not to waste it, for example, by building more glass skyscrapers totally dependent on artificial air, heating, cooling and light, where the thousands of airconditioners and lights go on at the same time, creating the peaks in demand that are the hardest to manage.

But we can't leave it to them. Just like we're opting for rainwater tanks and water-saving devices, what each of us does adds up. We can choose better designed passive solar houses that don't need airconditioners (trust me!), install solar hot-water systems, request 'green' electricity from energy suppliers, buy energy-efficient appliances, right down to compact fluoro light globes (no flickers, but choose warm white), and switch off lights not in use and appliances at the wall — even those little red power dots use electricity.

Let's switch on our brains instead.

I am especially attuned to this issue of mindless power usage and generation not only because I make my own, and because I'm concerned about global warming, but because I've seen what the excessive coalmines and the coal-fired power stations have done to *my* region. Its present is so horrific that a better future seems dubious. But I think of my granddaughter, and I have to try to turn the tide.

In the last ten years I've watched the once-clean country air of the mid-to-upper Hunter Valley turn murky with pollution and dust as open-cut coalmines have spread like the plague. Each time I descend from my mountain into the greyish-brown pall that hangs over the Valley, or see it as I approach from Sydney or the coast, I grieve. It hurts my heart and soul, offends my sense of rightness in the world. And I'm angry.

Mining has gone mad here: the markets are so hungry, the profits so big, that the companies have brought in their truly giant machines to bite kilometres-wide holes into the landscape, tossing all but the coal onto grey dust mountains higher than the hills were. Whatever the landscape was like before — what grew there, what lived on or under it — now it is all the same. Dead. A lunar landscape. The scars of the Hunter open-cut mines are so big they are visible from space. Look for yourself on Google Earth.

There are thirteen mines in one shire near me, and each year 30,000 tonnes of fine dust — the invisible, dangerous sort — is borne in its air. Two shires north, where there are no mines, it registers only 870 kilograms of such dust per year. A staggering difference.

Imagine you have several of these towering dust mountains right next to your town, just across the sports field, or your farm, just across that paddock. What on earth do the issuers of mining guidelines think happens at your place on windy days?

Farmers are being restricted or stopped altogether from drawing water from rivers to irrigate, yet the mines use massive amounts. In a drying climate, where will the water come from for all the new mines they are planning?

Long-wall underground mines might be less obvious, but they create subsidence, interfere with aquifers, and have caused whole creeks to disappear overnight, dam walls and land to crack open. BHP Billiton refuses to agree to a 1 kilometre safety zone from the Cataract and Georges rivers, critical to Sydney's dwindling water supply, instead mining as close as 30 metres in some cases. Why isn't the state government standing up to them?

The scale of what modern mines do, below and above ground, day and night, is oversized, with the profits and the damage accordingly so. 'Rapacious' is the only word for it.

In over-mined areas, the air, water and landscape are suffering. So are the people. Everyone talks about the increasing asthma, the all-year-round hayfever, the unexplained nosebleeds, the sleep deprivation from the noise, but it's not only physical. Dr Glenn Albrecht of Newcastle University has coined a term for the psychological damage he has observed: 'solastalgia' — the pain and helplessness experienced when one's home landscape is being destroyed, its solace removed.

I hear many heartbreaking stories of ruined lives and livelihoods, families and histories, dreams and plans. I've visited a beautiful heritage home and garden where the dust mountains have grown so near, so numerous, and so overwhelming, that nothing else can be seen in any direction.

'Ah well,' King Coal might say to the government, 'you can't make an omelette without breaking eggs. Perhaps we could offer the community money for a new sports shed?'

Pollution in these areas is an escalating disaster that nobody in power wants to know about. Instead they let King Coal do his own monitoring — of course he's trustworthy, he represents some of the world's biggest multi-nationals. The conclusions are always the same, as they repeat like Daleks, 'All environmental guidelines are being complied with.' Guidelines which they reckon are 'strict'. Well, this grandma's got eyes, and she reckons they're not half strict enough.

And the sad thing is that employment, the reason always touted locally as the up side for all the local damage, is short-term, unsustainable and overstated. Coalmining has become vastly more mechanised, so while coal production has more than doubled over the last twenty years, mining jobs have halved.

Many mineworkers live away from the polluted and coal-dependent towns, protecting their families and their property investment. Most admit they don't like what the mines are doing to the areas, but the money's good for their twelve-hour shifts: the 'golden handcuff'. Mines last fifteen to twenty years, less if the price of coal drops. When they close so will the towns, just as my old coalmining village did a century ago. People won't be able to move to find employment somewhere else, because they won't be able to sell their houses.

The mines will have destroyed the environment and threatened the viability of, if not ruined, many of the valuable rural industries like the vineyards and the horse studs, and the artificial hills and toxic voids they leave behind will have no appeal for tourists.

We need to be planning and initiating sustainable industries for employment *now*, to gradually wean areas like the Hunter off coal. We're way behind the smart countries — little Sweden's wind power industry alone provides 16,000 jobs. We could be clean, green and clever — instead of dirty, grey and greedy.

It would be nice if our local MPs took off their blinkers. But even if they did, the widest and worst damage from the Hunter Valley's coal frenzy, the CO_2 emissions, is invisible.

Carbon Valley, we're now called, the second biggest greenhouse gas producer in Australia, with our power stations and aluminium smelters. The next shire north is also a coalmining area, and home to two coal-fired power stations, belching far worse emissions into the atmosphere than what comes out of the squat towers beside the highway — 'WATER VAPOUR' the billboards explain, in case passers-by are suspicious. From the western end of my ridge, in the distance I can see the yellowish-brown lines of pollution from the other, taller chimneys — and there's no billboard to reassure us about them. Nor about the CO_2.

And they want to build a third station there. Burning coal. More CO_2. Surely no government will agree to that? Knowing the damage it would do to the planet? Of course not — if we lived in a sane world.

For government can't seem to say 'No' to coal, even while now saying, 'Yes, yes, we must do something about climate change.' Coal's toxic effect on the world is proven; it is self-destructive to continue to facilitate its use. Yet our state government hasn't been taking the carbon cost of proposed new coalmines into account when assessing their environmental impact. How irresponsible is that?

People agree, but shake their heads, shrug their shoulders. 'You can't fight the big boys with the big bucks.' Oh, but we have to try!

For it's not only the Hunter being trashed for mining profits, nor only coal that the country is being trashed for.

Now my neighbouring mountain country, the very beautiful Gloucester, Barrington and Stroud areas, their scenic alpine-fed creeks, and even the fragile, famous sub-alpine swamps of the Barrington Tops, like Pol Blue, are under threat from various types of mining. So are the stunning sandstone cliffs and gorges and the groundwater resources of the Goulburn River, just to the west of me, near Mudgee.

As with Anvil Hill, my mind boggles at why *exploration* applications are even considered in such places, let alone allowed to go further. Just because something worth money is under the ground doesn't mean it *has* to be dug up — at any cost.

All over the country governments are considering ludicrously self-serving proposals by the profit-makers — at the expense of our dwindling resources and irreplaceable treasures.

Like Lake Cowal, the biggest inland lake in New South Wales, a National Estate-listed wetland, home to endangered migratory birds, sacred heartland of the Wiradjuri Nation, critical to the already terminal Murray–Darling Basin — threatened by a Canadian open-cut cyanide leach gold-mining operation on its very edge. In the last 100 years Australia has managed to 'lose' 89 per cent of its wetlands. How can those entrusted with the care of our land be so careless with the rest?

Or the 20,000-year-old rock art, or petroglyphs, on the Burrup Peninsula in Western Australia, some of the most ancient and comprehensive in the world — threatened by the gas, oil and iron ore industries. When the National Trust recently nominated these unique, internationally significant carvings for inclusion on the National Heritage list, there was a huge fuss — because it might put developers off. Stonehenge is only 4500 years old. Have our governments lost their senses — or just their integrity?

We're in an unprecedented drought, with drier times ahead, and yet new coalmines, extremely high water users, are being blithely considered everywhere. The Moolarben proposal, which would be the third coalmine in the Mudgee Ulan area of New South Wales, would include three open-cuts and an underground mine and would waste 6.9 million litres of water a day to wash the coal. People mightn't be allowed to wash their cars or their driveways but hey, King Coal, go for it!

Small groups of passionate 'vocal locals' and environmentalists are fighting the mining giants in all these areas. But it's hard to believe in a fair go in the approval process, for locals or the environment, when we are beginning to discover how much money changes hands in advance.

For instance, instead of the old tendering process, BHP Billiton 'gave' the New South Wales government $100 million for the rights to explore the Caroona coal seam near Gunnedah. That's $91 million more than they needed to. As if they don't then expect a final go-ahead. As if the farmers' worries about subsidence from long-wall mining under their delicately balanced, rich agricultural floodplains are going to be heard as clearly as $100 million. As if it's not a *fait accompli* now the government has admitted that they had the Caroona coalfield in mind when planning a vast expansion of the coal-loading facilities at the port of Newcastle — but admit no responsibility for the consequent global expansion of greenhouse gases.

The New South Wales government assures us it's all above board, but there's something wrong with my telly — eyes slide sideways, forked tongues flicker.

As Edmund Burke said, 'All it takes for evil to flourish is for good men to do nothing'. Saving Tasmania's historic Recherche Bay from logging is what happened recently when enough good 'men' did something, and wouldn't let up.

A few years ago, I felt driven to 'do something' larger than my tree-planting and more effective than getting sad and angry. From writing letters to editors, then to politicians, I have ended up an 'electronic' activist, with my bush email receiving, sorting and sending on environ-mental and social justice information to the wider concerned 'greenish' community in the Upper Hunter, a two-way street that keeps me informed as well. It has to remain a mostly non-physical form of activism, as I am simply too far away, and can't afford the fuel, to travel to many meetings and protests. But I care fiercely. And I write.

In general I dislike and distrust politics — and politicians, apart from the few genuinely altruistic ones who dare to speak out, even against their party, as happened amongst the Liberals on immigration issues. Independents can often be what I'd call goodies, and I find a whole concentration of goodies in the Greens, like Bob Brown federally or Lee Rhiannon statewise, for example. Their names are known and respected because they continually stand up for people and principles, not power and profits and party politics.

I don't know where people like them, in or out of politics, find the strength to keep on battling for so long against the indifference and ignorance, the greed and the accepted corruption – that is of course not called so. And then there's the personal abuse and slander. Yet they don't give up and, most extraordinary of all, they retain hope and optimism.

I remind myself of what such people do daily, on behalf of all of us, whenever I feel like I can't spare the time to write another email to yet another MP whose office will fob me off with a policy statement, assuring me of their 'strict environmental regulations', and reminding me of the 'benefits we derive from the ... relatively inexpensive ... energy produced in coal-fired power stations'.

Relative to *what* is a $26 million per annum handout to just one mine considered inexpensive?

The great news of the year is that the hole in the ozone layer has been halted and is slowly healing. That only happened because the world's industry, government and science got together in the Montreal Protocol and set targets for phasing out products that emitted CFCs. You might have been vaguely aware of change in regard to fridges and aerosols, but it didn't hurt, did it?

We need to do the same to halt global warming. It's harder, because its fossil-fuel/energy causes are more deeply and broadly embedded in Progress. That's why countries driven by Big Business are refusing to listen to science, muttering instead about returning to the caves if we can't keep burning coal. Yet the writing on the wall is being read by some in Business, who see its connection with Profit: before investing, superannuation funds are now requesting carbon emission reduction plans from companies — for without them, they may have no future.

My granddaughter also gives me hope. She is observant about and interested in the natural world. Her father is a horticulturist and her grandfather is an entomologist; they also own a wildlife refuge. From them, and me, she not only learns to use the botanical names of plants and animals, but to look, to re-spect nature. At three, she would stop as we were walking and finger a part of a plant: 'Is that a bud or a seed, Grandma?' At four, she could play 'Spotto' on native plants as we drove through the national park in spring; we had chosen purple flowers, so we were yelling 'Hardenbergia!' 'Indigofera!' and giggling as our tongues tripped over our spottings.

The last time she was with me when I drove down the mountain to town, there'd been an almost gale-force southerly blowing the day before. As we reached the part of the descent where the view towards the Valley, usually with a very obvious pollution layer, becomes panoramic, she pointed down at it in astonishment. 'Look, Grandma!'

She took a few seconds to work out why it was so different. 'It's not yucky!'

Look what they've done to her world. Pollution is normal.

Think what they've done to her future — unless we tell them to stop. I'm trying, as are many others, but the number of voices has to swell, until we are so clamorous that we are louder than money, so broad-based that we can't be dismissed by politicians as green fanatics. Let's all start yelling from our verandahs or balconies: 'Put people and the planet before profit — give us back our future!'

On the wall by my desk, some years ago I'd pinned up a quote from writer Marcel Pagnol's autobiography; it had deeply impressed me at the time because it rang true with my own thoughts:

Such is the life of man. A few joys, quickly obliterated by unforget-table sorrows. There is no need to tell the children so.

I don't feel like that anymore. The paper on which it was printed is yellowed and nibbled by silverfish, but I leave it there to remind me of how life can look, and be, so different at different stages of one's own.

Despair is not a lasting option. My trees are growing, the frogs are croaking in the dam, joeys are leaping about the paddock, and a new grandchild is expected soon.

So I rejoice in the natural world around me, and write to make sense of life.

Oh, yes, and to try to save the world.

That's all.

POSTSCRIPT

JUST AS I WAS finishing this book, I came back from a week away to find Jess dead in the shallows of my little dam in front of the house. She was old, we'd known it must happen one day, she looked peaceful — but I sobbed, from shock, from guilt that I was away when it did, and for the pain this news would bring to my seven-months'-pregnant daughter.

She was heartbroken. Jess had been a part of her life, and of the mountain, for seventeen years. My daughter's first horse — frustrating, friend, savvy, stubborn, but never bad-tempered.

This was not a job that I or my Suzi could handle. And this time nor could my daughter. True friends came to my rescue in this awful and urgent task. Because Jess was special, we protected her, wrapped her in a tarpaulin shroud before we towed her gently through the bush to a resting place. Farewell Jess. Thank you friends.

POST-POSTSCRIPT

THERE IS ALWAYS A silver lining: I have a beautiful new granddaughter — and the mother quoll is back!

ACKNOWLEDGEMENTS

The traditional owners of these mountains; Nillumbik Shire and Parks Victoria, for the great gift of my three-months writers' residency at Birrarung; Lynda Wilson, editor and publisher of *The Owner Builder* magazine, for the unfettered use of my OB articles; Fred Baker, for his encouragement to write this book; Penny Walton, illustrator, friend, ex-OB subject, for introducing me to Exisle Publishing; Exisle's Anouska Jones, for her finely sympathetic editing, and the publishers, Benny and Gareth St John Thomas, for fostering my odd proposal and making it a reality.

REFERENCES

Any technical, botanical or zoological facts in this book are correct to the best of my knowledge, as told to me over the years by people who ought to know, or as referenced from my own sources.

Books:

Australian Museum, *The Complete Book of Australian Mammals*, 1983, Cornstalk Publishing.

Harry Frauca & Barbara Burton, *The Echidna*, 1974, Lansdowne Press Young Nature Library.

Gordon Ford with Gwen Ford, *The Natural Australian Garden*, 1999, Bloomings Books.

Raymond T. Hoser, *Australian Reptiles & Frogs*, 1989, Pierson & Co.

G.F. Middleton, *Build Your House of Earth*, (1953 A & R), 1975, Compendium.

Peter Slater, *A Field Guide to Australian Birds*, Volumes 1 & 2, 1970, 1974, Rigby.

J.B. Williams, G.F. Harden & W.J.F. McDonald, *Trees & Shrubs in Rainforests of New South Wales & Southern Queensland*, 1984, Botany Department, University of New England.

Websites:

www.theownerbuilder.com.au — *The Owner Builder* magazine

www.weavers.com.au — Weavers Design Group

www.watermarkliterarysociety.asn.au —Watermark Literary Society and Muster

www.echidna.edu.au/monotremes/echidna_watch.html — Pelican Lagoon Research Centre, Kangaroo Island

www.voiceless.org.au/ — Voiceless, the Fund for Animals

www.seedsavers.net — The Seed Savers' Network

www.bonzer.org.au — *Bonzer* online seniors' magazine

www.anvilhill.org.au — Anvil Hill Alliance

The Owner Builder articles referred to in the book appeared in the following editions:

'Confessions of a Bad Muddie' — Issue 109

'The Nah Mate Building Standard' — Issue 85

'Evolution of an OB Greenhouse' — Issue 88

'From Knoxie to Now' — Issue 115

Exisle Publishing is proud to introduce the Hourglass series. Hourglass books feature the true stories of ordinary women who have lived extraordinary lives. They are as varied as the women who love reading them, from the passionate and heart-wrenching to the humorous and uplifting, and range widely across continents and lifestyles. But they have one thing in common: they are all superb stories offering great reading.

Also available in this series:

THE GIRL WITH THE CARDBOARD PORT
Judith L. McNeil

Judith McNeil has lived a life that few of us can begin to imagine. She has faced tragedy and heartache, experienced crippling poverty and hunger and suffered unforgivable violence. But she has emerged a survivor, a woman with an indomitable will and the courage and resourcefulness to forge a new life for herself against all odds.

The death of Judy's father in a railway accident when she is only fourteen triggers a chain of events that will lead her first to the slums of Sydney and ultimately to far-flung Singapore and Malaya. Here, she finds friendship in the company of an Indian servant, love in the arms of a jungle warrior and hope in the laughter of her children.

Set against the backdrop of the political upheaval and widespread racial violence that swept through Singapore and Malaya in the early 1960s, *The Girl with the Cardboard Port* takes you into a world that few Europeans would have encountered. From glittering society balls to the isolation of a Malay kampong, from riches to poverty, Judy experiences a world of contrasts, often living in fear for her life and those of her children. And through it all, she has only one dream: to return home to Australia.

Raw and compelling, her story will linger in your mind long after the final page.

ISBN 0 908988 80 X